BEATRIX POTTER
1866-1943

The National Trust was able to co-publish this book with Frederick Warne
thanks to a generous grant from The Ford Motor Company.

BEATRIX POTTER
1866-1943

THE ARTIST AND HER WORLD

Judy Taylor, Joyce Irene Whalley,
Anne Stevenson Hobbs, Elizabeth M Battrick

F. WARNE & CO
THE NATIONAL TRUST

FREDERICK WARNE WITH THE NATIONAL TRUST

Published by the Penguin Group
27 Wrights Lane, London w8 5TZ, England
Viking Penguin Inc., 40 West 23rd Street, New York, New York 10010, U.S.A.
Penguin Books Australia Ltd, Ringwood, Victoria, Australia
Penguin Books Canada Ltd, 2801 John Street, Markham, Ontario, Canada L3R 1B4
Penguin Books (N.Z.) Ltd, 182–190 Wairau Road, Auckland 10, New Zealand

Penguin Books Ltd, Registered Offices: Harmondsworth, Middlesex, England

The National Trust, 36 Queen Anne's Gate, London SW1H 9AS

First published 1987
Reprinted 1987

Designed by Gail Engert

Cased edition ISBN 0 7232 3521 X

Paperback edition ISBN 0 7232 3561 9

Set in Linotron Goudy Old Style by Rowland Phototypesetting Ltd,
Bury St Edmunds, Suffolk

Printed and bound in Great Britain by William Clowes Ltd,
Beccles and London

British Library Cataloguing in Publication Data available

1 (half-title) Decorative border with blank inset: full-blown roses,
c. 1898–9

2 (frontispiece) Pigling and Alexander go to market: a rare and
shadowy self-portrait of Beatrix Potter with Kep, Aunt Pettitoes and
other inhabitants of Hill Top Farm. Alternative picture for *The Tale of
Pigling Bland*, p. 21, 1913

3 (title-page) 'When the cat's away the mice will play': unused vignette
of dancing mice for *The Fairy Caravan*, ?1929

CONTENTS

Acknowledgements   6

Publisher's Note   6

INTRODUCTION   7
Joyce Irene Whalley

1   THE STORY OF BEATRIX POTTER   9
    Judy Taylor

2   THE YOUNG ARTIST AND EARLY INFLUENCES   35
    Joyce Irene Whalley

3   FANTASY, RHYMES, FAIRY TALES AND FABLES   49
    Joyce Irene Whalley, Anne Stevenson Hobbs

4   FLORA AND FAUNA, FUNGI AND FOSSILS   71
    Anne Stevenson Hobbs

5   THE TALE OF PETER RABBIT   95
    Judy Taylor

6   THE LITTLE BOOKS   107
    Anne Stevenson Hobbs, Joyce Irene Whalley, Judy Taylor

7   CREATIVE YEARS AND THE LAKE DISTRICT   169
    Elizabeth M Battrick

8   LAKE DISTRICT FARMER   185
    Elizabeth M Battrick

9   BEATRIX POTTER'S LAKE DISTRICT   195
    Elizabeth M Battrick

AN APPRECIATION   207
Judy Taylor

Sources and Credits   209

Bibliography   214

Index   215

ACKNOWLEDGEMENTS

The contributors would like to thank John Clegg, Joan Duke, Gail Engert, Selwyn Goodacre, Mary Hobbs, Eileen Jay, Linda Lloyd Jones, Libby Joy, the Regional Director and staff of the National Trust North West Regional office, Natural History Museum, Mary Noble, Brian Riddle, Roy Watling and Derrick Witty.

The contributors and publishers are also grateful to the following for their kind permission to reproduce the illustrations in this book (for details of the sources please see pp. 209–13): Abbot Hall Art Gallery; The Armitt Trust; Book Trust (National Book League), Trustees of the Linder Collection; Winifred Boultbee; British Museum; Mary Burkett; Joan Duke; Betty Hart; Heaton Cooper Studio; John Heelis; Jean Holland; The Horn Book, U.S.A.; National Art Library, Victoria and Albert Museum (Leslie Linder Bequest); The National Trust; Rosalind Rawnsley; Heather and Alan Rhodes; J. Anthony Roberts; Frederick Rothenburgh; The John Ruskin Museum, Brantwood; Ruskin Museum, Coniston; Mortimer Shaw; Tate Gallery; Board of Trustees, Victoria and Albert Museum; Frederick Warne Archive; The Whitworth Art Gallery.

PUBLISHER'S NOTE

This book was commissioned as the official companion to *Beatrix Potter 1866–1943*, the exhibition shown at the Tate Gallery in London during the winter of 1987/88, which was sponsored by the Ford Motor Company in aid of the National Trust's Lake District Appeal.

The four contributors, who also selected the items for the exhibition, were chosen for their knowledge of particular aspects of Beatrix Potter's life and work. In some chapters their work was very closely shared. The contents list gives the broad division of responsibility and for a more detailed attribution for chapters 3 and 6, see below.

3 FANTASY, RHYMES, FAIRY TALES AND FABLES
Joyce Irene Whalley wrote pp. 49–54 and p. 57, paragraph 2, and Anne Stevenson Hobbs wrote the rest of the chapter.

6 THE LITTLE BOOKS
Anne Stevenson Hobbs: pp. 107–8, the introductory paragraphs; *The Tale of Two Bad Mice*; *The Pie and the Patty-Pan*; *The Story of Miss Moppet*, *The Story of A Fierce Bad Rabbit* and *The Sly Old Cat*; *The Tale of Tom Kitten*; *The Tale of Jemima Puddle-Duck*; *The Tale of Mr. Tod*; *The Tale of Pigling Bland*; *Tales of Country Life* and *Kitty-in-Boots*; *The Tale of Johnny Town-Mouse*; *Cecily Parsley's Nursery Rhymes*; *The Fairy Caravan*; *Sister Anne*, *Wag-by-Wall* and *The Faithful Dove*

Joyce Irene Whalley: *The Tailor of Gloucester*; *The Tale of Squirrel Nutkin*; *The Tale of Benjamin Bunny*; *The Tale of Mrs. Tiggy-Winkle*; *The Tale of Mr. Jeremy Fisher*; *The Roly-Poly Pudding*; *The Tale of the Flopsy Bunnies*; *Ginger and Pickles*; *The Tale of Mrs. Tittlemouse*; *Appley Dapply's Nursery Rhymes*; *The Tale of Little Pig Robinson*

Judy Taylor: *The Tale of Timmy Tiptoes*

Note on page and cross-references

All the page references for the Little Books refer to the reoriginated 1987 editions. The page references for *The Fairy Caravan* refer to the 1985 edition except for illustration 410 which appeared in all editions before 1985, when it was omitted.

The italic numbers in brackets which appear in the text are cross-references to illustrations in this book. These are only given when the illustrations do not appear on the same page as the text about them.

INTRODUCTION

Beatrix Potter offers us the unusual example of an artist in the English watercolour tradition who never exhibited her paintings and never sold a picture, as such, except to raise money for the purchase of Lake District land. She also had little formal training in her art. Yet on the rare occasions when an example of her work comes on to the market today, it commands a high price and her name is known world-wide. Undoubtedly the most familiar aspect of Beatrix Potter's art is her book illustration and there must be many people who would be surprised to learn that she produced anything else, so much has the attraction of the *Peter Rabbit* books overshadowed everything.

For the most part Beatrix was self-taught. She had copied illustrations from books from a very early age and this exercise had given her a training in the disciplines of drawing and observation. As soon as she was old enough, she became a regular gallery visitor. The Potters moved in a circle artistically aware of contemporary style, and discussions on art must have been commonplace among them. Beatrix herself studied the paintings at the exhibitions she visited with great care, making detailed notes about the various works in her journal. This gallery visiting was probably one of the most formative influences on her as a young artist. Almost as important was the family link with John Everett Millais, a close friend of her father's, which made her familiar with the concerns and problems of an artist.

Meanwhile Beatrix was developing her own style. Once she had decided to try and make some money from her art by designing greetings cards, she consciously imitated the style of card which the printing processes of the period produced. She developed her own dry-brush technique together with a meticulous attention to detail, painting the creatures she chose as her subjects in almost miniature fashion. Her subject matter was strictly limited right from the first – she rarely attempted anything she was not sure that she could draw well. There were no scenes with children in them on her cards, for instance, and in fact few 'scenes' at all. As a young child she had copied exotic pictures of leopards and other jungle creatures, but now she chose to concentrate on those animals that she and her brother had kept as pets or had studied at close hand – such as mice and rabbits, hedgehogs or squirrels. Moreover she had the confidence of knowing that she could paint these well because she had practised drawing such creatures in every detail, covering sheets of paper with claws and paws, heads and tails.

She could see, and make us see, beauty in the simplest things. Her microscopic paintings are not only scientifically accurate, but they can convince us that even unattractive creatures – or bits of creatures – have an intrinsic beauty. The same can be said of her fungi, or of her archaeological paintings. Although these are specialist subjects, the sheer painterly skill which Beatrix brings to her work makes us look at them in a new light.

Beatrix's painting later became much freer in style, and the meticulousness of the work she had produced for the chromolithographed greetings cards gave place to general studies using a more fluid line, frequently combining the use of watercolour with sepia ink outlines. The paintings of this period have great charm, and for the most part are devoted to natural history subjects and sketches of places she had visited. But she was always something of an experimenter in her art. From the 1890s for instance we have some fine examples of her work done in a grisaille monochrome, and at the same time she had begun to write the picture letters which were to play so important a part in the books later on. In these she made use of line drawing, filling pages with lively and entertaining sketches.

Beatrix Potter's first illustrated book was privately published in 1901. She had discovered her ability to compose and write simple attractive stories, and her solitary reading and regular journal entries had given her a command of good English and a lucid style. Beatrix usually reworked her earlier sketches for publication, but sometimes she found she could not recapture the first flush of originality, and then an older painting was used. The published pictures portray yet a further stage in her development, for they manage to combine something of the earlier meticulousness with the more fluid painterly style of her later period. These paintings certainly have outlines, but they are never the somewhat intrusive ones of her late-nineteenth-century 'sepia-ink-and-watercolour' period. It is very interesting to look at a work like *Appley Dapply* (*see p. 153*), published in 1917, where there is a combination of both the earlier and the later work, showing clearly her changes of style. As late as the publication of *The Tale of Mr. Tod* (1912) (*see p. 145*) she was still experimenting, for in this book the black-and-white drawings are surrounded by a frame, and the pictures themselves are drawn with a heavy black line that is reminiscent of woodcuts.

Beatrix married in 1913 and turned her attention to farming in the Lake District. She had little inclination to continue with book illustration, and her eyesight was no longer good enough for detailed work. But she still sketched for pleasure, and her work became much more impressionistic. It is these later paintings, together with her many other landscapes, that place Beatrix Potter firmly in the English watercolour tradition.

This book is a companion to the Beatrix Potter exhibition held at the Tate Gallery in November 1987 to raise money for the National Trust's Lake District Appeal. The wide range of Beatrix Potter's interests has resulted in her work being regarded in many different ways. To some she is a writer or an artist or a lively diarist of the late nineteenth century. To others she is the great benefactor of the National Trust or a sheep farmer or a mycologist. In order to provide a focus it was decided to concentrate on Beatrix Potter's Lake District connection, with special emphasis on her art, and the contributors have tried to represent every aspect of this. For example, all the Peter Rabbit books are included but those set in the Lake District are treated in greater detail.

By emphasizing the many facets of Beatrix Potter's work, the contributors have shown that while for many people she will always be one of the finest writers and illustrators of children's books, there is also a great deal to interest those who have never seen anything more than the book pictures. Indeed, just looking at the detailed study and preliminary sketching that went into the creation of the familiar books may, in itself, say more about the art of Beatrix Potter than any amount of writing on the subject.

J.I.W.

1

THE STORY OF
BEATRIX POTTER

4   *Rupert Potter (1832–1914)*

5   *Helen Potter, née Leech*
(1839–1932)

Helen Beatrix Potter was born at 2 Bolton Gardens on Saturday, 28 July 1866, the first child of Rupert Potter, barrister-at-law, and of his wife, Helen Leech, who was 27 years old.

The Potters were a well-to-do, middle-class couple, owing their comfortable situation to the Lancashire cotton trade. Rupert's father, Edmund, had made a considerable fortune as a calico printer, setting up his own printing works in Glossop in the early 1820s, and introducing machine printing to an industry that until then had known only the time-consuming use of hand blocks. In 1829 Edmund married Jessie Crompton and their seven children were born in the next eleven years, Rupert, their second son, in 1832.

By the middle of the decade Edmund Potter and Company was a vast printworks, renowned not only for the quality of its printing but also for the facilities afforded to its workers, for Edmund Potter was an enlightened employer, building a school and a library for his child workers and providing cheap fresh food for everyone who worked for him. In 1861 he followed his close friends, John Bright and Richard Cobden, into politics when he was elected Liberal MP for Carlisle. Also in that year Edmund left Lancashire and moved with his wife to London, content to leave his printworks in the expert care of his eldest son, Crompton.

His second son had also been expected to join the family business, but soon after gaining his degree at Manchester New College Rupert Potter set his heart on becoming a barrister and in 1854 had enrolled as a student of law at Lincoln's Inn. Three years later he had been called to the Bar, and had set up as an equity draughtsman and conveyancer with chambers in Lincoln's Inn. In 1860 he had moved his chambers to New Square where they were to remain for the next thirty years.

On 8 August 1863 Rupert Potter married Helen Leech, an old family friend. She was one of the five daughters of John Leech, who had been a prosperous cotton merchant in Stalybridge until his death two years earlier. Helen brought with her to the marriage a generous legacy from her father, and the couple bought a house in Upper Harley Street, where they lived and entertained in considerable style until Helen was expecting their first child. They moved into a four-storeyed,

newly-built terrace house in a quiet Kensington square in 1866. The houses in Bolton Gardens, suitably enough, had generous gardens; in the mews there were stables for the horses and coach houses for the carriages. Mature trees were a reminder of how recently the area had been open country. Number 2 Bolton Gardens was to be the Potter family house for the next fifty years.

When Helen Beatrix was born the small band of servants in the house was joined by a young nurse, Miss McKenzie, from the Scottish Highlands, about whom Beatrix wrote many years later: 'She had a firm belief in witches, fairies and the creed of the terrible John Calvin (the creed rubbed off but the fairies remained).' A room on the third floor was turned into a nursery and child and nurse began their separate life there together, leaving only for walks in the park or when Miss McKenzie took her charge downstairs to see her parents on special occasions or to say goodnight. Beatrix depended for everything on her nurse, who brought her up with strict and spartan attention.

To avoid confusion with her mother, the baby was called Beatrix, or quite often just B.

Beatrix's parents were totally absorbed in their London lives. Having left the country behind her, Helen Potter was enjoying the social round, holding elaborate and elegant dinner parties for her husband's friends and driving out in the carriage to leave her card with the ladies of Kensington. Rupert Potter had become quite a gentleman about town, allowing his practice to be looked after by others while he spent much of his time at his club, the Reform, where he felt at ease among fellow Liberal sympathizers. He had always been interested in painting and in drawing, keeping a sketchbook himself while

7 *Beatrix Potter with her mother, Helen*, R. Potter

8 *Beatrix Potter with her father, Rupert*, R. Potter

9 (above) *No. 4 bedroom at Camfield Place*, ?1890

10 (right) The great cedar at Birds' Place, Camfield, *The Fairy Caravan*, p. 51, 1929

he was a student, and now he indulged his interest, visiting art galleries and exhibitions, and adding to his own picture collection. He had a particular liking for the work of Randolph Caldecott and bought his original drawings whenever the opportunity arose.

Rupert Potter's other great enthusiasm was photography, the relatively new art form which had caught his attention some years before, and now he began to take it up seriously. He photographed everything – the ever busy and ever changing London streets, his long-suffering family, the countryside when they were all on holiday. He soon became a skilled photographer and was elected to the Photographic Society of London. Although he never photographed professionally, Rupert Potter often worked for his friend, John Everett Millais, providing him with photographs of his sitters as portrait references and sometimes even with a landscape or two for the backgrounds.

Meanwhile Beatrix was growing fast and when she was nearly 6 she was joined in the nursery by her brother, Walter Bertram, named after his uncle but called Bertram by the family. After having the undivided attention of her nurse for so many years, Beatrix found that she often now had to provide her own amusement. She had always been surrounded by the books which her parents supplied to the nursery in a steady stream but she had also discovered a love for drawing and painting, a direction in which she was much encouraged. And Beatrix began to see more of her parents. She found her mother remote and even a little frightening but she became increasingly fond of her father, writing letters to him whenever they were separated and posing with him in his delayed-action photographs.

One of Beatrix's real favourites in the family was her grandmother, Jessie, whose husband Edmund had retired from politics and calico printing and bought a large country property in Hertfordshire. It was an easy journey from London to Hatfield and Rupert Potter frequently took his young family to stay there. Camfield Place became a dearly-loved haven for both the children, who relished the freedom of the extensive garden and who soon discovered the delights of the farmyard.

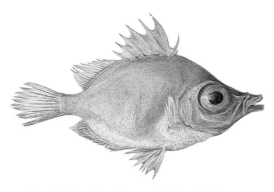

11 Boar fish found at Weymouth (*detail*), 1895

But Camfield was not their only escape, for twice a year the Potters went on holiday – for two weeks in April to a seaside hotel on the south coast and for three whole months in the late summer to a rented home, when the entire household, including the groom with the horse and carriage, left London. Bolton Gardens was closed and shuttered. Like his father before him, Rupert Potter favoured Scotland for this longer holiday, and invited friends from London and Manchester to join the party – John Millais with his wife and daughters, John Bright and William Gaskell. While the adults fished the river for salmon or stalked the estate for deer, the children explored the woods and played on the wide beaches of the river.

From the time she was 5 until she was 15 Beatrix spent every summer in Perthshire at Dalguise House, an elegant mansion overlooking the Tay near Dunkeld. It was a place of magic and enchantment for the little girl, a place where her senses were first awakened to the sights and sounds of the wild life around her, the bark of the roe-deer, the scent of the heather. She explored the woods on the extensive estate, and she drew and painted all that she saw. When Bertram was old enough he

12 (above) *Beatrix Potter with William Gaskell*

13 (right) *After the salmon fishing at Dalguise*, R. Potter

14 Posy of wild flowers

15 *Portrait of Beatrix Potter*, R. Potter

joined in her expeditions and together they picked wild flowers, watched the birds, caught rabbits and tried to tame them. It was at Dalguise that Beatrix's deep love of nature was instilled.

It was always hard to return to London after the freedom of the country, particularly as London for Beatrix meant lessons. Her governess was a Miss Hammond, who happily allocated a generous portion of the timetable to art without neglecting the basic necessities of 'reading, writing and arithmetic'. By the time she was 12 and Bertram had joined her in the classroom, Beatrix was showing enough talent to have special instruction from a drawing teacher, and Miss Cameron taught Beatrix for the next five years. She received advice about her painting from other directions, too, even from John Millais, whom she saw when she visited his studio with her father, and for a short time she had lessons from a 'Mrs A.' – never identified – with whom she disagreed on nearly everything.

By her mid teens Beatrix was starting to escape the confines of the third floor of Bolton Gardens but she remained a lonely child, for close friendships were discouraged by her parents and she had only young Bertram for companionship. They were fond of each other, though, and together they had established almost a menagerie in the schoolroom. The creatures were smuggled downstairs to the garden for the occasional airing. At

16 *Beatrix Potter with her brother, Bertram, at Camfield Place*, R. Potter, November 1878

17 Pineapple with the lizard
Judy, 1883

18 Two skulls (*detail*), ?1887

one time there was a green frog, two lizards, four black newts, a
ring-snake and two salamanders, soon to be followed by a bat, a
dormouse and a tortoise. The children closely observed the
behaviour of their pets, recording their measurements, noting
their characteristics, even boiling them when they died so they
could study their skeletons. But above all they drew them,
covering page after page with meticulous drawings.

It was at this time, too, that Beatrix started her journal – a
secret journal written in code of her own invention designed to
keep her record from prying eyes, particularly those of her
mother. Although the code was a simple one of substitution of
letter for letter it was to remain undeciphered for over eighty
years – and even Beatrix found it hard to read in later life.

In 1882 Rupert Potter was faced with the disappointing
news that their beloved Dalguise House, the only summer
home that the children could remember, was no longer available and that they must look elsewhere to spend their long
holiday. Breaking with family tradition, Rupert chose the Lake
District where he took a large house on the west side of Lake
Windermere, the imposing mock-Norman Wray Castle.
Although his Grandfather Crompton had at one time owned a
sizeable amount of property in the Lake District, it was the first
introduction to that part of the country for the Potters of
Bolton Gardens and they warmed to it quickly, finding echoes
of their beloved Scotland in the fells and lakes and tumbling
becks. For Beatrix that first visit to Windermere marked the
start of an association with the Lake District that changed the
course of her life.

As had been the custom in Scotland, family friends came to

19 *The 16-year-old Beatrix Potter*, R. Potter,
15 October 1882

20 *A Potter family boating party on Lake Windermere*, R. Potter, September 1882

21 *Beatrix Potter with Hardwicke Rawnsley and his son, Noel, at Lingholm*, R. Potter, 2 July 1885 or 1887

stay at Wray Castle and Rupert Potter surrounded himself with those with whom he could discuss politics and religion, painting and literature. One of the regular local visitors to the house was the vicar of the village of Wray, Hardwicke Rawnsley, a good-looking married man in his early thirties, a poet and a keen athlete. Rawnsley was leading the fight to preserve the natural beauty of the Lake District from the incursions of both industry and tourism. He was also preparing to form the Lake District Defence Society, which was the forerunner of The National Trust. The Rev. Hardwicke Rawnsley had a great effect on Beatrix, then 16. He admired her artistic talent, encouraged her growing interest in geology and archaeology, and impressed upon her his conviction of the importance of conservation and the protection of natural beauty.

In April of the following year, when Bertram was 11, it was decided to send him away to boarding school. The children's governess, Miss Hammond, took the opportunity to announce that as Beatrix had overtaken her in academic prowess, she would now leave the Potters' employ. The proposed changes left Beatrix with mixed feelings. She would certainly miss the company of young Bertram, and she had grown deeply attached to Miss Hammond, but perhaps at 17 the time had come for her to finish with lessons altogether and to concentrate on the one thing she cared most about, her painting. But her mother had other ideas and the day before Bertram left for school Mrs Potter appointed Miss Annie Carter to be Beatrix's companion and to teach her German, a language Miss Carter had learned while working as a governess in Germany.

Beatrix's companion was only three years older than she was

22 *Beatrix Potter with Bertram and Rupert Potter at
Coniston Bank*, R. Potter, September 1890

and the two young women soon became close friends. In her
over-sheltered life it had been almost impossible for Beatrix to
develop any relationship with contemporaries, other than one
or two cousins who occasionally came to tea, but here was
someone of her own age with whom she could go out to
exhibitions, walk in the park and, above all, talk, sometimes
in German, sometimes in English. Beatrix's journal for the
next few years sparkles with energy and enthusiasm and shows
a young lady emerging from her cloistered childhood. She
spent more time with her father, too, going with him on his
rounds of the galleries, and she often visited her recently-
widowed Grandmamma Potter. In one exciting week she even
accompanied her parents to Edinburgh, travelling up on *The
Flying Scotsman* 'at a great rate at times'.

Whatever new experiences Beatrix was enjoying there were
always two things that she never neglected – her animals and
her painting. She looked after Bertram's bat while he was at
school: 'It is a charming little creature, quite tame and
apparently happy as long as it has sufficient flies and raw meat.'
She bought some new lizards and she mourned the death of
Punch, the green frog they had kept for 'five or six years'. But
most important of all to Beatrix was her art:

It is all the same, drawing, painting, modelling, the ir-
resistible desire to copy any beautiful object which strikes
the eye. Why cannot one be content to look at it? I cannot
rest, I must draw, however poor the result, and when I have
a bad time come over me it is a stronger desire than ever, and
settles on the queerest things, worse than queer sometimes.
Last time, in the middle of September, I caught myself in the
back yard making a careful and admiring copy of the swill
bucket, and the laugh it gave me brought me round.

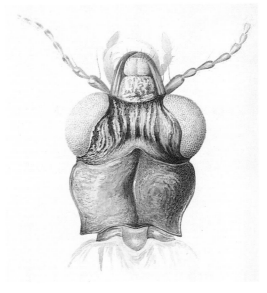

23 Microscopic study of a beetle (*Notiophilus
bigutattus*) (*detail of head and thorax*), 1887

The years when Annie Carter was at Bolton Gardens were probably the happiest time that Beatrix had ever known but they ended abruptly in June 1885 when Annie announced that she was leaving to prepare for her marriage the following year to Edwin Moore, a civil engineer. Although Beatrix was devastated, the loss of her companion was tempered slightly with the news that all lessons were at an end. On the other hand she now found herself alone with her parents for the first time in her life. Her journal records her increasing involvement in the household discussions of politics, and details her opinions of the pictures in the latest exhibitions at the Royal Academy or the Tate Gallery. She kept in close touch with the new Mrs Moore, and when occasionally Mrs Potter could spare the carriage, Beatrix drove to the Moores' small house in Bayswater with gifts for the expected child.

For the next five years the Potters spent their summers in the Lake District, mostly at Lingholm, a house magnificently sited on the wooded shore of Derwentwater, near Keswick, looking across to St Herbert's Island and beyond to Walla Crag. The woods were alive with red squirrels, the lake was perfect for fishing and boating, and Beatrix loved every moment of it. The air was good for her, too. While she had suffered from frequent colds and headaches all her life, she had recently been more seriously ill with rheumatic fever, which had affected her heart, and she needed to rebuild her strength.

In London, the menagerie on the third floor had been augmented by a rabbit, christened Benjamin H. Bouncer or Bounce for short. Benjamin was a source of great amusement for the whole family – when they got used to him, but for Beatrix he was the perfect model. She sketched and painted him from every angle and in every pose and he served as the model for her first commercial art.

Following a suggestion from her brother, she sent some of her rabbit drawings to Hildesheimer & Faulkner, a greetings-card publisher, who to her amazement and delight sent her a cheque for £6 by return, with a request for more. The company then made cards from some of her drawings, and others they used as illustrations to a set of verses by Frederic E. Weatherly in a booklet called *A Happy Pair*. At 24 Beatrix had begun her professional career. Her successful sale of drawings was followed by many more, until Beatrix was supplying regular card designs to Hildesheimer & Faulkner and illustrations for booklets and annuals to Ernest Nister. With the confidence this gave her, Beatrix then sent some sketches and a booklet to a number of children's book publishers, among them Frederick Warne, who, although they returned them as unsuitable, expressed an interest in 'any ideas or drawings in book form'. It was an area that Beatrix had not yet considered but she already thought that one day she might try her hand at it.

For the summer of 1892 the Potters returned to Scotland for the first time in eleven years, taking a small house in Birnam,

24 *Beatrix Potter with Benjamin*, September 1891

25 *Portrait of Beatrix Potter*, A. F. Mackenzie, Birnam, ?1892

26 *Strobilomyces floccopus*
(Old Man of the Woods),
September 1893

not far from Dalguise, called Heath Park. The family's spirits
were at a low ebb. Bertram was being sent to Oxford in the
hope that it might distract him from a worrying tendency to
drink too much; Beatrix was badly missing her grandmother,
who had died the previous September, and they were all
having to face the inevitable sale of Camfield Place.

Heath Park was too small for the usual Potter holiday guests
so everyone settled down to their own amusements. Rupert
and Bertram fished together and then went their separate ways
with camera and easel. On some days Mrs Potter and Beatrix
drove out in the pony cart to visit friends from the Dalguise
days, on others Beatrix indulged in her new interest in photography, or sketched and painted the surrounding landscape
and made meticulous watercolour studies of the many species
of fungus she found in the local woods. She also ensured regular
exercise and outings for Benjamin, whom she had brought
with her from London in a basket, and she wrote letters to
Annie Moore, and sent her pictures for her fast-increasing
family. The Scottish air worked its magic and when the time
came to head south the Potters were ready for the winter.

They holidayed in Scotland for the next two summers and it
was on one of these visits, from a house in Dunkeld called
Eastwood, that Beatrix wrote the letter to 5-year-old Noel
Moore that was to become one of the most famous letters ever
written. It began: 'My dear Noel, I don't know what to write to
you, so I shall tell you a story about four little rabbits whose
names were Flopsy, Mopsy, Cottontail and Peter.'

The faithful Benjamin had been replaced by Peter Piper, a
rabbit with a great liking for performing tricks, a talent that
Beatrix encouraged for the entertainment of visiting children.

27 *Portrait of Noel Moore*, Baker,
Cambridge, December 1910

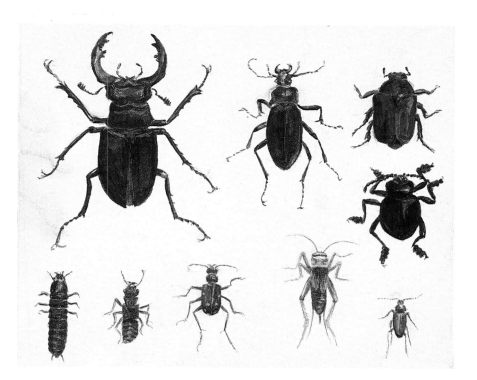

28 Nine beetles, *c.* 1885?

29 *Portrait of Beatrix Potter*, Delmar Banner, 1969

Like Benjamin, Peter proved to be an invaluable model for Beatrix and she made sure that he was kept comfortable – in a box with a rug before the fire in the old schoolroom. He was also a source of amusement and a considerable friend to her for, though she was nearing 30, she was alone for much of the time. She left Bolton Gardens now and then, to visit cousins in Gloucestershire and Denbigh or to accompany her parents on their spring excursions to Weymouth and on their annual holidays, but most of the time Beatrix spent in London. Her interests had always been varied and now to her drawing and photography she had added the study of fossils and insects, making regular visits to the Natural History Museum. She was taking lessons in Platinotype printing, learning Shakespeare's plays by heart – 'I learned six more or less in a year' – and for some time she had been making a study of spores, experimenting with cultivating new spores and making detailed drawings of the slides under her microscope. Entirely on her own and without help from anyone she was becoming extremely knowledgeable on the subject.

One day, Beatrix's uncle, Sir Henry Roscoe, suggested that she might bring her drawings to Kew Gardens where he would introduce her to the Director, his friend Mr Thiselton-Dyer. The result was a ticket to visit and to study at Kew, an opportunity Beatrix accepted with alacrity and one that she made much use of. After a great deal of work she became convinced that she had discovered a way to grow spores. But it was when she sought help at Kew to prove her discovery that she came up against a wall of professional jealousy. Her claims were virtually dismissed. Beatrix persisted, detailing her research in a paper entitled, 'On the Germination of the Spores

30 *Portrait of Marjorie, Winifred, Norah and Joan Moore, 1900*

of *Agaricineae* by Miss Helen B. Potter'. The following year, on 1 April 1897, her paper was presented to the Linnean Society of London, not by Beatrix, as ladies were not allowed to attend the Society's meetings, but by the very man at Kew who had earlier been so dismissive of her claims (*see also p. 91*).

One of the delights of Beatrix's life in London were her visits to the Moore family who had moved, some years before, into a house on the edge of Wandsworth Common. There were now six children under thirteen and Annie was virtually bringing them up single-handed, as Edwin was often abroad for long spells. Beatrix was fascinated by this large, bustling family, their life so different from anything she had ever known, and she much admired the way that Annie coped, instilling discipline with a firm but loving hand. The children looked forward to Beatrix's visits, too, for more often than not she arrived with a rabbit or a basket of white mice which she let loose in the room for them to play with. The picture letters that Beatrix sent when she went away or whenever they were ill were kept especially carefully by them all, the oldest girl, Marjorie, tying hers into a bundle with yellow ribbon.

The Potters now spent every summer in the Lake District, making sure that their chosen home was always near to water. Holehird overlooked Lake Windermere, Eeswyke in Near Sawrey was on Esthwaite, but their favourite house of all

31 Mouse dancing a jig, *The Story of Miss Moppet*, p. 36, 1906

32 (above) Fossils, some found at Nanny Lane above Troutbeck (*detail*), 1895

33 (right) *Aleuria (Peziza) aurantia* (Orange Peel Fungus) among fallen leaves, October 1893

remained Lingholm. On most days Beatrix and Bertram drove out together through the valleys and woods in the pony and trap, Beatrix in search of fossils or fungus, Bertram seeking a good vantage point from which to paint. Beatrix was growing to love this countryside and she wrote enthusiastically in her journal of 'the ideal beauty of Coniston', of 'the wonderful view over Troutbeck Tongue. There is a largeness and silence going up into the hills.'

Hardwicke Rawnsley remained a close friend of the family and particularly of Beatrix and, although he was a very busy man, they saw much of him. He had moved from Wray to be the vicar of Crosthwaite, a village just the other side of Keswick from Lingholm, and with his wife had set up a school for the industrial arts. As well as being Honorary Canon of Carlisle and Honorary Secretary of the newly-formed National Trust for Places of Historic Interest or Natural Beauty, he was a prolific author, writing sonnets and guides to the Lake District and a widely popular collection of verses for children. It was because of this last publication that Beatrix turned to her old friend for advice when, in 1900, she decided to write and illustrate a book for children herself: *The Tale of Peter Rabbit and Mr. McGregor's Garden* 'by H. B. Potter'. It was based on the letter written all those years ago from Dunkeld, borrowed back from Noel Moore and copied out into an exercise book.

Canon Rawnsley agreed that Beatrix's story might well find a publisher and agreed to help her. Their enthusiasm began to ebb only when time and again the book was returned to them without an offer. There was one expression of interest but only on condition that the size of the book was enlarged – and that was something that Beatrix refused even to consider. At last she lost patience. If no publisher would take the book, then Beatrix would pay to have it printed and publish it herself. On 16 December 1901 *The Tale of Peter Rabbit* by Beatrix Potter was ready, in an edition of 250 copies, most of which the author (and publisher) gave away, though selling a few at 1/2d each – 6p in today's money.

Meanwhile, Hardwicke Rawnsley had not given up hope of

finding a commercial publisher for Beatrix, even going to the length of rewriting her story himself in rhyme, and he had attracted the attention of Frederick Warne, to whom Beatrix had sent her drawings ten years before. To his considerable disappointment they asked for the rhymes to be replaced 'by simple narration', and also for all the illustrations to be in colour. Beatrix was easily able to supply the former but she was hesitant about the colour until persuaded that Warne would still be able to publish the book at a price that children could afford. She also had to allow time for her parents to become accustomed to the idea that their daughter was in a position to earn some money of her own. Even though Beatrix was in her mid-thirties, as the unmarried daughter of the house her first loyalty and duty was expected to be to her parents.

The Warne edition of *The Tale of Peter Rabbit* was published on 2 October 1902, all of its first printing of 8,000 copies having been sold even before publication.

Meanwhile Beatrix was arranging for the private publication of a second book, a tale she had written as a Christmas present for Freda Moore the previous year, based on a true story she heard while staying with her cousin in Gloucestershire. When she had prepared Freda's version Beatrix had painted twelve watercolours for the book but now she redrew the pictures in black-and-white, for so much colour would be too expensive for her small edition. She had 500 copies printed of *The Tailor of Gloucester* and distributed them herself, sending one copy to Norman Warne, her publisher.

Following the success of *Peter Rabbit*, Warne were anxious for Beatrix to do a second book for them but Norman Warne found *The Tailor of Gloucester* too long and with too many rhymes and Christmas carols holding up the flow, and he suggested that they publish a considerably shortened version. Beatrix had half expected that and although she agreed to his request she had already started another book altogether, this time a story originally written for Norah Moore about some naughty squirrels. Beatrix worked on both *The Tale of Squirrel Nutkin* and *The Tailor of Gloucester* while she was staying with her cousin at Melford Hall in Suffolk in the late spring. The books were published within two months of each other, both in time for Christmas 1903.

All Beatrix's dealings with her publishers were through Norman Warne, the youngest of the three brothers who had taken over the firm in Bedford Street, Covent Garden, from their father. It was with Norman that she discussed her contracts and to him that she sent her ideas. He in turn saw that her proofs were sent on time and that her instructions for alterations were carried out. They exchanged letters nearly every day, whether Beatrix was in Bolton Gardens or in the Lake District and their friendship was deepening. Norman, the youngest of a family of six, lived with his widowed mother and his unmarried sister, Millie, in the Warne family house in

34 Mr Tod looks up at Melford Hall, from 'The Fox and the Stork', ?1919

35 *Portrait of Norman Warne*

36 *The north side of Bedford Square*, drawn from
No. 8, the home of the Warnes, November 1905

Bedford Square. He was a gentle, good-looking man, undoubtedly his mother's favourite and warmly cared for by her
and Millie. He was intrigued by Beatrix, admiring of her
undoubted talent, and he looked forward to her increasingly
frequent visits to his office – though she never came without a
chaperone. He invited her to Bedford Square to meet his
family and she and Millie struck up an immediate friendship,
discovering that they had much in common.

Beatrix was enjoying this new aspect of her life very much,
even though she was working harder than she had ever done
before. She was increasingly responsible for the running of
Bolton Gardens and always loyal to the sometimes unreason-
able demands of her mother. Her own work she had to fit in
whenever she could. She had made a Peter Rabbit doll, which
she observed 'would be in demand at Harrods', and she was
preparing a new book, a sequel to *Peter Rabbit*, about his cousin
Benjamin Bunny. By the end of 1903, with sales of *Peter Rabbit*
over 50,000 copies, her royalties were mounting up and she
bought a field in Near Sawrey, close to Lakefield (now
Eeswyke), one of the Potters' Lake District holiday houses.

Beatrix was just finishing *The Tale of Benjamin Bunny* when
she called on Norman for some practical help. Knowing that
he was good at carpentry she asked him if he would make her a
new cage for her mice. She wanted one with a glass side to it so
that she could draw the mice as they scurried up and down to

their nest, for she had an idea for a book about two mice who raided a doll's house. The model for the house would be the one that Norman had recently made for his niece, Winifred, and Beatrix planned to journey down to Surbiton to draw it. Norman was delighted to help her and he invited Beatrix to lunch with his sister and her family, a visit that was distinctly frowned upon by Mrs Potter who was beginning to sense that her daughter's friendship with Mr Warne had gone far enough.

38 'Once upon a time there was a very beautiful doll's-house', *The Tale of Two Bad Mice*, p. 8, 1904

The Tale of Two Bad Mice was published, with *The Tale of Benjamin Bunny*, in September 1904 and by the end of the year there were 30,000 copies in print. Meanwhile Beatrix was already at work on two more books. For some years she had kept a pet hedgehog called Mrs Tiggy-winkle, whom she took everywhere with her in a cardboard box, and the creature was the perfect model for the washerwoman heroine of one book, a story Beatrix had first written four years before while staying at Lingholm. The second book was to be about a Pomeranian dog called Duchess, a cat called Ribby and a rather special pie with a crust held up by a patty-pan. As well as the two books, Beatrix was also designing wallpaper and devising a Peter Rabbit board game. She had little time to worry about her mother's disapproval.

For support in her work Beatrix turned to Norman, the one person who always gave her encouragement. His admiration for her over the years had turned into something deeper and, in the summer of 1905, he ventured to propose marriage. Beatrix was overjoyed and accepted at once but she had not foreseen her parents' reaction. Their beloved only daughter, admittedly now nearly 39, was their prop and stay, they relied on her to look after them, to take them on holiday, and here she was proposing to marry 'into trade'. They would do everything in their power to prevent it.

Poor Beatrix was torn in two. While acknowledging her duty to her parents, she was much attracted to this gentle man and she was determined to marry him. After some argument and discord, a compromise was reached. Beatrix would wear Norman's ring but no announcement would be made and no one outside the two immediate families would be told about the engagement.

It was a difficult and emotional time for Beatrix and she

found distraction and solace in her work. *The Tale of Mrs. Tiggy-Winkle* and *The Pie and the Patty-Pan* were finished and in proof before she set off to stay with her uncle in Wales. When she called at the office to say goodbye to Norman she discovered that he was not there, having been taken ill a few days before. She was never to see him again. On 25 August 1905 Norman Dalziel Warne died of pernicious anaemia at his home in Bedford Square. He was 37.

Beatrix was devastated, her shock made all the worse by the suddenness of the tragedy. She was unable to talk to anyone about her grief, for no one knew of her relationship with Norman, or if they did they disapproved, and the thought of returning to Bolton Gardens and facing the obvious relief of her parents was more than she could bear. She was rescued by Millie who invited her to stay in Bedford Square, and together they sought distraction from their loss in Norman's young niece, and visited his grave in Highgate Cemetery. From Bedford Square Beatrix went to the Lake District, to Near Sawrey, where earlier in the year she had bought a working farm called Hill Top. She had arranged for the farm manager, John Cannon, to stay and she went to see how he was getting on. Their discussions about pig farming and the accuracy of the butter scales proved to be ideal distractions.

Norman's work at Warne had been taken over by his brother, Harold, and before she left for Sawrey Beatrix had persuaded him to let her go ahead with an idea for a book about

39 (left) 'Butter and milk from the farm', *The Pie and the Patty-Pan*, frontispiece, 1905

40 (above) *Beatrix Potter at Hill Top, Near Sawrey*

41 Heads of pigs (*detail*), ?1910

42 *Beatrix Potter with Bertram and Rupert Potter at Lindeth How*, R. Potter, 11 August 1911

43 The Puddle-Ducks of Sawrey, *The Tale of Tom Kitten*, p. 35, 1907

a frog. In Sawrey she had the opportunity to make sketches of suitable backgrounds – and of frogs. *The Tale of Mr. Jeremy Fisher* was published the following July, and for Christmas 1906 two further Beatrix Potter titles were added to the Warne list, a pair of panoramic picture books for younger children, *The Story of A Fierce Bad Rabbit* and *The Story of Miss Moppet*.

Beatrix was now spending more and more of her time in the Lake District, sometimes for just a few days snatched away from the household routine, sometimes for the longer summer holidays with her parents. She had alterations made to Hill Top so that she could stay there when she was on her own without disturbing the Cannons and she began to be more seriously involved in the running of the farm. She and John Cannon had decided to breed sheep, choosing to concentrate on Herdwicks, a hardy breed native to the area but disappearing from the fells due to the slump in the demand for carpet wool. On her choice of Herdwicks Beatrix was much influenced by the founder of the Herdwick Sheepbreeders' Association, her old friend Hardwicke Rawnsley.

The next few years were extraordinary ones for Beatrix. She was in her early forties and at the height of her productive powers, and she used every moment of her waking hours to the full. Her parents still expected her to accompany them on their spring holidays and to take them away from London for the long summer months. Fortunately for Beatrix the latter were now spent regularly in the Lake District but the Potters were not entirely in sympathy with her farming interests and found her frequent visits to Hill Top an irritant. Her books published at that time reflect her involvement in the farm and her pictures show her love for the countryside round about. *The Tale of Tom Kitten* is set in the house and garden of Hill Top, as is *The Roly-Poly Pudding* (later to be called *The Tale of Samuel Whiskers*). *The Tale of Jemima Puddle-Duck* is set on the farm, and *Ginger and Pickles* in the village. Only *The Tale of the Flopsy Bunnies* breaks the pattern and that has for its setting the garden of Gwaynynog, the house of her Uncle Fred Burton in Denbigh where she had been staying when she heard the news of Norman's death. She went back there every year and had built up a good collection of sketches which proved invaluable when she eventually came to do this sequel to *Peter Rabbit* and *Benjamin Bunny*.

In 1909 Beatrix bought a second farm in Near Sawrey, Castle Farm, which was not far from Hill Top and had a cottage that afforded a fine view over her holding. She was now the owner of a considerable amount of land in and around the village and in all her property dealings she took the advice of William Heelis, a partner in a firm of local solicitors, who kept her informed of land coming on to the market and attended sales on her behalf. William Heelis was becoming intrigued by this lady from London who shared his love for the country in which he had been born and brought up. In the ensuing years

44 Beatrix Potter with her ducklings

45 (below) The front cover of Peter Rabbit's Painting Book, 1911

46 (below right) Early Peter Rabbit merchandise, Derrick E. Witty, 1986

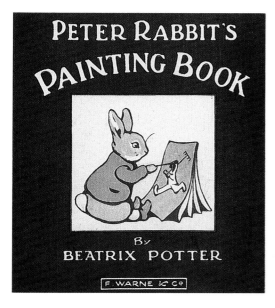

his intrigue turned into admiration and then affection, and in the late summer of 1912, William Heelis asked Beatrix to be his wife.

Beatrix had also grown very fond of this kind and understanding man and as there was no doubt at all in her mind that she wanted to marry him, she accepted his proposal. However, once again she had not foreseen that there would be opposition from her parents. Rupert Potter was now 80 and not at all well; his wife was aware that, should their daughter marry, they would have to find someone else to look after them in their declining years.

The last few years had taken their toll on Beatrix, too, and she was not sure whether she was strong enough to persuade them to let her go. She now had seventeen books in the Warne catalogue, as well as a painting book and a whole range of merchandise, from china tea-sets to children's slippers. *The Tale of Mrs. Tittlemouse* had been published in 1910, *The Tale of Timmy Tiptoes* in 1911, and Beatrix had delivered to Harold Warne the text and illustrations for a longer book than usual, *The Tale of Mr. Tod*, a story set in the hills around Sawrey. Beatrix was exhausted and during the winter she fell ill, with a serious illness that once again affected her heart. It took her many weeks to recover and she was forced to spend most of the time lying on her back resting. Being Beatrix, she used the time to invent a story about an adventurous young piglet called Pigling Bland.

Gradually Helen and Rupert Potter's opposition to their daughter's marriage began to weaken, helped not a little by Bertram's revelation that he had been married for seven years, his long absences from home not being due to his supposed 'painting expeditions' after all. So Beatrix's wedding preparations were put in hand; alterations were begun at the cottage at Castle Farm where Beatrix and William Heelis had chosen to make their home – and Beatrix delivered her new book to her publisher.

47 'Quite a speckled pig': Cross-patch in bed with measles, attended by Aunt Pettitoes and Beatrix Potter. Unused picture for *The Tale of Pigling Bland*, 1913

The Tale of Pigling Bland was published just before Beatrix Potter married William Heelis at St Mary Abbot's in Kensington on 14 October 1913. After a short honeymoon in London the couple went up to Sawrey, but the next few months were difficult ones for them. Rupert Potter's health had worsened and he now became seriously ill. Beatrix made eight journeys from Sawrey to London in the first four months of 1914 and her father died on 8 May. She brought her mother up to stay in lodgings in Sawrey just as the country was plunged into the war that was to change the whole condition of a nation.

The four years of war were just as depressing and heartbreaking for everyone at Sawrey as in London, although the family were fortunate to suffer no direct loss. Willie continued his practice as a solicitor from his office in Hawkshead, while Beatrix concentrated on the farms, infuriated by the bureaucracy and by the weather. At the same time she was anxious about her publishers who appeared to be using the war as an excuse not to pay her royalties, although she knew that her books were still selling in their thousands. Her fears were realized when on 27 April 1917 Harold Warne was convicted of forgeries amounting to £20,000 (some half a million pounds in today's money) and sent to prison for eighteen months. Frederick Warne was on the edge of bankruptcy.

As one of the company's most important authors, whose work was a major asset, and as someone who so nearly became a Warne herself, Beatrix was asked for help by the third Warne brother, Fruing, who was faced with saving the business. It had been four years since Beatrix had produced a new book, partly due to her unease about the company and partly because of her family commitments, but now she agreed to do what she could, though she certainly had no time to write or illustrate an original story. *Appley Dapply's Nursery Rhymes* were a selection from a book that had been in the making since 1902 and, together with two new painting books, it made a strong contribution to the depleted fortunes of Frederick Warne. In 1919 part of the money owed to Beatrix was paid in allotted shares, a move that tied her even more closely to her publisher.

48 *Beatrix Potter with William Heelis on their wedding day*, R. Potter, 14 October 1913

49 *Beatrix Potter with Kep at Castle Cottage, Near Sawrey*

There was another new book in 1918, *The Tale of Johnny Town-Mouse*, this time a story, rather than rhymes, and retold from an Aesop fable. The illustrations were clearly set in Sawrey and in Hawkshead and Beatrix had to fit in her work on them between the demands of the farm and attending her brother's funeral, for Bertram had died while working in his garden at Ancrum. He was only 46 but his years of drinking had taken their toll.

The following year Beatrix persuaded her mother to leave London permanently and to settle in the Lake District, buying for her Lindeth How in Windermere, a house in which they had stayed one summer. Though Helen Potter was in good health, she was entering her eighties. Having her nearby would make it easier for Beatrix to keep an eye on her and she and Willie would be able to settle down to life in Sawrey.

And it was not all work. Willie was an active golfer and a good bowler, he enjoyed country dancing and a day's shooting. Beatrix did not dance but she often went with Willie to watch and to draw, and she was becoming increasingly involved in village activities. She helped to establish a nursing trust linking three local parishes and she was a member of many of the local committees. She was never happier, though, than when she was with her animals. 'I have cows and sheep and horses, and poultry. I look after the poultry and rabbits and

50 The hen house, *The Tale of Pigling Bland*, p. 41, 1913

pony and my own particular pet pig . . . I seem to be able to tame any sort of animal.' There was little time left for new books and somehow there was no longer the urge to produce them any more.

Frederick Warne on the other hand felt rather differently. There had been no new Beatrix Potter books for three years now and, though the company was beginning to get back on its feet, something was needed from its star performer. As long ago as 1907 there had been discussions about both French and German translations of a number of the Potter books and now Warne decided to publish French language editions of *Peter Rabbit* (*Pierre Lapin*) and *Benjamin Bunny* (*Jeannot Lapin*), advertising them as 'the new Beatrix Potters' for 1921. When Beatrix agreed to their publication she could not have foreseen the avenues that they were to open for her.

One day in 1921 she was visited by an American librarian who had been sent to France to help reorganize the children's libraries devastated by the war. Anne Carroll Moore was the Superintendent of Children's Work in the New York Public Library and having long been an admirer of Beatrix's work she had bought fifty copies of each of the French editions for the new libraries. Now she wanted to meet the author. Beatrix had always discouraged personal publicity and usually refused to meet any fans but Miss Moore's work intrigued her and in this instance she agreed. The meeting was a great success and Beatrix was stimulated by talking to someone who knew from experience that nothing was too good for children, to a woman who had achieved considerable status in her chosen profession. It was the start of a friendship that was to last for the rest of Beatrix's life. Anne Carroll Moore even persuaded her not to keep her readers waiting any longer for a new book and *Cecily Parsley's Nursery Rhymes* was ready for publication in time for Christmas 1922.

After the book was finished Beatrix once again turned her attention to farming and in particular to sheep farming. In

51 Head of a sheep

52 *Beatrix Potter with Harry Lamb at the Eskdale Woolpack Show*, M. C. Fair, 1931

53 Fleecy Flock's wool shop, *The Tale of Little Pig Robinson*, p. 72, 1930

1924 she added to her property, buying one of the most spectacularly situated hill farms in the Lake District, Troutbeck Park Farm. To look after the sheep there, the majority of them her favourite Herdwicks, she appointed a new shepherd, Tom Storey. Beatrix now had two large flocks of sheep, the old pedigree flock on the low ground in Sawrey and the main flock up on the fells above Troutbeck. In the following spring a thousand ewes were lambed in Troutbeck alone. London seemed a long way away and the pressures of publishing no longer important.

It was two years before Beatrix worked on another book, and during that time she was never idle, whether it was walking the fells to look for lost sheep, or journeying across Lake Windermere on the ferry to Bowness to visit her mother. She welcomed an increasing number of American visitors to Hill Top, which she kept solely as a place in which to draw and to display her collection of fine furniture and china. She took Willie's brother, Arthur, into Castle Cottage and nursed him until he died. Although she did complete *Peter Rabbit's Almanac* for Frederick Warne in 1927, it was not published until the following year, and she was not happy with the way it was produced. Her heart was with her sheep and together with Tom Storey, whom she moved from Troutbeck to Hill Top, she began to breed Herdwicks for showing. Within a short time she was regularly winning cups for her ewes and in due course she became a respected judge at local agricultural shows. By 1930 Beatrix was the first woman President of the Herdwick Sheepbreeders' Association.

In 1929 an American publisher, Alexander McKay of David McKay, Philadelphia, persuaded Beatrix to allow him to publish a long short story she had been writing for years about a guinea pig. Beatrix found great difficulty in doing the illustrations for *The Fairy Caravan*, 'My eyes have lost the faculty for seeing clean colours', but she eventually managed to complete seven colour plates and to supply a host of line drawings.

Frederick Warne were understandably angry that Beatrix had not offered the book to them for publication, but she insisted that as it was clearly set in and around Sawrey it was too autobiographical and revealing for her to allow it to be seen in England – though when it was ready she presented specially bound copies of the American edition to all her local friends.

The Fairy Caravan was followed only a year later by *The Tale of Little Pig Robinson*, again commissioned by David McKay but this time also published by Frederick Warne, though they chose to leave out twelve of the drawings. The income from her increasing list of books enabled Beatrix to buy an important new property which was in danger of being split up, the Monk Coniston Estate, some 4,000 acres stretching from Little Langdale to Coniston. She then immediately sold over half of it to the National Trust, promising that the rest of the estate would come to them on her death in memory of her Grandfather and Grandmother Crompton, who had once owned land in Coniston.

Beatrix was by this time in her mid sixties and her mother in her nineties. Mrs Potter had kept remarkably well, cosseted and protected by her faithful servants in Lindeth How, but now she was fading away, literally dying of old age. She died just before Christmas 1932, and her death severed Beatrix's last link with her family life in London.

The 1930s for Beatrix were filled with responsibilities towards the tenants and their cottages on her land, with sheep and cattle sales in the district, and with discussions with the National Trust over the transfer back to them of the management of the Monk Coniston Estate. She found time too to keep an eye on the large Heelis family of nephews and cousins, and to invite her own cousins and their children to Sawrey for the holidays. It was during one of these visits that Beatrix so admired the courage and stamina of her cousin Stephanie's Pekinese dog that she acquired two Pekinese puppies for herself, Tzusee and Chuleh. Both Beatrix and Willie became very attached to the Pekes and hated being separated from them, even for a day.

In the late 1930s Beatrix's health began to worsen, and in April 1939, just as Hitler was marching into Czechoslovakia, she was admitted to the Women's Hospital in Liverpool for a hysterectomy. Not expecting to survive her operation, Beatrix

54 *Beatrix Potter with Tzusee and Chuleh*

wrote movingly to her next-door neighbours, asking them to look after Willie and to urge him to marry again. 'The misfortune is that I have acquiesced in such slovenly untidy-ness [sic] and unpunctuality that I am afraid that no old maidly lady would put up with it and he is too old to remodel.'

Though gravely ill for some days after the operation, Beatrix called on all her strength and slowly over the following weeks she recovered and was able to return to Sawrey. By June she was in Troutbeck watching the men clipping the sheep and herding the cattle into the fold: 'A fine sight, about 30 black cows with their calves at foot, and a magnificent white bull.' And like everyone else in the country, Beatrix was preparing for the inevitable war, looking out her blackout curtains from the last war and laying in stores of sugar and dog biscuits.

The first few months of the war made little impact on Sawrey and the sound of the occasional aeroplane passing high overhead brought everyone outside in great excitement, but as the months turned into a year the shortages and the restrictions began to be felt. Willie was on the War Agricultural Committee and was a reserve policeman; Beatrix started breeding rabbits to help with the meat ration. Both of them had been victims of the 1940 influenza epidemic that had swept the country and Beatrix had reluctantly to admit that she was beginning to feel old. She now leaned heavily on a stick, her bowed figure a familiar sight all over the district, for she still regularly supervised the work on her farms.

In December 1941 the Japanese attacked Pearl Harbor and the United States was in the war. For Beatrix the news brought a certain relief for it meant that she no longer need be critical nor regretful in her letters to her friends across the Atlantic.

55 Timmy Willie goes to beg a little milk,
The Tale of Johnny Town-Mouse, p. 48, 1918

56 *Beatrix Potter judging at
Keswick*, British Photo Press,
Barrow-in-Furness

57 *Beatrix Potter with a young visitor (Alison Hart) at Near Sawrey*, Reginald Hart, September 1943

Her readers kept up a regular flow of enthusiastic fan letters, and her friends were now sending food parcels as well as books. The food was especially appreciated, particularly the lemon juice, for though Beatrix was certainly not starving she was increasingly a victim of colds, 'flu and bronchitis. In September 1943 bronchitis struck again, and this time she found it hard to shake off. What was worse, it was affecting her heart, weakened by her childhood rheumatic fever. She was still confined to the house in mid-December, frustrated but cheerful. 'If an old person of 77 continues to play these games – well it can be done once too often. I have plenty to do indoors and the little dogs are great company – most efficient footwarmers.'

Ten days later Beatrix had a relapse and on the evening of 22 December 1943 she died. Her husband was by her side and though heartbroken he requested that there would be no mourning, no flowers and no letters. After her cremation in Blackpool on the last day of the year, Beatrix's ashes were scattered by her favourite shepherd, Tom Storey, on the land she loved so much.

In her will, Beatrix left nearly everything to Willie for his lifetime, but she stipulated that the royalties and rights in her books should go to Norman Warne's nephew, Frederick Warne Stephens. Her farm and property of over 4,000 acres she gave to the National Trust, who strive to preserve this unique landscape, timeless evidence of the reality of so many of her books.

J.T.

2

THE YOUNG ARTIST AND EARLY INFLUENCES

Trying to assess the various influences on the work of an artist is rather like trying to unscramble an egg. If the egg has not been very well scrambled it is possible to trace some of its constituent ingredients – a little white among the yellow, for example – but for the most part it has become something quite different from the sum of its parts. In the work of Beatrix Potter we can sometimes catch a glimpse of this influence or that, especially when she was young, but for the most part the artist she became was the well-scrambled result of all she had seen and absorbed.

The young Beatrix Potter produced as many paintings and drawings as most children of her age, but this early work is of interest because we know how her art developed and want to understand its beginnings. If Beatrix Potter had just become a writer, her work with pencil or paintbrush would have evoked little comment. For whatever we like to say about her earliest surviving paintings and drawings, they are no more remarkable in themselves than the work of any intelligent 8- or 9-year-old, but unlike most children Beatrix Potter's interests were not

58 (above) *Foxgloves and periwinkle*, 9 February 1876

59 (right) *Huts on a hillside*, October 1877

60 Grapes and peaches,
October 1883

dissipated as she grew older, and she continued to work at her art. By the age of 12, for example, she was already showing considerable talent, while the work done in her early teens was remarkably mature. By the time Beatrix was 16 her work could be considered on its own merit. Anyone who could produce a painting as accomplished as *The Library, Wray Castle*, executed when she was 17, needs no excuse on the score of age.

Beatrix Potter was born into a family which had a lively interest in the fine arts. Her father and mother both sketched, her relatives, including her parents, collected pictures and for all of them gallery-going was a regular event, in which Beatrix participated as she got older. It was also quite a bookish background – at least as far as her father was concerned – and Beatrix herself was encouraged to read, enjoy and look after the books she was given. Hers was a lively and alert mind, a view which is confirmed by the entries in the early years of her journal, which she started when she was about 14.

Her family was probably the most important influence on Beatrix, especially during her formative years. Much has been written in the past about Beatrix's repressed upbringing, which is only now being gradually disproved to some extent. The ruler of her young life was undoubtedly her nurse – this was typical for all children of her age and class – but she had some contact with her parents and the young Beatrix seems to have been an attractive, merry and outgoing little girl. Her shyness and withdrawal came later. We know little of her early relationship with her mother, though surviving photographs show them in a reasonably happy association – again, the

61 *The Library, Wray Castle*, July 1882

change may have occurred as she grew older and her mother became more demanding. But her relationship with her father, especially when she was a very young child, was delightful as some of the early letters between them show.

We should not be put off by the fierce and whiskered appearance of Rupert Potter, since he merely conformed to the style of the day. He was a man of considerable intelligence and literary and artistic taste, and not without a sense of humour – which Mrs Potter may well have lacked. He was just the man to appreciate a lively and intelligent daughter, who no doubt was constantly asking questions and seeking information. A child, moreover, who was likely to be influenced by a father who took an interest in her – which Rupert Potter undoubtedly did, as the many photographs he took of Beatrix at various ages prove.

One of the more remarkable survivals among the Beatrix Potter material now in the Victoria and Albert Museum is a sketchbook which belonged to Rupert Potter as a young man. It bears the inscription 'R. Potter Sep 1 1853 Broughton in Furness, Dinting Lodge Glossop' and contains a wide range of pen-and-ink drawings. It is likely that a number of these were copied from books, or journals such as *Punch*, but one suspects that some of the pictures may well have been adapted by Rupert Potter to suit his own fancy and sense of humour – which is in evidence here. Even more remarkable, we find a very real foreshadowing of Jemima Puddle-duck, in the illustration of a flying duck wearing a bonnet. Was this taken from a book in Rupert's library – and did Beatrix see it? These various caricatures and drawings might be considered as the mere *jeu d'esprit* of a young man, except that he took the trouble to buy the sketchbook and then to preserve it.

But it is obvious that Rupert maintained his interest in actually making pictures – though one can never be quite sure how much was copied from existing illustrated books and how much he was merely influenced by their style. There exists a

62 *A corner of the schoolroom, 2 Bolton Gardens,* 26 November 1885

63, 64 Two pages from Rupert Potter's sketchbook, 1 September 1853

number of very fine drawings by him in the Victoria and Albert Museum collection, and also in other collections, and we know that he designed and painted some plates for the children's nursery. Beatrix says of him at a later stage: 'He can draw very well, but has hardly attempted water-colours, and never oil.' Perhaps one reason why he largely gave up art was because he realized that he lacked any technical training, and so felt frustrated. Certainly Beatrix implies that he easily became impatient with the technical difficulties of artists, mainly, she thought, because 'seeing Mr Millais paint so often and so easily would make a man hard on other painters'.

We are very fortunate in that Beatrix – and her family – were hoarders and did not willingly destroy things. As a result we possess two of her early sketchbooks, done when she was aged 8 and 9 respectively. It is very hard to look at them dispassionately, without being influenced by the knowledge of the artist she was to become. The first of these sketchbooks was not the sort that can be bought in a shop. It was one Beatrix made herself, out of sheets of paper, including some family writing-paper. Even at that early age she knew what a sketchbook was, and knew that she wanted one. The sketches it contains are good for an 8-year-old, but not outstanding. A few of the drawings are taken from things she could see around her, but the majority have been copied from books, which allowed her qualities of patience and application to come to the fore. The sketchbook was made at Dalguise during one of her long summer holidays, and it must have offered a useful occupation

65 A group of four dogs, R. Potter

66 (left) Page from sketchbook (age 8), 1875

67 (above) Page from sketchbook (age 9), 1876

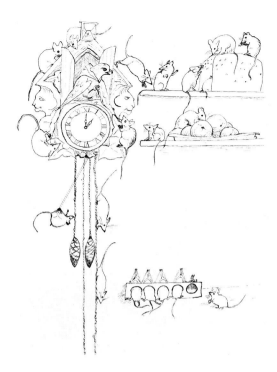

68 Drawing copied from *The Pipits* by Mrs Blackburn, sketchbook (age 10), 1876

69 Narcissus, a very early painting

to the lonely little girl during the many wet summer days which occur in that part of Scotland. But she obviously paid attention to what she drew: her caterpillar paintings, for example, are accompanied by written out information about them (150).

By 1876 her interests had widened and her next sketchbook has a considerable variety of drawings, some original and others taken from books. But what is especially noticeable about this sketchbook are the drawings of animals – and rabbits at that – clothed and active. There are rabbits skating, rabbits in a coach, rabbits on a sledge. They may well have come from one of her children's books, though if this was so the source has not yet been traced. But even if the drawings were second-hand, it does not detract from the fact that the young Beatrix chose to copy them. Also in this sketchbook are paintings of flowers and birds and, rather surprisingly, part of a Japanese print – a very fashionable object at that time.

Another sketchbook from later the same year, when she was 10, shows a further range of copying which once again reveals the books she was looking at and those which especially impressed her. We have a delightful drawing of a clock with some mice, taken from Mrs Blackburn's *The Pipits*, and a good copy of 'Mrs Bond' from Walter Crane's *The Baby's Opera* (81). There are also exotic scenes of animals, suggesting that she had access to her father's books too. We know from her journal of her joy in receiving a copy of Mrs Blackburn's *Birds drawn from Nature* as a tenth birthday present, and how she 'danced about the house with pride'. This particular anecdote, dating from the time when she later visited Mrs Blackburn in 1891, is one of the few glimpses of her own childhood that we get from Beatrix, as she recalls her younger self with her 'grimy little hands', which she had to wash before she was allowed to handle her new treasure.

To judge by the surviving drawings and painting, her most common subject was flowers, no doubt because they were available in town and country alike. But they must also have formed part of her formal training in art – indeed *The Art of Flower Painting* was among her early books. From 1878 to 1883 she studied with a Miss Cameron, and after her last lesson in May of that year she wrote:

> I have great reason to be grateful to her, though we were not on particularly good terms for the last good while. I have learnt from her freehand, model, geometry, perspective and a little water-colour flower painting. Painting is an awkward thing to teach except the details of the medium. If you and your master are determined to look at nature and art in two different directions you are sure to stick.

Beatrix Potter already had a mind of her own where art and nature were concerned, even at the age of 17. Later the same year she took a further series of lessons from a 'Mrs A.', which she confessed to finding rather disappointing. Apart from these two periods, Beatrix relied almost entirely on her own natural talent, aided by her frequent visits to galleries and her acute powers of observation.

A very important influence on Beatrix from the age of at least 16 was her regular gallery-visiting, often accompanying her father. The annual visit to the Royal Academy Summer Exhibition was for many people just a social event and the opening of the London season, but not for the young Beatrix. She went round the pictures with her catalogue, marking up her various points about the paintings and entering them in her coded journal. In the early years these comments are the clever remarks of a very young person, and made her smile at her younger self later on. But gradually they became much more informed (often with a touch of dry humour), and there can be no doubt that she learnt a lot from this constant and detailed study. In 1882 there was a portrait of her cousin Kate by Briton Rivière: '*Cupboard Love*, Kate Potter and Figaro and a slightly deformed pug. After all one has heard, it is not as bad as I expected. Should not have known Kate, but it is rather a pretty picture. The chief part of it, however, is taken up by the cupboard.' In 1883 she went to the first of her Winter Exhibitions at the Academy and was brought face to face with old masters for the first time. 'I never thought there *could* be such pictures', she enthused. But that did not stop her critical appraisal of them. Then again, father and daughter would go to various smaller private galleries, and her opinions here were also carefully recorded in her journal.

This suggests that Rupert Potter himself taught her a lot about pictures and how to look at them. As she got older there must have been some lively discussions between them, though one suspects that whatever Beatrix felt and confided to her journal, she may well have been more submissive to her father's opinion in public. This discussion about painting, and art in general, was probably commonplace in the Potter household, especially as Bertram was soon old enough to join in.

Bertram was born when Beatrix was nearly 6, which is quite a considerable age gap when thinking of brother and sister relationships. In this family, however, brother and sister were thrown very much together as they were both educated at home until Bertram was 11, and they had few young friends apart from cousins. So that, in spite of the fact that by the time Beatrix was 12 and becoming quite skilled in her drawing and Bertram was only a little boy of 6, they do seem to have shared a lot of activities together. Bertram too was encouraged to draw – and he had his sister's example before him as well as his father's. They drew each other: Beatrix did some sketches of Bertram at the age of about 9 and they show that from the start she had problems with figures and faces. Bertram had much more talent in this direction, and in one of his surviving sketchbooks – made when he was about 7 or 8 – there are some of his earliest recordings of his sister and mother. Like the rest

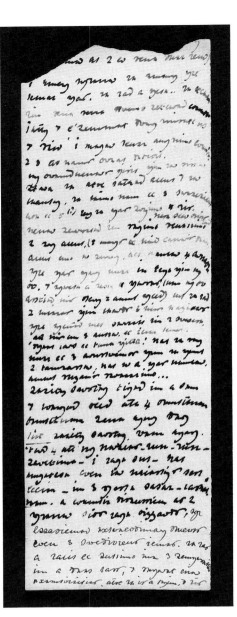

70 Fragment of code writing as used in the journal, including the 'Cecily Parsley' verse, c. 1884–6

71, 72 Drawings by Bertram
Potter (age 8 or 9)

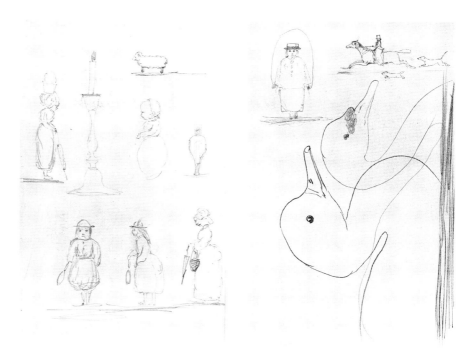

73 Study of ducks near a
river bank, Bertram Potter

74 Transfer print, *Mother rabbit
and five babies*, 1880

of the family he also made copies from the illustrated books of
the period, in neat, precise pen-and-ink sketches, though
occasionally he too indulged in flights of fancy.

They both tried their hand at making lino cuts and in using
various transfer methods, and at making prints. It would
appear that for this purpose they copied book illustrations,
since the same picture appears in work by both children and
their father. It was obviously a hobby which at that moment
they all shared. The prints are not especially good, but they are
a further example of the all-pervading interest in art in all its
forms. Bertram, who later took up art as a career, also did a
certain amount of etching, but we do not know that any work
by Beatrix in this medium survives. Although she tried her

75 Study of a rabbit (probably Benjamin Bouncer), 1880

hand at oil-painting, it is obvious that from the beginning her real love was watercolour. Watercolour is a very difficult medium for a young artist since, unlike oils, there can be no alteration once the paint has met the paper. On the other hand it has a spontaneity and a freshness which must have appealed to Beatrix at all stages of her career.

One of the features of the Potter nursery was that pets of all kinds were tolerated, and Beatrix and her brother took full advantage of this fact. Rabbits were always favourites among the smaller animals, and there is a charming letter to Beatrix written by her father from Dalguise in 1874, in which he mentions among other things 'the bunnies' he has seen on the lawn. Not only did Beatrix and Bertram keep pets but they also used them as subjects for drawings whenever the countryside of their holiday homes was denied to them. The very 'fine drawings of rabbits which Beatrix made in her early teens show her growing artistic competence as well as indicating her constant practice.

Bertram shared his sister's intense interest in the natural world and, like her, he had his share of pets. Perhaps their choice of favourites shows a subtle difference between their characters, since on the whole Beatrix went for gentler creatures such as mice and rabbits, while Bertram chose the biting and fighting jay which travelled with him. However, they obviously had many natural history interests in common. On one occasion when he was away, Bertram wrote to his sister (in reply to a letter from her): 'I suppose from what you say you will have to let lose [sic] the long-eared bats, as they will not eat meat. It is a great pity they are not easier to feed. As for the other, I think it would be almost wrong to let it go, as we might never catch another of that kind again. If he cannot be kept alive as I suppose he can't, you had better kill him, & stuff him as well as you can.' Nothing sentimental about either Bertram or Beatrix in their attitude to animals here! Moreover, Bertram reminds Beatrix to measure the animal carefully before she stuffs it, and he goes into considerable detail about the actual stuffing itself. No wonder they both fitted in to the life of breeders and farmers when they grew up.

76 Two studies of a bat with its wings spread (detail), 1885

Rupert Potter's real love was for the new art of photography. When a young man this must have appealed to him as a wonderful new invention with exciting possibilities – 'from today painting is dead' he may have echoed – and perhaps he felt that he too could have a place in this new science, which required both patience and money in its early stages. Judging by the number of frail sepia prints which have survived, the Potter household must eventually have been bulging with Rupert's photographs. Every holiday was well recorded, and from every angle. His family was expected to pose in all sorts of places and positions. It must be remembered that photography in its early years was not a matter of a quick snap but was a slow and laborious process. That Rupert was technically competent is obvious, and is further indicated by the number of times he appeared in his own photographs – which required elaborate setting up. It is also proved by the quality of his prints, many of which he made himself. But more important from the point of view of Beatrix's development were his 'artistic' compositions, where it was not just a case of posing a pretty picture.

In due course (and not surprisingly) Beatrix herself took up photography, inheriting one of her father's old cameras, and the pair of them would go off loaded with equipment on photographic expeditions. She learnt much of the art of composition from her father, as well as appreciating the usefulness of the photograph in storing up some of her summer scenes for winter painting. It is interesting to note that Rupert's ability was recognized in various ways. He was early voted a member of the Photographic Society of London, and he was often called upon by his friend John Everett Millais to

77 *Tenby*, R. Potter, April 1900

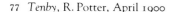

78 Newlands, near Keswick
(or Broad How, Troutbeck),
Bertram Potter, 1898
(*see also p. 164*)

79 *Landscape with trees and cliff*,
Helen Leech, undated

provide photographic models for the painter's own work.
Though he may not have continued his personal artistic
endeavours, there is no doubt that he was very proud of his
daughter's achievements, having his own copies of her little
works specially bound for his library.

Bertram does not seem to have shared his father's and sister's
interest in photography but remained true to his early love of
sketching. Eventually he decided he would be an artist, and an
artist he became – until he became a farmer in the Borders.
From the pictures which have survived he appears for the most
part to have been a competent but not inspired painter of
landscapes. It could be that his technique was not particularly
good, since many of his larger paintings, most of them in oils,

appear dark. But his sketches and etching show much greater ability. Nevertheless, he lacked the talent of his sister, and probably realized this only too well, settling down contentedly with his Scottish wife on the farm at Ashieburn.

We know little about Mrs Potter's interest in art, except that like most girls of her age and class she had instruction in the art of painting in watercolours and several of her works in this medium survive. She undoubtedly went the rounds of the fashionable exhibitions, for whatever else we may deduce about Mrs Potter we can assume she was always in the mode. But for the most part she appears in her many photographs as a well-dressed, precise and authoritative person, who only rarely permitted herself the liberty of a smile in front of the camera. She gives the appearance of a woman who would not suffer dirty or mischievous children very gladly, and Beatrix herself makes frequent reference later in her journal to her mother's difficult ways – though always admitting that she herself might be something of a difficult daughter.

But her family was not the only influence on Beatrix and her art. She was an avid reader, as we can tell from her journal, and her early sketches show that she had access to some of her father's illustrated books, including works on natural history. There may be hints of other children's books still hidden in her early sketches, but one which is quite clear is the copy from Walter Crane's *The Baby's Opera*. Crane was very popular at the time when Beatrix was young and it would not be surprising to find that such an up-to-date Aesthetic Movement artist was represented in the Potter household.

More important, because of its influence on her own art, was the work of Randolph Caldecott and she shared her appreciation of this artist with her father. There is an amusing passage in her journal for February 1884 (when Beatrix was nearly 18): 'Papa has become very extravagant. He went on the sly the other day and bought two little drawings of *The Frog*.' (This was Caldecott's *A Frog He Would A-Wooing Go*.) She also indicates that he had already acquired three coloured drawings from *Three Jovial Huntsmen*. They must have discussed Caldecott's work between them, and his pictures were presumably among those displayed on the walls of the house in Bolton Gardens, along with Mr Potter's other purchases which she mentions. Certainly two prints from one of Caldecott's toy books still hang at Hill Top to this day, and they have the maker's label on the back of the frame, indicating that they too came from the London house.

Randolph Caldecott was probably the most obvious influence on Beatrix Potter's own art. She knew his work from a young age, her father admired him, and his talent was very much in sympathy with her own. Sometimes we can see a direct reflection of the older artist in Beatrix's work, at other times it is just an indefinable way of handling colour or composition. *A Frog* is a particularly good example to consider. If

80, 81 'Mrs Bond' from *The Baby's Opera*, Walter Crane, 1876 (top), and (above) Beatrix's copy of it from sketchbook (age 10), 1876

82, 83 Two illustrations from *A Frog He Would A-Wooing Go*, Randolph Caldecott, 1883.

we look carefully through the pages of this particular Caldecott toy book, we continually see a foreshadowing of Jeremy Fisher, and even perhaps of Mr Jackson, while the rat with his hands comfortably crossed on his fat tummy is certainly the brother of Samuel Whiskers. Caldecott used a clear but light-toned palette, as did Beatrix, in contrast to the brighter colours of Walter Crane. He also made use of the space surrounding his pictures, whereas Crane tended to decorate every part of the page. It is interesting, too, to consider the line drawings by both Caldecott and Beatrix Potter, and the expressive economy which both brought to their pen-and-ink sketches. This shows up very well when we look at Caldecott's cat who is clearly saying, of the thievish knave in *The Queen of Hearts*, 'He went that-a-way', although he doesn't speak. In the same way Beatrix can also convey actions without words, as in the drawing of the petrified Tom Kitten confronting Samuel Whiskers. These are specific instances, but more general links between the two artists can be made by anyone who makes a careful study of their work. One important difference, though, lies in the fact that Caldecott's countryside was far more of an idealized unlocated place than Beatrix Potter's ever was.

There were a number of other artists, particularly illustrators, whom Beatrix greatly admired without consciously imitating or being directly influenced by them in any way. She mentions in her journal the death of Richard ('Dicky') Doyle, and adds: 'I have always from a little child had a great admiration for his drawings in the old *Punches* . . . I consider his designs as good and sometimes better than Leech's.' A little later the same year, 1883, she visited exhibitions by Hablot K. Browne ('Phiz') and Gustave Doré, finding the first by far the most interesting, although adding 'I consider Doré one of the

84 Illustration from *The Queen of Hearts*, Randolph Caldecott, 1881

greatest artists in black-and-white'. These were all illustrators in the English tradition, but we know that she also studied and copied the works of certain painters, because these copies have survived. There are, for example, several paintings in the Linder Bequest which are after John Constable sketches in the Victoria and Albert Museum, and she may well have copied other painters though chance has not preserved these copies. That she did this sort of work at all is indicative of how much she was self-taught, in spite of her several spells of formal instruction in art. What she needed from her teachers was technical know-how; the rest she could gain from her critical gallery-visiting and her own innate ability.

Another influence on the young Beatrix Potter was probably Rupert Potter's close friendship with the painter John Everett Millais, though it is surprisingly difficult to decide how important this family friendship was. It gave her a close insight into the private as well as the professional life of an artist, which does not come the way of many young people, and she must have listened with interest to talk about the progress of the pictures he had in hand. Then she went to see them exhibited – and very critical of them she often was, at least in the privacy of her journal. In 1886 there was a Special Exhibition of Millais' work at the Grosvenor Gallery and a journal entry gives Beatrix's opinion. 'Millais will doubtless paint some noble pictures yet, but on the whole his work seems to have passed its prime.'

Millais himself appears to have taken a casual interest in his friend's young daughter and her work, which Rupert was obviously ready to show him, and he consulted with Millais on the best teachers for Beatrix. When Millais died in 1896 Beatrix wrote in her journal: 'I shall always have the most affectionate remembrance of Sir John Millais, although un-mercifully afraid of him as a child . . . I had a brilliant colour as a little girl, which he used to provoke on purpose . . . He gave me the kindest encouragement with my drawings (to be sure he did everybody!) . . . but he really paid me a compliment for he said "plenty of people can *draw*, but you and my son John have observation".'

As a result of the friendship with Millais, Beatrix followed his career and his paintings with great interest, and her father often provided Millais with photographs for the work in hand. 'He wanted a photograph of a running stream to assist him with the landscape in the Drummer, and of course, as it was wanted, papa had the greatest difficulty in finding any. I should have thought we had them in every variety, however we found a few.' This not only says something about Millais but it also gives a charming picture of quite a modern aspect of relations between Beatrix and her father in the use of 'we'. One can see the pair of them searching through the piles of holiday photographs for just the right 'running stream' while Millais' messenger waited anxiously below.

85 *Portrait of Sir John Millais and Rupert Potter in the garden at Dalguise*, R. Potter, September 1880

In spite of this close link with Millais, there is little sign of his influence on Beatrix herself, except where he acted as an advisor on teachers of drawing and was a general encourager of her talent. Possibly this was because from the beginning she herself had an inclination to the small and intimate in her art, and found that when she tried larger works or oil-painting she was less sure of herself. Far more likely to have influenced her than any of his large-scale paintings were Millais' book illustrations, done for the most part earlier in his career. His *Little Songs for Me to Sing* may well have been given to her as a child – indeed one or two of the illustrations in this book depict little girls looking not unlike a very young Beatrix Potter!

Lessons for Beatrix did not stop until her last governess left to get married in 1885, but her art lessons had been over for some time. Over the next few years her style changed and she experimented in various ways until she found her true métier.

86 'Mary's Lamb' from *Little Songs for Me to Sing*, illustrated by John Millais, 1865

87 View from Bolton Gardens, June 1882

In the final analysis, however, though we can pick out certain strands of art which *may* have influenced her development as an artist, Beatrix was basically herself. Always keenly aware of the art and artistic trends around her, she absorbed and transmuted these to produce a very personal art – the art of Beatrix Potter.

J.I.W.

3

FANTASY, RHYMES, FAIRY TALES AND FABLES

Beatrix Potter's earliest fantasy drawings appeared in her childhood sketchbooks, but there is quite a gap between the childish pictures of rabbits wearing clothes and skating, and her more mature work. As she continued with more serious studies she grew out of this type of drawing and her natural history studies occupied a considerable amount of her time and energy, together with a special interest in fungi and in geology. In addition to painting the objects of her studies, she also drew her pets, the houses in which she stayed and their furniture, and the countryside around them. Only very occasionally was there something more imaginative. Nevertheless Beatrix was interested in children's books. She had young cousins, and after her last governess, Annie Carter, left to get married, she kept in close touch with her growing family. She took her pets to show the young children and presents were forthcoming at all the appropriate moments – and these must surely have included books for the children.

The actual date at which she again began to produce her imaginative paintings is very difficult to determine. Although Beatrix usually signed her work, if only with her initials, she was less inclined to date it, but many of her best imaginative paintings date from the 1890s. The main reason for this sudden burst of energy was the need for money.

By 1890 Beatrix Potter was a young woman in her early twenties and her brother was in his late teens. Bertram had managed to achieve a certain independence from the family, having gone away to school, and he was about to go up to Oxford. Beatrix, however, was still very dependent on her parents and was reluctantly becoming ever more absorbed into her mother's household affairs. A little money of her own, she felt, would give her at least an illusion of independence. The only thing she had to sell was her art, but she was by no means sure how she should go about it and she dared not consult her parents. But from Bertram she had enthusiastic support and help. In her journal for 1890 she mentions that she and Bertram particularly needed the sum of £6, and later she states

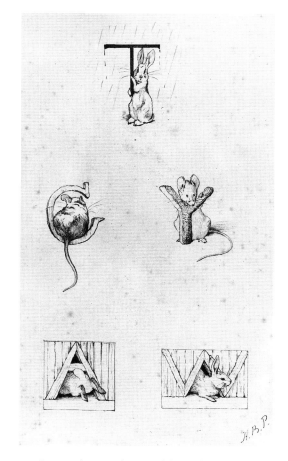

88 Designs for some letters of the alphabet

49

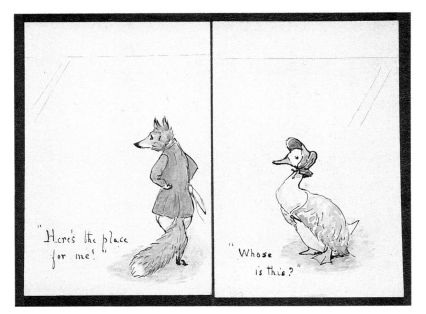

that they wanted to buy 'a printing machine, price £16'. 'We decided that I should make a grand effort in the way of Christmas Cards,' she wrote, 'and if they fell flat, as usual, we would take the matter into our own hands.' Within the family she was already in the habit of providing Christmas or menu cards and trifles for special occasions, but now she and Bertram were trying them out with serious intent. 'The cards were put under the plates at breakfast and proved a five minutes wonder. I referred to them the other day and found my uncle had forgotten their existence, but he added with laughable inconsistency that any publisher would snap at them.'

No help was forthcoming from the family, 'so in the beginning of February I began privately to prepare Six Designs, taking for my Model that charming rascal Benjamin Bouncer our tame Jack Hare'. The cards were ready by Easter 1890 and Beatrix and Bertram found the addresses of five publishers of greetings cards. Her first choice was Marcus Ward, who sent back her work by return of post. They turned down Raphael Tuck because 'it is such an absurd name to be under obligations to'. Finally Bertram had his way, and delivered the designs to Hildesheimer & Faulkner on his journey to Oxford for his examination. To their great delight, a cheque for £6 was received, together with a request to see more. Beatrix Potter was launched on her career as an artist-illustrator.

This small success proved a great stimulant to Beatrix and she set about making other similar sketches. Later in the year her uncle escorted her to the offices of Hildesheimer & Faulkner so that she could show them her work in person. At the time Mr Faulkner said little to her, but she got the impression that he found her designs amusing, although only committing himself so far as to say they 'should be able to do business'. She was given the opportunity to look through some of the printed examples of cards which Hildesheimer &

89, 90 From a set of dinner cards used at Melford Hall

91 Design for a Christmas card

92 Design for a Christmas card, probably intended for Hildesheimer & Faulkner

Faulkner produced: 'Some of the flowers and landscapes were lovely, and they have one lady that draws animals better than I, but not humorous, most of the comic ones were poor, though my Uncle observed there was nothing vulgar.' She was also shown a small children's book, no doubt with a view to her producing something similar.

The result was a number of delightful sketches which she either offered to Hildesheimer & Faulkner, or drew with a similar publisher in mind. Beatrix's style reflects the state of colour printing at that time, because she was trying to produce pictures that would reproduce adequately in the medium then available. Later she changed her style to take account of the improvements in the field of colour printing. Most of the cheaper colour printing was done by chromolithography, which gave at best somewhat muted colours, and at worst rather muddy ones. Beatrix suited her palette to match the colours available – muted reds, fawns and greys – though occasionally we do see some brighter clearer colours in use. She also adapted her technique to this quite miniature style of painting. She used a fairly dry brush, which gave her a precise fine line. This dry-brush technique was especially admirable for rendering the fur of small animals, such as rabbits and mice, but unfortunately, though the style and colour of these paintings reproduced quite well, it was impossible when printing cheap long runs of greetings cards or booklets to convey anything of the fine quality of the original work.

93 An early design for Hildesheimer & Faulkner: a Christmas card in the form of a mouse's nest, showing the inside and the outside

As she got older Beatrix Potter developed a more fluent style in her painting, with less use of the precise dry-brush technique and more of colour wash. Standing somewhat apart from the greetings card type of drawings are two pictures which show how the artist could adapt well-known places as backgrounds for some of her more fantastic paintings – something she was to develop and which was to characterize many of the Peter Rabbit books, where part of the pleasure lies in the fact that they are set in a still recognizable background, be it building or landscape. 'The Rabbits' Potting Shed' is exquisitely painted in a grey wash with pen-and-ink and white highlights and shows the rabbits solemnly going about their business, but the potting shed is the very one from Bedwell Lodge – there is a painting done in 1891 to prove it. (The Potters stayed at Bedwell Lodge in Hertfordshire in the summer of 1891.) The same applies to 'The Mice in their Storeroom' which is set firmly in a passage at Bedwell Lodge, and both are treated with great care and seriousness. There is no 'talking down' here, to either the animals or the observers.

Among the most delightful sequences of paintings which Beatrix Potter produced was *The Rabbits' Christmas Party*. This too has been painted with loving care and great inventiveness of detail. The rabbit under the umbrella in the first picture makes us wonder if Beatrix Potter unconsciously recalled Renoir's *Les Parapluies*. This set of four pictures was given to her aunt, Lucy Roscoe.

94 The potting shed at Bedwell Lodge, 1891

95 (below) 'The Rabbits' Potting Shed', 1891

96 (right) 'The Mice in their Storeroom', 1891

97, 98 Two illustrations from
The Rabbits' Christmas Party: the
guests arriving and going home

In quite a different vein was the set of sketches for 'A Frog he would a-fishing go', which Beatrix Potter sold to Ernest Nister in 1894, as a little booklet. The illustrations were eventually used with a text by someone else, signed 'C.B.', and Beatrix later bought her sketches back from Nister. They contain the first hint of Jeremy Fisher, and her tentative preliminary sketches have survived, showing how she set about the work.

It was not surprising that when she came to write to young children she should ornament the letters with just such sketches as she was working on at that time, and even make up tales about them, for the picture letters and the drawings were all done for the most part during the 1890s. The most famous, of course, resulted in *Peter Rabbit* (*see p.* 95), but in 1900 she wrote to Marjorie Moore from Tenby and illustrated her letter with scenes from the seaside. During this period she also produced a few 'toy pictures'. The last two decades of the nineteenth century saw a great fashion for 'movables': books where some part of the picture could be made to move by pulling a cord, lifting a flap or turning a wheel. Beatrix's were activated by the human hand alone, usually by lifting up a flap. She painted and made these toy pictures, with all their parts, by herself, so that each one is unique and its survival due entirely to the loving care given to it by the original recipient. One of the best-known is 'Benjamin Bunny & Son Greengrocers', showing the shop front and Benjamin Bunny. It was made for a young Potter relation, Walter Gaddum, in 1891.

99 (above left) 'The frog jumps into his boat' from 'A Frog he would a-fishing go', a booklet offered to Ernest Nister in 1894

100 (above) A page from a picture letter addressed to Marjorie Moore from Tenby, 24 April 1900

101, 102 'Benjamin Bunny & Son Greengrocers': a 'movable' toy picture where the lids lift up to reveal the contents of the barrel and basket

A year before her death Beatrix Potter wrote to the *Horn Book Magazine* that she had never illustrated another author, but memory had played her false. From about 1893 she tried her hand at illustrating favourite books for her own amusement. Comments in her journal on Phiz and Doré show that she had meditated on the problems of illustration, especially of the ancient writers: 'Flaxman and Turner are perhaps the only artists who have succeeded . . .' She never attempted the classics, and her immersion in Shakespeare (whose works she learnt by heart in chunks, pacing up and down on sleepless nights) produced only a handful of drawings inscribed with a line or two from the plays. 'Fishes come bite!' (337) has another title – 'The Rain it Raineth Every Day' (from *Twelfth Night*) – and beneath a study of cowslips and bluebells are lines spoken by a fairy in *A Midsummer Night's Dream*: 'The cowslips tall her pensioners be.'

Fairies, fairy tales and fantasy literature, especially the humorous or frightening bits, attracted her most and her choice was dictated by the books available. 'When *I* was a little girl, *I* was satisfied with about six books, three dolls, and a stuffed cotton pig.' But she saw far more than six books, not all of them instructive, and the grown-ups read them too. She chose well-known and much-illustrated works which appeal to adults: Lewis Carroll, Edward Lear, 'Uncle Remus' and, above all, traditional rhymes and stories.

Folklore had become fashionable by the late nineteenth century, and antiquarianism was rife (even Beatrix's parents went to costume balls). Fairy painting was now a major artistic preoccupation – for Millais too. Newly translated folktales from all over the world flooded into England, headed by the *Märchen* of the German Romantics. Some of Beatrix's designs are Germanic in style but most are original in concept: 'Thank goodness, my education was neglected and the originality was not rubbed off.' Just as she practised the art of writing in her journal, and animal drawing from dead or living models, she tried to strengthen her handling of the human figure by copying from artists such as Otto Speckter or Ludwig Richter. Human subjects were never her forte, and she preferred to concentrate on animals, plants, interiors or gardens. As in the animal fantasies, she drew from life: Peter was the model for both Brer Rabbit and the White Rabbit. A few pictures appear singly in the two printed rhyme books, *Appley Dapply's Nursery Rhymes* and *Cecily Parsley's Nursery Rhymes* (see pp. 153, 158), and a painting for 'Three little mice sat down to spin' was redrawn for page 47 of *The Tailor of Gloucester*, but most were never published.

'Three little mice' reached an advanced stage of preparation as an illustrated booklet, but in spite of the accurate and

103 'Three little mice sat down to spin', *The Tailor of Gloucester*, p. 47, 1903

104 'Three little mice sat down to spin': illustration for first line of that verse, *c.* 1892

105 'What are you at, my fine little Men?': illustration for third line of 'Three little mice sat down to spin', *c.* 1892

exquisite drawing no publisher could be found. Six paintings were done, one for each line (the last two lines had been omitted). There was a coloured title-page with mice and distaffs, and six text pages embellished with sepia drawings of appropriate household and sewing accoutrements: oil-can, ink-pot and quill, buttons, bobbin and thimble, ending aptly with padlock, keys and candle-snuffer. An extra page showed spinning wheel and distaff: one text page was tried out in line and watercolour. Before painting, Beatrix made detailed pen-and-ink outlines to be used as a guide. The spinning mice exist in several variants, some with ten mice, some with six and some with two. The bentwood chairs originate in bedroom No. 4 'where I always slept' at Camfield Place (9) – Beatrix loved to record old houses and furniture.

106 'The Day's News'

Not only industrious and virtuous mice, but dining or dancing mice (and rats) figure in letters, fantasy pictures and the 'Tales' (158). They dance boisterously in a banned *Tailor of Gloucester* illustration (229), triumphantly in *Miss Moppet* (31), joyfully at mouse-parties in *The Fairy Caravan* and – most delightfully of all, holding up their tails – in *Mrs. Tittle-mouse*. The play-rhyme 'Tingle, Dingle, Dousy' is illustrated with yet another dancing mouse.

Mice were also the subject of fantasy paintings: a mouse reading a newspaper, mice playing cards and the superb painting of a mouse in its nest (93). Rabbits too came in for their share of attention: the *Happy Pair* booklet illustrations were published in 1890 with verses by Frederic Weatherly, a prolific writer of doggerel; and there were also two gentlemen rabbits dressed in eighteenth-century greatcoats, walking earnestly together in the snow, and rabbits with their sledge (111). *Changing Pictures*, published by Ernest Nister in 1894, also has a rabbit on the cover. A beautifully painted jackdaw, carrying a sweep's brushes, was done for the firm of Ernest Nister (112). The importance of these creatures, in spite of their clothes, is the accuracy of

107 Dancing mice, *The Tale of Mrs. Tittlemouse*, p. 57, 1910

108 (below left) An illustration for *A Happy Pair*, published by Hildesheimer & Faulkner in 1890

109 (below centre) One of the illustrations submitted to Hildesheimer & Faulkner for *A Happy Pair*

110 (below right) Design for Hildesheimer & Faulkner, Christmas 1894, subsequently the frontispiece to *Appley Dapply's Nursery Rhymes*

111 (above left) Possibly a Christmas card design

112 (above) A jackdaw drawn for Ernest Nister, 1892

113, 114 A sketch (far left) for part of the cover of *Changing Pictures* (left), Ernest Nister, 1894

115 (below) A sketch originally offered to Ernest Nister

their depiction as animals, and the complete seriousness with which they were painted. Some ideas she put on paper for her own pleasure, but others were done in the hope, no doubt, that at some time they would attract a publisher.

Most of the early rhyme pictures are populated with mice, too. In 1893 Beatrix made a booklet of the ancient rhyme 'There was an old woman who lived in a shoe'. In the better-known *Appley Dapply* design the mouse and her family spill out of an elaborately beaded turquoise-blue shoe – here the children scamper and play (116), or are whipped by the 'old woman' inside the distant shoe (a fertility-symbol). The mouse knitting peacefully in *Appley Dapply* illustrates the end of the rhyme, when the children are in bed (117). The cradle with varying numbers of mouse babies was finally redrawn with four inside for *The Tale of Two Bad Mice* (118). 'I saw a ship

She had so many children.
She didn't know what to do!

116 (top left) From 'There was an old woman who lived in a shoe', 1897

117 (above) 'A mouse knitting', the version which appears in *Appley Dapply* between 1955 and 1987

118 (left) Hunca Munca and babies, *The Tale of Two Bad Mice*, p. 48, 1904

a-sailing', a later rhyme given to Marjorie Moore, had mouse sailors and rabbit passengers, and 'The captain was a guinea-pig – The pilot was a rat'. She wrote at the end: 'I think the words are lovely. Just imagine the white mice letting down the bags of comfits into the hold!'

In a 1900 picture letter Beatrix records a visit to the British Museum to see a delightful old book full of rhymes – almost certainly *Tommy Thumb's Pretty Song Book* (c.1744): 'I shall draw pictures of some of them whether they are printed or not.' The rhyme book planned for 1905 was delayed by other work and by the death of Norman Warne. It metamorphosed into an abridged collection of mainly original verses – *Appley Dapply's Nursery Rhymes* – but some of the unused rhymes with their rough sketches survive in manuscript. Apart from a fortune-telling chant about 'Big Box, little Box, Band-Box, Bundle' (drawn with faces and legs), the protagonists are flora, fauna and the elements: pigs and guinea pigs, guinea fowl and geese, moon and clouds. *Cecily Parsley's Nursery Rhymes* has eight rhymes, seven traditional. Though heterogeneous collections of verses and drawings from different periods, the published rhyme books contain some outstanding work.

At least six of the 'Tales' are based on fables, fairy tales and nursery rhymes. Beatrix had *The Tailor of Gloucester* printed

the captain

The ship

The passengers embarking

And the passengers were rabbits
Who ran about, pit pat!

All of which will have to be carefully drawn, but I think the words are lovely. Just imagine the white mice letting down the bags of comfits into the hold!

119 From 'I saw a ship a-sailing', ?1905

privately, guessing that Warne would want to cut out her favourite rhymes. Each had been chosen for some reference to the story and the connections had to be guessed. Some, like 'Hey Diddle Diddle', are quoted only as fragments, and origins are noted at the end of the manuscript. The final printed version has 850 fewer words of rhymes, and only six are quoted in full. *Squirrel Nutkin*, which revives the mediaeval riddle-game tradition, originally had more of the rhyming riddles. Several were removed because they bored Beatrix's young cousins, but the nine which remain are an essential part of the story, their answers integrated into the text. The original *Mrs. Tiggy-Winkle* also had to be trimmed, but one or two verses remain – as in *Pigling Bland*.

The sound and rhythm of old rhymes intrigued Beatrix as much as old names and rural customs. In later life she owned a number of rhyme books: Halliwell, Cecil Sharp, Baring Gould; and in Scotland during 1894 she read Chambers's *Rhymes and Fairy Tales*. Otherwise traditional rhymes are mentioned far less often in her journal than fairy tales.

Fairies and ghosts were very real to Beatrix all her life. At Dalguise 'everything was romantic in my imagination. The woods were peopled by the mysterious good folk. The Lords and Ladies of the last century walked with me along the overgrown paths.' At Camfield she used to look out into the stable yard and wonder if there was an enchanted Prince below, 'but he made no sign'. Like Robert Louis Stevenson she had a Highland nanny who steeped her in tales. The journal is full of references to myth and legend: the White Lady of Avenel, the Red Etain of Ireland, the mediaeval lady on a gravestone with her hair in side-cushions 'like Cinderella's proud sister'. During that long summer spent in the haunted Scottish borders 'the whole countryside belonged to the fairies'. Hedgehogs were fairy beasts, and haunted the ruins of Dryburgh Abbey. Small fleecy clouds were Mother Holda's flocks, and wild grey storm clouds the horses of Woden and Thor, or so they believed 'in realms that still reverence the stork and the ladybird, and where childhood clings to the cult of Red Riding-hood and Puss-in-boots'. In a jocular context, she compared herself to a fairy-tale princess being transformed into a white rabbit, or to 'riddling the ashes à la Cinderella' for a lost microscope lens (it was found in the last spoonful but *one* out of the dustbin). The toadstools below Oatmeal Crag seemed to be fairies 'singing and bobbing and dancing in the grass'.

The Tailor of Gloucester was her 'pet book' not just because of the nursery rhymes but because mice play the part of benevolent fairies, 'an honest unashamed imitation of Puck, Robin Goodfellow & the Scottish Brownie'. In the original, 'true' story the Tailor believed that fairies had done his work.

Late in life, after her creative years were thought to be over, Beatrix still felt the urge to write, inventing new tales and

120 Cinderella's carriage at the door, *c.* 1895

rediscovering old favourites. *The Fairy Caravan* for instance was inspired by the mysterious dance of the fell ponies (*see p. 165*). In 1932 she wrote: 'I should like to do a set of fairy tales in thin volumes.' The idea never came to fruition.

'Cinderella', best-known of all fairy tales and ancient by Perrault's time, is more than twice as long in the Potter version (*c.* 1930), with minutely described backgrounds and some unexpected details. The curfew times are earlier than midnight, and Cinderella must be cured of grubbiness and unpunctuality. The setting is the kingdom of Nowharra where 'the Palace drowned in sunshine that seemed always afternoon'. Instead of a pumpkin there was 'the most beautifullest gold coach, harnessed with rabbits driven by a whiskered rat, attended by mouse link boys and on the backboard hung four lizard footmen'. In drawings she made at least forty years earlier, the coach *is* a pumpkin – and the clock, a fine piece with a broken pediment, stands at midnight. The coach waits at the palace door in a blaze of light; one rabbit licks its paw and a mouse adjusts the harness. Another picture is a remarkable study in atmosphere, in which format is suited to subject. Mice peep out of windows and pour down the steps of half-timbered houses, and on the back is written: 'Cinderella's Coach going to fetch her from the ball. Intended for *moon*light.'

121 Cinderella's pumpkin carriage goes to fetch her from the ball (*detail*), *c.* 1895

122 'He amused himself with step-dancing over the shadows', *The Fairy Caravan*, p. 137, 1929

The weird effects of moonlight fascinated her too in *Mr. Tod*, and in the favourite *Fairy Caravan* vignette of a pony trotting through a shadowy moonlit wood straight from Walter de la Mare. Writing in her journal of some designs planned at the same time as the early Christmas card sketches, but more elaborate, she mentioned intending to work them out into a little book some time. 'They were taken partly from the *Cinderella*': a tantalizing hint that she must have made a whole set of pictures for this tale.

For 'The Sleeping Beauty', first of Perrault's stories, Beatrix made several drawings between 1898 and 1902, for pleasure and practice, after woodcuts by the German artist Richter. 'The doves asleep upon the house-tops' of a mediaeval German town foreshadows *The Faithful Dove* (*see p. 168*), on the manuscript of which is written 'The doves also slept there on the roof'. Here the setting is Rye, stranded in its marsh and dozing 'through the lazy summer days like the Castle of the Sleeping Beauty'. To her drawing Beatrix added in gothic script the title 'Dornröschen' – 'Thorn Rose', the German 'Sleeping Beauty' – which implies that Grimm was her source. Other illustrations include 'The Briar Rose' (a castle set in thorns), 'The Prince coming into the Courtyard of the Palace' and 'The Old Woman at the Spindle'; all are fashionably framed in roses (*see p. 154*). 'Little Ida's Flowers' from Hans Andersen shows dancing flowers with a tulip border, and his 'China Shepherdess' (1900) is drawn in a medallion partly framed by an ink sketch of a cottage. The 1905 Book of Rhymes was intended to have similar borders: daisies for the mole rhyme, and clover with grass and button mushrooms for the fungus rhyme. A set of charming but unfilled flower frames still awaits its subjects (1).

'Puss in Boots' is the most famous animal helper tale, again known before Perrault. Beatrix shows the cat-hero presenting a rabbit to the King, following closely Speckter's title-page for *Das Märchen vom gestiefelten Kater*. The letters of the title have metamorphosed into bird-laden branches in which hang the boots, and a miniature Puss is chased by a coach with galloping horses. Two latter-day Pusses in Boots are Simpkin entering the Tailor's house with snowy boots and a pipkin of milk, and

123 'The doves asleep upon the house-tops': design for 'The Sleeping Beauty', 1899

124 'Puss in Boots': design for title-page or cover, 1894

the hunting cat of 'Kitty-in-Boots', an unpublished tale with an Esthwaite Water background (334).

'The White Cat', taken from the Countess d'Aulnoy (Marie Catherine de la Motte), she treated in the English sporting print manner, selecting as always sympathetic subjects. Kittens collect game for the White Cat's supper: an early episode of the story. The brown-coated kitten appears again in a Nister booklet, *Pinkie, Winkie, and Wee*, as 'The sporting cat'. Beatrix made designs for more tales: 'The Yellow Dwarf' and 'Tom Thumb' but, surprisingly, not for 'The Frog Prince'. Her 'Red Riding Hood' is visualized in long hair and cap, climbing over a stile, and greeted by the wolf. In Queen Victoria's reign the 'Arabian Nights' and other Eastern tales became as popular as Grimm through the translations of Richard Burton and others. Beatrix illustrated 'The Forty Thieves', without the people, in

125, 126, 127 Three sporting kitten designs for 'The White Cat', ?1894

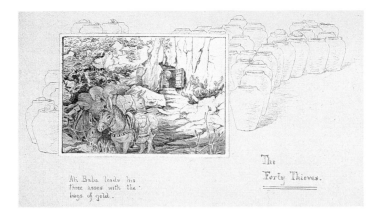

Ali Baba leads his
three asses with the
bags of gold.

The
Forty Thieves.

128 Three asses outside Ali Baba's storehouse:
design for 'The Forty Thieves', *c.* 1895

a scene of asses bordered by pots. All these early designs were based on familiar styles and techniques – the wood and steel engravings of picture books, the colour plates of natural history books – in muted colours and a miniaturist's manner.

By 1896 Beatrix had come to know Sawrey, where she wrote: 'The great, dull fir-woods recall one's childish fancies of wolves, a very striking background they would make for Grimm's Fairy Tales.' But it was Perrault's 1695 version of her favourite 'Red Riding Hood' that she rewrote fifteen years later, with its classic dialogue, and in which the wolf eats all. In a late *Fairy Caravan* setting this story is told by the ewe Habbitrot, who learnt it from a swallow from France: 'It is old, and sad.'

Several original fairy tales were invented as well: fragments of 'Peermingle, the story of a cockle-shell fairy', 'Llewellyn's Well' (written at Gwaynynog), 'The Fairy in the Oak' – later adapted for the last chapter of *The Fairy Caravan*. Another tree-felling story told of the troll-like Oakmen, turned out by woodcutters but rehoused in Mrs Heelis's new plantation (*see p.* 153). Perrault was once more the source for her bleak 'Bluebeard' story, *Sister Anne* (*see p.* 167).

Beatrix Potter's approach to fairy tales was a realistic one – yet she never lost her sense of mystery. 'I do not remember a time when I did not try to invent pictures and make fairy-tales – amongst the wild flowers, the animals, trees and mosses and fungi – all the thousand common objects of the country side; that pleasant unchanging world of realism and romance, which in our northern clime is stiffened by hard weather, a tough ancestry, and the strength that comes from the hills.'

Animal moral tales proliferated in the nineteenth century, refurbished or copied *ad nauseam* – but Aesop, over-used, came back to life with the inventiveness of artists such as C. H. Bennett and Walter Crane. Fables lend themselves to illustration, with their dramatic simplicity and lack of psychological complexity. Likewise, the symbolic qualities of animals have ancient roots. Beatrix always went back to the origins: her

creatures, from the cunning Tod to the resourceful Benjamin, are descendants of Aesop's fable bestiary. Her common sense and wisdom, like Aesop's, are based on observation of human behaviour – but animal behaviour interests her as much.

In the best English tradition, Beatrix produced some refreshingly inventive versions of fables in new settings. A reference in her journal for 1895 anticipates the helpless lambs in *The Fairy Caravan*: 'It is curious to see a shepherd in a smock frock of butcher blue, a sheep in wolf's clothing.' Better-known is *The Tale of Johnny Town-Mouse*, with its warning about the danger and extravagance of urban life. In 1919, badgered by her publishers, she suggested a new collection of nursery rhymes. Rebuffed, she sent another Aesop story, 'The Tale of Jenny Crow'. Starting it just before crow shooting, she had 'hopes of both models & pies'. Colour work was an effort now, and only a handful of drawings was completed, Caldecottian in style and palette. Another rebuff – 'it is not Miss Potter, it is Aesop' – provoked an explosion: 'I never have cared tuppence either for popularity or for the modern child; they are pampered & spoilt with too many toys and books. And when you infer that my originality is more precious than old Aesop's, you *do* put your foot in it!' And later: 'You don't suppose I shall be able to continue these d...d little books when I am dead and buried!! I am utterly tired of doing them, and my eyes are wearing out.' And she added: 'My foxes are not up to much either.' Warne hurriedly gave way, but the fable book never appeared in print.

Now called 'The Tale of the Birds and Mr. Tod', it was a

129 (left) A fox in sheep's clothing at Wilfin Beck, *The Fairy Caravan*, p. 70, 1929

130 (above) The mice take refuge in the coal cellar, *The Tale of Johnny Town-Mouse*, p. 36, 1918

131 'The Fox and the Crow', ?1919

conglomeration of fables with a renamed 'Fox and Crow' at its centre, 'The Folly of Vanity', which tells of a 'vain and foolish' bird in the Jemima mould. It contains some gems of Potter prose: 'Something blue black and shiny twinkled amongst the oak leaves. It was Miss Jenny Crow', whom Mr Tod addresses in an amusing adaptation of the La Fontaine original: 'Beautiful black lady bird, elegant as a newly tarred railing!'

As part of this miscellany, or separately, Beatrix retold several other fables: 'The Frog's King', 'The Idle Shepherd Boy' ('Wolf! Wolf!') – with an excellent description of a working sheepdog – and 'Sour Grapes', with its punch line 'That is *Not* a fat pigeon!' But pigeon and grapes are drawn respectively plump, and 'dripping with ripeness'. 'The Ant and the Grasshopper' was expanded into 'Grasshopper Belle and Susan Emmet', which Beatrix began to rewrite twenty-three years later, not long before her death. The Ant is true to type: 'A rusty black gown with tight black sleeves, a black net cap with two long bows like horns, a sharp set nose, a wide crooked chin, and near sighted eyes, had Miss Susan Emmet.' This image can only have come from the *petit-bourgeois* housewife of J. J. Grandville's influential *La Fontaine*. She also wrote versions of 'The Hare and the Tortoise', featuring Alderman Ptolemy ('I am a Grecian box-tortoise'), and 'The Dog and the Bone', about a spaniel called Nettie. In the manuscript collection, 'King Stork' leads on to 'The Fox and the Stork', for which Beatrix made a complete set of drawings. Seven finished and three unfinished watercolours survive. They show Mr Tod and King Stork in the setting of Melford Hall, with its oak-panelled walls, corkscrew stair and red-brick tower (34). Another fable was incorporated into *The Fairy Caravan*: a re-enaction of 'Belling the Cat' in the meeting of Sawrey rats chaired by Alder-rat Squeaker – a twin of Samuel Whiskers.

Beatrix Potter was well-acquainted with the immortal 'Uncle Remus', a former slave – like Aesop – whose African stories in an American setting include variants of familiar fables and trickster tales. Fables were a safe weapon against authority where escape – or opposition – was impossible for the unheroic hero who had to survive where fate had planted him. Brer Rabbit, the wily animal-hero and cunning trickster of the brier patch, gives hope to the oppressed but is sometimes tricked himself. Several tales, myth-like, are savage and malevolent, but their impact is always softened by the wise old Negro storyteller.

The first of ten collections, *Uncle Remus: his Songs and Sayings*, was published by Joel Chandler Harris in 1880; it appeared in England within a year. *Uncle Remus* appealed to nineteenth-century children, hemmed in by authority. Mark Twain called it 'the oracle of the nation's nurseries'. However subversive, it was not kept from Beatrix. The eminent Liberal statesman and Quaker John Bright, a memorable orator and

132 "That is *Not* a fat pigeon": 'The Fox and the Grapes', ?1919

133 The meeting chaired by Alder-rat Squeaker from 'Belling the Cat', *The Fairy Caravan*, p. 167, 1929

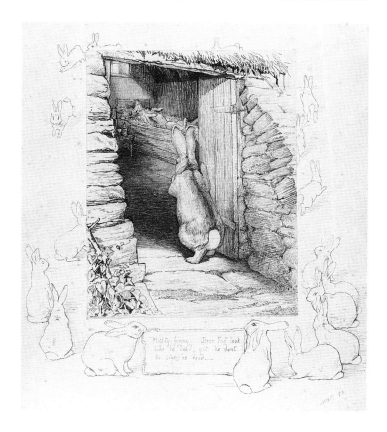

134 'Brer Fox and Brer Rabbit', from 'Mr Wolf makes a Failure', *Uncle Remus* (chapter xi), 1893

reader of poetry, used to fish with Rupert Potter, and liked children. He met 'Brer Rabbit' for the first time at the Potter household, and was 'very much taken' with it. 'When papa showed it to him he used to read it aloud till the tears ran down with laughing.' Its shrewd humour and virtuosity of language must also have appealed to Beatrix, with her sensitivity to nuance and tone of voice and her fondness for dialect – in this case authentic American dialogue.

The impact of these tales on the modern animal fantasy tradition and writers such as Potter, Rudyard Kipling, Kenneth Grahame and A. A. Milne cannot be overestimated. Thanks to 'Uncle Remus', talking animals took their place in children's literature. He revealed to Beatrix that stories could be made out of the everyday material of an uneventful life – but her beasts are real ones, not just people in disguise.

Between 1893 and 1896 Beatrix made a set of eight designs for *Uncle Remus*, each bordered with expertly-drawn rabbits and a few lines of text; she called them 'subject drawings'. Five were illustrations to the 1880 collection. The first, 'Brer Fox and Brer Rabbit' (from 'Mr Wolf makes a Failure'), shows Brer Fox looking unconvincingly dead, watched by a thoughtful Brer Rabbit. Its frame is a twin to 'The Rabbit's Dream' (*157*): rabbits sit or run round the picture and hold up the text in their mouths. In 'The Awful Fate of Mr Wolf' Brer Rabbit cruelly finishes off Brer Wolf, imprisoned in a chest, by pouring on

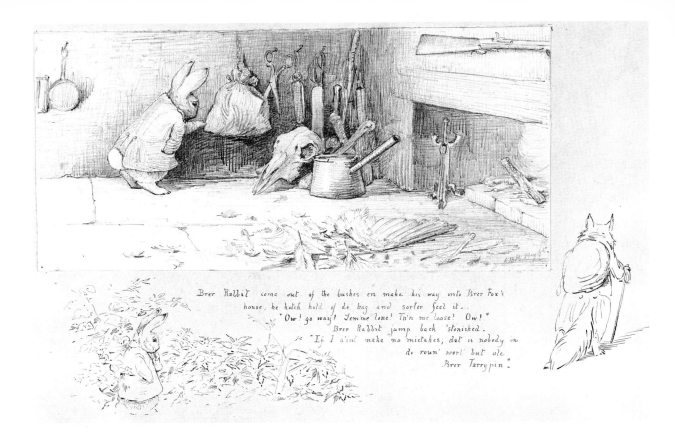

Brer Rabbit come out of the bushes en make his way into Brer Fox's
house, he hotch hold of de bag and sorter feel it..
"Ow! go way! Lemme lone! Tu'n me loose! Ow!"
Brer Rabbit jump back 'stonished.
"Ef I a'int make no mistakes, dat is nobody in
de roun' worl' but ole
Brer Tarrypin."

boiling water – the little rabbits are triumphant. 'Brer Fox goes a-hunting' appears in two instalments, complementary designs drawn a year apart. Brer Fox twice finds Brer Rabbit shamming dead: in the first Brer Fox is seen from behind and in the next he shows off his handsomely buttoned shooting costume (can it be Peter Rabbit's fir-tree behind?).

Four more drawings were done, three for *Nights with Uncle Remus* (1883). 'How Mr. Rabbit saved his Meat' is a more complicated tale: 'Brer Rabbit steals Brer Wolf's fish' (Beatrix's title) and then his meat, resorting to the old trick of digging in a cow's tail as if the whole cow were buried. In 'Mr Benjamin Ram' the hero prepares to play a last tune on his wonderful fiddle, scaring away the wolves. The story 'In Some Lady's Garden' tells how Brer Rabbit, alias Mr Billy Malone, persuades a little girl to let him into her daddy's garden, and runs off with the vegetables. A grisly illustration to 'Brother Rabbit rescues Brother Tarrypin' shows Mr Fox's den, strewn with bones and feathers; the invisible terrapin hangs in a sack. In 1927, referring to an American piracy of *Peter Rabbit*, Beatrix observes that its illustrations follow the American portrait of Brer Rabbit rather than hers of Peter. Certainly her *Uncle Remus* designs were not in the American tradition.

Beatrix was attached enough to 'Brer Rabbit' to hang a duplicate drawing in the entrance hall at Hill Top – and her own tales are full of Remus reminders. Lavender is 'rabbit-tobacco'; there are Puddle-Ducks and even a Molly Cottontail;

135 In Brer Fox's den, from 'Brother Rabbit rescues Brother Tarrypin', *Nights with Uncle Remus* (chapter LXX), 1895

and Brer Fox with a 'spell er de dry grins' resembles Mr Tod. In the Tar-Baby story Brer Rabbit goes 'lippity-clippity, clippity-lippity – dez ez sassy ez a jay-bird', but Peter goes 'lippity-lippity' in a more subdued manner. The Southern rabbits raid a garden in true Benjamin style. Brer Fox feigns illness in a rocking chair, wrapped up with flannel – just like Miss Moppet in the handkerchief. In one story a pan and carving knife are set out with evil intent, just as in *The Tale of Mr. Tod*. In fact, Beatrix wrote of *Mr. Tod* that its chief defect was being an imitation of *Uncle Remus*. Both storytellers loved to make subtle jokes, and the same could be said of Beatrix Potter as 'Uncle Remus' said of himself: 'Well, I tell you dis, ef deze yer tales wuz des fun, fun, fun, en giggle, giggle, giggle, I let you know I'd a-done drapt um long ago.'

Alice in Wonderland was given to Beatrix at a much more tender age than 'Uncle Remus' – by an Oxford friend of her father. The grown-ups proceeded to discuss whether she was old enough, or the book too old, but Beatrix immediately lost herself in John Tenniel's pictures. In 1927 she writes 'Dickens, and Alice-in-Wonderland, have been illustrated once for all', yet she had long before joined the ranks of Carroll illustrators.

As far as we know she made only half a dozen *Alice* drawings. Though clearly indebted to Tenniel, she chooses different scenes: the little Lizard Bill, for instance, revived by guinea pig gardeners with an audience of mouse, guinea hens and the White Rabbit. As always, and unlike Tenniel the caricaturist, she avoids human subjects. Alice herself never appears – though we do get a glimpse of the King's feet in 'The Trial of the Knave of Hearts' (almost the same viewpoint as the 'Puss in Boots' design (124) where only His Majesty's crown and ink-pot are visible). The anthropomorphized White Rabbit, evidently a favourite Carroll character, enters splendidly

136, 137 Two designs for *Alice in Wonderland*: 'The little Lizard, Bill', 1893 (for chapter IV) and 'The Trial of the Knave of Hearts', 1894 (for chapter XI)

dressed and fleeing down a long panelled corridor. An atmosphere of nightmare is evoked, foreshadowing Tom Kitten's passage through the dark chimney: a common fantasy. The White Rabbit's attitude is repeated in a place-card which shows Peter Rabbit nervously pulling on his gloves (90). Apparently Beatrix never illustrated *Through the Looking Glass*, but a gesture is made to Tenniel's sheep in Mrs Flock, keeper of the wool shop in *Little Pig Robinson* (53).

Carroll and Beatrix Potter both sent witty letters to children; so too did Edward Lear. Beatrix owned his *Book of Nonsense* and for years was fascinated by 'The Owl and the Pussy Cat', illustrating a shortened version in booklet form as a compliment to Lear, that other great artist of natural history. At the end is a seascape with island and setting sun: an idea born in Ilfracombe as early as 1883, it was revived for *Little Pig Robinson*. A curly-tailed pig on board ship reminded her of Lear's rhyme, which she illustrates again in an 1894 picture letter sent to Eric Moore from Falmouth. Chapter II begins: 'You remember the song about the Owl and the Pussy Cat and their beautiful pea-green boat?'

Beatrix even attempted a limerick in the Lear manner for the 1905 Book of Rhymes: called 'The Monster', it begins 'There once was a large spotted weevil'.

To Warne's suggestion ten years later that she might illustrate another writer, Beatrix replied: 'With regard to illustrating other people's books, I have a strong feeling that every outside book which I did, would prevent me from finishing one of my own . . . I will stick to doing as many as I can of my own books.' Her early animal fantasies were to blossom into a finished story, the first of nearly thirty – and it was as her own illustrator that she was most in sympathy with the text.

J.I.W.   A.S.H.

138, 139   Two designs for *Alice in Wonderland* (chapter II), ?1895: 'The White Rabbit, splendidly dressed' (left) and 'The Rabbit . . . scurried away into the darkness as hard as he could go' (centre)

140   (right) From 'The Owl and the Pussy Cat' by Edward Lear, c. 1893

141   From a picture letter sent to Eric Moore, 28 March 1894 (*detail*)

4

FLORA AND FAUNA, FUNGI AND FOSSILS

'It sometimes happens that the town child is more alive to the fresh beauty of the country than a child who is country born.' On holiday at Dalguise Beatrix and her brother escaped into a new and enthralling world. Back in London, isolated in their nursery, they kept pet animals, tried to tame house mice and boiled down the bones of specimens, even articulating the skeleton of a fox. (One packing list reads 'Spirit bottle, Virgil, 2 bird's skeletons'.)

Beatrix bought a rabbit – Benjamin – in a paper bag from a bird shop; 'his existence was not observed by the nursery authorities for a week'. Animal invasions were tolerated more than human ones – but Beatrix and Bertram seem to have been too occupied to notice the lack of companionship. A family of snails was reared in a plant pot and a daily record kept: they had 'such a surprising difference of character'. An 1898 design shows a 'whimsical snail' burying eggs and sowbugs, its hole drawn in section. Beatrix was also much taken with lizards, especially 'the little lizard Judy' who came from Ilfracombe. A juvenile still life shows Judy next to the pineapple which Beatrix was attempting to paint against all the odds. Seeing it threatened at a dinner party she exclaims: 'I felt fit to kick under my chair.' (*17*) Judy laid an egg which died, and she

142   The lizard Judy against an unfinished background, 1884

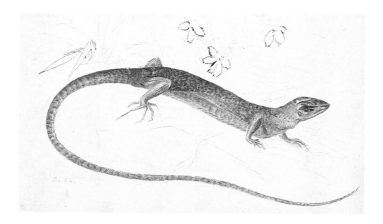

herself died in 1884 at Minehead, commemorated in the Lizard Bill illustration (*136*). 'I have had a great deal of pleasure from that little Creature.'

Amphibians were just as interesting. Surprised to discover that newts squeak, Beatrix notes the difference between their breathing system and that of frogs and toads. The newt collects air in its throat, then rises to the surface and lets out the air by opening its mouth wide with a snap. The name 'Sir Isaac Newton' (the newt in *The Tale of Jeremy Fisher*) celebrates both the animal and the pioneering scientist! Her knowledge of amphibians is illustrated in *Jeremy Fisher* and *Mrs. Tittlemouse*, where each creature keeps its natural attributes. Jeremy cannot stay long under water but must pop up for air from under his lily leaf. His limbs are articulated so that he moves by leaps and bounds, whereas Mr Jackson (the toad in *The Tale of Mrs. Tittlemouse*) can sidle along a dry ditch; also, toads can sit in an upright chair and are capable of huffing and puffing (*313*).

Travelling with a menagerie had its disadvantages. In 1896 Bertram went to Birnam with a dog, a jay, a kestrel and a hat-box full of chemicals, and on journeys Beatrix found the rabbit hutch 'a great resource . . . it is surprising what it will hold'. Spring brought reviving holidays by the sea, and discoveries of new sorts of fish and shells. At Falmouth in 1892 Beatrix discovered forty-nine cowries and four little blue-caps in an hour on the last morning – and an unknown seaweed. Weymouth was as productive of fish as of fossils (*see p. 92*). There she picked up an 'odd yellow-black toad-like dead fish' and 'a strange little red fish which I painted', staring and globular (*11*). A striking study of lobster claws was done much earlier, probably at Eastbourne.

Some animals were copied from natural history books. A great event was the present on her tenth birthday of Mrs Blackburn's *Birds drawn from Nature* (*see p. 39*). (Some years after, Beatrix remarks that Mrs Blackburn's birds do not 'stand on their legs so well as Bewick's, but he is her only possible rival'.) Birds interested her greatly: she writes about them in her journal, lists them on holiday and in 1888 writes to *The Times* on the habits of hawfinches. Some of the earliest drawings extant are a group of dead bird studies; others show blue tits, young thrushes, blackbird and guillemot – and the Moores' parrot. In 1902 she drew a thrush 'picked up dead in the snow' at Woodcote, home of her uncle Sir Henry Roscoe (*see p. 85*), recording it from several angles with a naturalist's eye and a clear, transparent palette.

At the Zoological Gardens Beatrix made sketches of magpies as models for Dr Maggotty in *The Pie and the Patty-Pan*, putting rusty nails into a bottle of ink. She made notes on the colour of their feathers: parts are 'very blue' and parts green; the tail is more than half of the overall length and the nose 'a little hookier' than in jackdaws. Sketched earlier at the Zoo

143 Study of male newt in the breeding season, ?1886

144 Studies of a thrush 'picked up dead in the snow' at Woodcote, Surrey, 1902

were a roe-deer and its fawn; Beatrix studied deer in their natural state too, in Perthshire. She comments rather unfairly on 'that ugliest of animals, the red deer hind', as silly a countenance as a dishorned Ayrshire cow.

The Potters lived near enough to the newly opened Natural History Museum for Beatrix to be allowed to visit it alone. She found it rather formidable, a dictionary of species unhelpful to the novice. 'I never saw anything so fearful as the stuffed animals': she drew them none the less. The roe-deer's head was 'drawn from a stuffed specimen, natural size', probably at the

145 (above) 'Dr. Maggotty's Mixture', *The Pie and the Patty-Pan*, p. 49, 1905

146 (right) Roe-deer at the Zoological Gardens, 1891

147 Head of a ram, ?1895

Museum – as was a ram's head in the same technique of minute greyish-white brush strokes, producing a bold overall effect.

The Museum's entomological and fossil collections attracted – and frustrated – Beatrix most of all. Studying their 'Index' collection of insects, which she described as 'an extreme example of museum labelling run mad', she concluded that perhaps the subject was 'beyond the wit of mortal man, even be he FRS [Fellow of the Royal Society]'. A couple of months later, needing advice and being 'not in a good temper, I worked into indignation about that august Institution . . . They have reached such a pitch of propriety that one cannot ask the simplest question . . . The clerks seem to be all gentlemen and one must not speak to them. If people are forward I can manage them, but if they take the line of being shocked it is perfectly awful to a shy person.'

At least she could learn how to mount specimens and prepare microscopic plates. With the help of Bertram's microscope she was studying the magnified wing scales of Painted Lady and Small Tortoiseshell butterflies, and the Privet Hawk Moth (*Sphinx ligustri*), complete with caterpillar and chrysalis – but for the tales of *Mrs. Tittlemouse* and *Tom Kitten* she draws the Red Admiral. Several studies of caterpillars survive, but none so early as those in a sketchbook inscribed 'Dalguise 1875' (66). At the age of 9 she was making extensive records of birds' eggs, butterflies and caterpillars, accompanied by remarks on their habits.

Beatrix Potter's insects were drawn to scale with the care of a professional: their scientific accuracy is as great as their aesthetic attraction. The fine dry-brush technique parallels that of early imaginative paintings such as the 'Three little mice' (*104, 105*). Copied perhaps, and certainly drawn with a myopic intensity worthy of the Pre-Raphaelites, are two sheets of beetles (*28*) – but other studies are very much all her own work. *Carabus nemoralis* (Ground Beetle), as seen in *Mrs. Tittlemouse*, is examined microscopically at different

Painted Lady Butterfly.
Vanessa Cardui.
Scales on lower side of wing highly magnified.

Small Tortoise shell Butterfly.
Vanessa Urticae
Scales on upper side of wing highly magnified

148 (left) Microscopic studies of *Vanessa cardui* and *Aglais urticae* (Painted Lady and Small Tortoiseshell butterflies), *c.* 1887

149 Red Admiral butterfly, *The Tale of Mrs. Tittlemouse*, p. 44, 1910

150 (left) Observations on caterpillars and their habits, from sketchbook (age 8), 1875

151 Microscopic studies of *Carabus nemoralis* (Ground Beetle), *c.* 1887

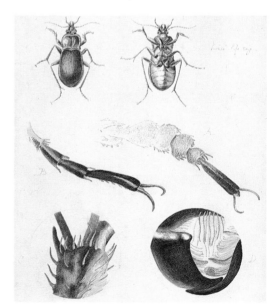

Tiger moth.

1. The caterpillar of the Tiger feeds on the nettle and both hawthorn and is found in June they are covered with black, white and red. They are found by road sides and lanes.

Drinker.

2. The cat. is a dark brown with orange dots. I dont know what it eats, but I think it is the flowering nettle. It is found by hedges in May and June.

Bombycidal

3. The caterpillar eats sloe, it is a rare moth, the caterpillar is brown with yellow rings, it is hairy and found in June.

Yellow tail

4. The cat. feeds on hawthorn, it is yellow with a blue line along its sides and black dots. It is found on hedges in June.

magnifications and from above and below (*151*). Another beetle reveals its highly-magnified head and thorax painted in watercolour (*23*). Ants and damselflies, freshwater creatures or gnats and mites, all are minutely observed. Anxious for accuracy, she altered the description 'water-boatman beetle' in *Jeremy Fisher* to read 'A great Diving-beetle came up underneath the lily leaf'.

Beatrix made at least a dozen drawings of spiders, including an almost human tarantula. The lithograph of *Linyphia triangularis*, marked with the scale of magnification, shows enlarged details of claw and mouth, and a holly leaf drawn with spider and nest below. Provided with instructions to the lithographers West & Newman, it probably dates from 1895, when she began to prepare twelve plates for Miss Martineau of the Natural History Museum. Only three are known; they include another Privet Hawk Moth and a 'trial run' of miscellaneous items. Beatrix modestly doubted whether they were of any educational value 'because they were not drawn with design'.

There was a limit even to Beatrix's toleration of wild life. Finding bugs at a Torquay hotel in March 1893, she remarked wryly 'it is possible to have too much Natural History in a bed!'

Penetrating beneath the skin of mammals too, she drew skulls and skeletons (*18*). Cows were submitted to X-ray treatment and drawn again to show off their sweeping

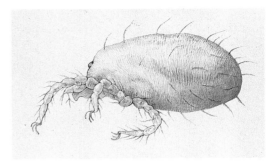

152   Microscopic studies of a mite (*detail*), c. 1887

153   Microscopic studies of *Linyphia triangularis* (Sheet Web Spider), ?1895

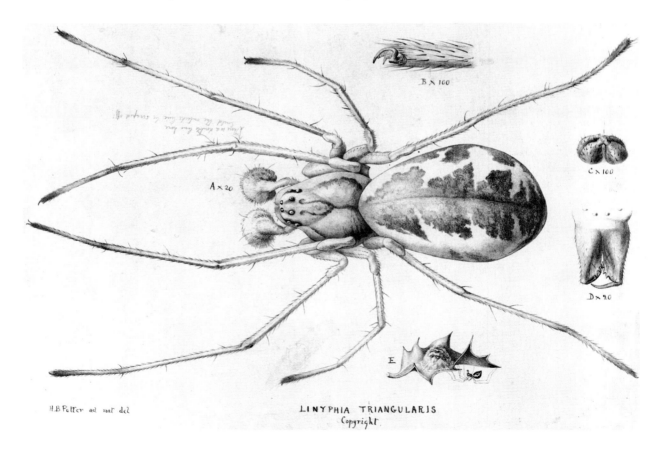

B × 100

A × 20

C × 100

D × 20

E

H.B.Potter ad nat del

LINYPHIA TRIANGULARIS
Copyright

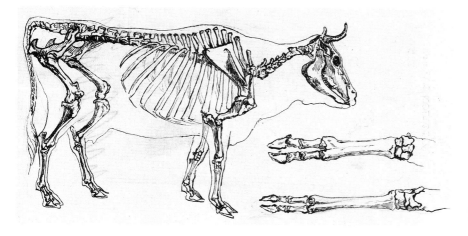

eyelashes. In 1895 she was 'dusting and mending our little bone-cupboards, when that containing the collection of British mice descended bodily upon my head amidst a shower of glass eyes. I caught the skeleton of a favourite dormouse, but six others were broken and mixed. I mended them all up. I thought it a curious instance of the beautifully minute differences and fittings together of the bones.'

Bertram specialized in birds and bats; the latter hung upside-down in parrot cages. His jay travelled 'crammed into a little box, kicking and swearing. Mamma expressed her uncharitable hope that we might have seen the last of it.' The jay discovered how to open the bat-box and destroyed one of the bats 'in a disgusting fashion'. In 1884 when Bertram returned to school he had left her 'the responsibility of a precious bat . . . I had no idea they were so active on their legs, they are in fact provided with four legs and two wings as well, and their tail is very useful in trapping flies.' (76) Bertram wrote to her about its health and inevitable death (see p. 42).

(see p. 42)

Bat populations are now only 5 per cent of their level at the beginning of this century: Beatrix drew several varieties at Dalguise and Lingholm, and at Camfield where at dusk 'the bats hawked up and down between the wall and the kitchen window'. Occasionally there was 'the excitement of a great grey "raat baat" sweeping over the roof with a piercing twitter'. At Gwaynynog she wrote a story, never finished, about two bats: 'Flittermouse and Fluttermouse' love twilight and 'have little blinking winking eyes like small black beads'. The bats are painted sitting or hanging with every detail lovingly observed – especially the ears of a long-eared bat.

Rabbits' ears are portrayed with the same sensitivity, in 'The White Rabbit' (138, 139) and the studies of Benjamin's fine head (156). Beatrix acquired an intimate knowledge of rabbit nature: 'Rabbits are creatures of warm volatile temperament but shallow and absurdly transparent.' Though 'regular vermin', she discovered that their personalities are as diverse as humans'. Benjamin was 'a noisy cheerful determined animal, inclined to attack strangers'; Peter was calmer and more clever. One study of Peter shows the characteristic position adopted

154 (left) Skeleton of a cow, possibly a copy (*detail*)

155 (above) Side view of a bat with folded wings, 1885

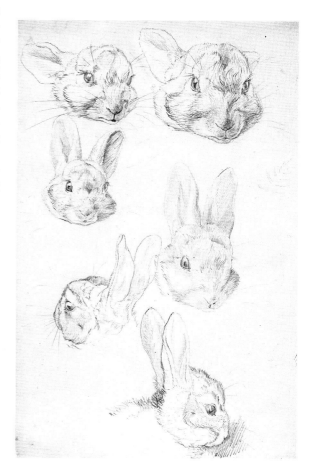

156 Six heads of Benjamin Bunny, 1890

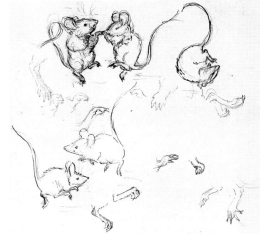

by a cold rabbit, its forepaws tucked backwards under the fur (*198*). She noticed too that rabbits rub their chins on objects to show contempt (probably a form of marking).

Perhaps because Beatrix had pleasant dreams, she was fascinated with the subject of sleep. There are white mice tucked up in brass bedsteads (*37*), 'The peculiar Dream of Mr Samuel Whiskers [her tame rat Sammy] upon the subject of Dutch Cheese' and the celebrated 'Dream of Toasted Cheese' (*182*). Especially interesting is 'The Rabbit's Dream', which shows Peter dreaming of himself asleep in No. 4 bedroom, Camfield Place, surrounded by his different sleeping positions. Beatrix practised making timed drawings of rabbits – washing, stretching or scratching – but she covered even more sheets with drawings of mice.

All her life Beatrix found mice fascinating subjects – she became a little tired of rabbits – and she drew all sorts of mice, voles and dormice. A wood mouse with magnificent whiskers and a long curly tail was painted in 1886 as a Christmas present for a friend; and a double study of the same Mrs Tittlemouse variety was given to her cousin, Ulla Hyde Parker. Beatrix recalls: 'When I was a child I had a favourite dormouse – a sleepy little animal – so we used to say "Wake up, wake up, Xarifa!" In the real poem [by John Gibson Lockhart] it is "Rise up! . . ." So that was how she got her curious name of Xarifa

157 (left) 'The Rabbit's Dream', *c.* 1895

158 (top) Sketches of mice, *c.* 1897

159 (above) Wood mouse, 1886

160 Studies of Xarifa, a hazel dormouse (*detail*), 1887

Dormouse.' In *The Fairy Caravan* Beatrix describes Xarifa's infancy at Birds' Place, Camfield. '*Poor Miss Mouse*, otherwise *Xarifa*' died in 1886; a sheet of studies dates from the year after. 'I think she was in many respects the sweetest little animal I ever knew.'

Beatrix also records the appearance of a live dormouse at a lunch party – at the Pagets' house, where on another occasion she found relief from society in a visit to the guinea pigs. The Pagets lent her guinea pigs with grand names and pedigrees; unfortunately one died (*see p. 159*). She used them as models, and was accused of caricaturing Mr Paget. Her drawings were published as a Christmas card and, thirty years later, in *Cecily Parsley* (263).

Pigs she loved too (41), admiring at Putney Park the Pig-wig variety, 'a splendid breed of black Berkshire pigs'. Dogs, sheep and horses were never caricatured; she confessed to finding them difficult to draw. When asked why she had never written about dogs, Beatrix replied 'I *have*! but I could not do them justice. I can manage to describe little rubbish, like mice and rabbits – dogs, sheep and horses are on a higher level.' Her feelings about cats were ambiguous, but it is a myth that she disliked dogs – though even after a succession of sheepdogs she writes: 'I respect dogs to a certain extent, but I don't think they are moral characters.' A particular favourite was the spaniel

161 (left) Guinea pigs in a basket: design for a Christmas card, 1893

162 (above) Studies of a cat, ?1903

163 'Old Dimond' with the carrier's cart, *The Tale of Johnny Town-Mouse*, p. 12, 1918

164 (above right) Pony Billy (Pony Dolly) crosses the ford, *The Fairy Caravan*, p. 127, 1929

165 Six heads of rams

Spot, who caused great amusement by his insistence on riding in carriages, if necessary other people's. In *The Tale of Johnny Town-Mouse* and later, in *The Fairy Caravan*, Beatrix celebrates memorable horses and ponies whom she had encountered in real life.

Beatrix always noticed sheep (51), commenting throughout her journal on Southdown sheep at Rye, Highland sheep at Birnam, the 'great Ram Sale' of Border Leicesters at Kelso in 1894, the ugly crossbreds, Dorset sheep and Cheviots. In 1895 she is struck by the sheep on Elterwater Common – 'of shortest wool and every colour' – probably Herdwicks, which grow lighter with age. Forty years later, now an expert on the Herdwick, she was sent a Christmas card showing six handsome rams with curly horns: 'From the herdwick gentlemen of Eskdale to Mrs Heelis's herdwick ladies of Sawrey, wishing them every success in 1934!'

Interested in animals as personalities, but also by their behaviour, she records it with scientific detachment – as for instance the hibernation pattern of her pet hedgehog Mrs Tiggy-winkle (254). This was not dependent on weather alone, but under the creature's own control: it could induce a cataleptic state in under an hour. Mrs Tiggy-winkle was a 'scrupulously clean little animal' who, if obliged to model for too long, began to bite, and who drank milk 'like anything, out of a doll's tea-cup!' In the case of Brock the badger, Beatrix made one of her few mistakes. Badgers and foxes are not natural enemies, and by nature badgers are more fastidious than foxes – but Mr Brock goes to bed in his boots.

Beatrix enjoyed anecdotes about animals: the fox caught in a snare which shammed dead like Brer Fox, or the one she pictures curled up asleep in a pig-sty with the pig. She caricatured herself with a favourite pig (*see p. 150*), and compared other people with animals. 'How amusing Aunt Harriet is, she is more like a weasel than ever.' Beatrix satirized the world about her, and unmasked animal qualities sometimes all too obvious in human beings. Her Gloucestershire cousin, Mr Hutton, must have been a forebear of Mr Jackson: 'He had

w in some more genteel n...

166 Beatrix Potter (Mrs Heelis) with a favourite
pig, 1924

on large gaiters and seemed hungry.' Johnny Town-mouse was
a caricature, as was Mr Tod, the archetypal 'wolf', and the
guinea pig threatened by over-solicitous friends, economical
but eloquent in word and line (357).

The anthropomorphism is never stereotyped or exaggerated:
Sir Isaac Newton is both amphibian and old gentleman, and
the genteel Tabitha Twitchit, epitome of respectability, is all
cat. Many pictures can be read on two levels and demand a
certain degree of sophistication – though Beatrix was never
one to write with an eye on the grown-ups. Young children are
quite capable however of understanding what lies beneath the
surface. To a child, talking animals are in any case more
interesting than human beings; observing animals, they learn
to understand people.

On a more conscious level, Beatrix loved to entertain
children with her pets and anecdotes, and to share her discoveries – the escapades of a tame owl, the cuckoo-like habits
of puffins. But most of the discoveries remained shut up in her
journal, whether observations on animal behaviour or theories
about the behaviour of glaciers. She compared the flight of a
meteor to photographs of a bullet's trajectory, and pondered
the laws of physics: 'Force is said to be interminable. I sometimes reflect what may happen when Peter Rabbit stamps,
which is one of the most energetic manifestations of insig-
nificance which has come under my notice.' Considering
photographic images and the relationship of sound- and
colour-waves, she wondered if our hands and, especially, our
memories retain impressions varying in depth, from 'sight,
sound and shock'. 'There is no such thing as extinction of
energy.'

Self-taught, she was aware of her creative, laterally-
thinking approach: 'It may just be that one sees [things]
because one has an open mind, not in a groove.' Like the gift of
memory, it remained with her into an old age remarkable for
advanced and unorthodox attitudes to problems such as sheep-
dipping or treatments for cancer (*see pp. 182–3, 89*).

Stalking roe-deer in 1892, she was inspired to a typically
penetrating observation – on the arrangement of eyes in man
and other animals. Bats and rabbits, for instance, have 'an
absolute gap between the two planes of vision . . . It would
follow logically that those whose eyes are most sideways would
rely most on their ears.' Beatrix relied on her eyes and her
profound knowledge. Her creatures, scrupulously observed and
anatomically correct, are drawn with unsentimental realism –
except that the unsavoury details are glossed over or relegated
to the journal. They behave in character and live in the right
sort of burrows, only slightly over-furnished. The smaller
creatures leave the most lasting impression, and are drawn
from their own field of view – nowhere more so than in *Johnny
Town-Mouse*, where loud noises and huge objects threaten
(*130*). Beatrix constantly reminds us that 'Nature, though

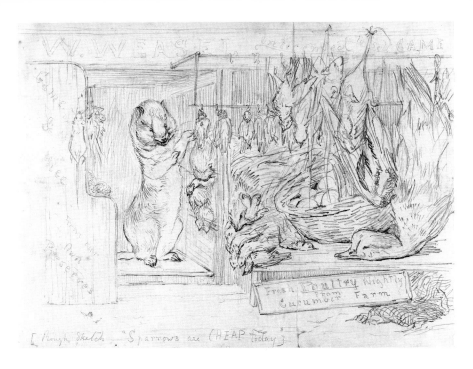

167 'The Weasel's Poultry
Shop', c. 1891

168 (below left) Study of a
weasel, Camfield, 1888

169 (below) 'The Squirrel's
Gift', c. 1890

never consciously wicked, has always been ruthless'. She
writes with the objectivity of a countrywoman: 'I see no reason
why common-sense should not foster a healthier appreciation
of beauty than morbid sentimentality.'

Several drawings which represent the borderline between
observation and imagination reflect both unsentimentality
and expertise. The self-satisfied proprietor of 'The Weasel's
Poultry Shop' is 'Unlicensed to sell GAME'; birds and mice
hang in the window, labelled 'Sparrows are CHEAP today' and
'Fresh *Poultry* Nightly'. Like the toy picture shop (*101, 102*)
this drawing was probably a Christmas present. Beatrix also
made straightforward studies of weasels and stoats, finding a
dead stoat difficult to draw.

Red squirrels, like bat populations, had not yet declined in
number at the start of this century. 'The Squirrel's Gift', set
probably in a Scottish forest, appears to have been touched up
for publication. Two drawings of squirrels on a log, front view
and back view, fit perfectly together to make a greetings card.
The annual rings of the tree are clearly shown. Trees interested
Beatrix both scientifically and imaginatively; she wrote several
serious articles on trees and timber and also two fairy tales,
'The Fairy in the Oak' and 'The Oakmen'.

The 'Tales' teem with a variety of fauna and flora. Apart from the main actors there is a procession of supporting characters, especially in *Mrs. Tittlemouse* and *Jeremy Fisher*. Part of the decor, rather than of the drama, are the dead mole and mice of *Squirrel Nutkin* and the house-fly settled on the doll's house roof in *Two Bad Mice*.

Gardens, and the food which grows in them, play a central part, from the Bad Rabbit's carrot or Peter Rabbit's radishes to the broad beans and onions of *Benjamin Bunny* – not forgetting the Flopsy Bunnies with their decaying marrows and soporific lettuce. The paraphernalia of gardening are in evidence everywhere: wheelbarrows, waterbutts, watering cans, sieves and swills – and the 'still life' of Mr McGregor's rubbish heap. Beatrix often drew fruit better than flowers. There is soft fruit – blackcurrants and strawberries – and wild fruit – elderberries

170, 171 Two squirrels on a log: card design (front and back view), *c.* 1895

172 Broad bean in flower: background study for *The Tale of Benjamin Bunny*, 1903

173 (left) Timmy Willie and strawberry, *The Tale of Johnny Town-Mouse*, p. 58, 1918

174 Study of a pine-cone (*detail*), 1895

175 Study of foxgloves, possibly for *The Tale of Jemima Puddle-Duck*, 1908

176 'The Veal and Ham Pie', *The Pie and the Patty-Pan*, p. 23, 1905

and blackberries, pine-cones and crab-apples. She loved bluebell woods, drawing them for *Cecily Parsley* and *Mr. Tod*, and for *The Fairy Caravan*, where they are lyrically described. Foxgloves mask the crude hut of Mr Tod, and Benjamin Bunny sports a carnation in his buttonhole. Cultivated flowers run riot in the luxuriant cottage gardens of *Tom Kitten* and *The Pie and the Patty-Pan*: nodding bleeding hearts or neat box hedges, tiger lilies, pansies, pinks and poppies. Geraniums usually appear on window ledges (294), but sometimes as flying objects.

Like all Victorian young ladies Beatrix had to fulfil her quota of flower paintings. Of the more conventional examples, several were done in the Lake District: for instance wild yellow balsam (*Impatiens noli-tangere*) at 'Derwentwater, also Coniston'. Later she writes of the 'peculiar blue' of snow on white frost: 'I know no colour like it except that milky lemon-blue which you find in the seed of wild balsam.' Sprays of sweet bay are inscribed: 'Direct light from this side' and 'Against the light. The veins in the leaf are slightly transparent. There has been no sunshine & evergreen leaves show very little transparent light without it.' Arrows point to the direction of the

177 (below left) Sprays of sweet bay, 1900

178 (below) 'Duchess in the porch', *The Pie and the Patty-Pan*, p. 35, 1905

179 (above) Study of a daisy plant

180 (right) 'Dinner in Mouseland', c. 1900

181 Cecily Parsley makes cowslip wine, *Cecily Parsley's Nursery Rhymes*, p. 10, 1922

light. Beatrix usually examined individual plants, but there are some delightful mixed bunches too: Duchess standing in the porch with an outsize 'tussie-mussie' (in *The Pie and the Patty-Pan*); a group of wild flowers in an outdoor setting (*14*). Daisies, drawn plain or coloured, are aptly chosen for miniature settings – in *Mrs. Tiggy-Winkle* or *Johnny Town-Mouse*, or (as a pot-plant) in the fantasy 'Dinner in Mouseland'.

The gardens were soon to be peopled with animals, the flowers their accessories, but Beatrix remained the complete botanist, writing on the medical properties of elder – which, like cowslips, she made into wine, à la Cecily Parsley. Owning an early edition of Gerard's *Herbal*, she knew of other remedies, among them Peter Rabbit's camomile tea. The herb pudding offered to Johnny Town-Mouse must have been the cleansing Easter Ledger Pudding (based on bistort, with dandelion, nettle or lady's mantle), still a springtime dish in the Lake District. Her greatest expertise however lay in the field of mycology.

Beatrix first discovered fungi at Dalguise, but early encouragement came from her 'discreet uncle' Sir Henry Roscoe, who had married Rupert Potter's younger sister Lucy. The Roscoes gardened and farmed at Woodcote in Surrey; their youngest daughter Dora had a gypsy caravan in which the two cousins used to paint animals and plants. Mr McGregor may have been partly inspired by their bad-tempered head-gardener, plagued with rabbits. The cultivated, cosmopolitan and broad-minded atmosphere of the Roscoe household had a profound effect on Beatrix. She spent several Christmases there, drawing birds in the snow and special pictures for her favourite aunt (*97, 98*), and she found refuge at Woodcote soon after Norman Warne's death in 1905.

Sir Henry Roscoe, FRS and Vice-Chancellor of London University, was a great educationist and a specialist in the sewage pollution of rivers, collaborating with Joseph Lunt and

182 'A Dream of Toasted Cheese', 1899

Frank Scudder. To honour the publication of Roscoe and Lunt's popular *First Step in Chemistry*, Beatrix presented her Uncle Harry with 'A Dream of Toasted Cheese' (*182*), making sly reference to a statement in the book on NH_3 (ammonia gas): 'The peculiar pungent smell of this compound is noticed if we heat a bit of CHEESE in a test-tube.' Roscoe was highly tickled, and reproduced the drawing, 'as original as it is humorous', in his autobiography. The learned mouse perched on the Bunsen burner (Roscoe had studied and worked with Bunsen) appears elsewhere, reading a newspaper (*106*) and on the *Tailor of Gloucester* cover. Industrious mice in the background manipulate test tubes and retorts, and sit in scale-pans: a few are familiar from the sheets scattered with mouse studies.

Some time before the 'romantic elopement' to Kew with Uncle Harry (*see p. 90*), Beatrix had renewed her acquaintance with 'that learned but extremely shy man' Charles McIntosh, the most important influence on her study of funguses – as they were then called. As postman at Dunkeld he observed fungi, ferns and mosses on his daily fifteen-mile walks. 'Modern habits and machines are not calculated to bring out individuality or the study of Natural History': Charlie's successor had a tricycle. In 1887 Rupert Potter had sent him the newly-published *British Hymenomycetes* by an acknowledged authority, the Rev. John Stevenson of Glamis.

Long ago at Dalguise it had been 'an amusement to hop from puddle to puddle on the strides of Charlie's hob-nailed boots'. Meeting him again, now retired, at Birnam in 1892 – and reminded of a 'damaged lamp post' or 'a scared startled scarecrow' – Beatrix discussed fungi with him. 'He was certainly pleased with my drawings, and his judgement . . . gave me infinitely more pleasure than that of critics who assume more, and know less than poor Charlie. He is a perfect dragon of erudition, and not gardener's Latin either.'

Beatrix was already painting fungi in 1888; 'by lucky intuition' she had chosen two species in which Charlie was interested: 'he became quite excited and spoke with quite poetical feeling about their exquisite colours'. He collected fungi for Beatrix to paint, posting them to London in the winter. She was not the first naturalist to be discouraged by the foxy smell of Stinkhorn (*Phallus impudicus*). Still addressing Charlie formally in the third person, she hopes he will not send 'a horrid plant like a white stick with a loose cap which smells exactly like a dead sheep'. Charlie McIntosh taught her the importance of correct nomenclature and the study of living specimens. She became knowledgeable about her finds, and grew in confidence over the identification of obscure species, even questioning Stevenson about *Lyophyllum decastes*. In the grounds at Eastwood she found an extremely rare fungus, similar to a pine-cone: *Strobilomyces floccopus* or Old Man of the Woods (*26*). Stevenson confirmed Charlie's identification, 'a very good find'. (Mr Massee at Kew saw it only once, in

183 *Leccinum melanea* and *Leccinum scabrum* (*detail* showing the former), Lingholm, October 1897

184 *Amanita muscaria* (Fly Agaric) with polypody fern and lichen, *c.* 1895

a wood near Watford.) Beatrix painted it on 3 September 1893, the day before she sent Noel Moore the Peter Rabbit picture letter. Could Mr McIntosh have been another, less irascible forebear of Mr McGregor?

Beatrix's studies of fungi were unusually detailed for her time, especially for an amateur, but Charlie suggested that she 'might make them more perfect as botanical drawings by making separate sketches of sections showing the attachments of the gills; the stem if it be hollow or otherwise, or any other detail that would show the characteristics of the plant more clearly'. She incorporated these suggestions into later drawings – as in the view of cap, gills and longitudinal section of the whole fructification of *Leccinum melanea*. Beatrix lamented 'Now of all hopeless things to draw, I should think the very worst is a fine fat fungus', and according to her Sawrey friend Miss Hammond she always claimed to have ruined her eyes doing the fungi and microscopic work.

Beatrix produced over 300 drawings of which any mycologist would be proud today, without modern aids such as a camera lucida, and keeping an exact record of the timing of spore germination. The fungi are often shown in their natural settings: grass, ferns and leaves. *Amanita muscaria*, the 'fierce red fly Agaric', is drawn with polypody fern, mosses and the lichen *Peltigera canina*: an example of her interest in mosses and ferns as well as lichens and fungi. *Amanita muscaria*, which

brought about the horrid end of a less fortunate fungus-illustrator in Dorothy L. Sayers' *The Documents in the Case*, she found near Lingholm in 1897 and painted with *Amanita crocea* (Yellow Grisette), a fungus of northern birchwoods. *Peziza aurantia* from the Woods of Strathallan nestles among fallen leaves (33); she recorded it again in Berwickshire. 'There was a great growth of crisp yellow *Peziza* in the moss, and a troop of gigantic *Cortinarius*', which she finds again by Smailholm Tower, 'brittle and graceful on bleached horse-dung in the bog'. At Coldstream she was 'overtaken with funguses, especially *Hygrophorus* [Wax Cap]', and in Hatchednize Wood 'the fungus starred the ground apparently in thousands . . . I found upwards of twenty sorts in a few minutes, . . . and joy of joys, the spiky *Gomphidius glutinosus*, a round, slimy, purple head among the moss, which I took up carefully with my old cheese-knife, and turning over saw the slimy veil. There is extreme complacency in finding a totally new species for the first time.' At Wray Castle in autumn 1895 she discovered *Lepiota friesii*, on a rubbish heap near the shrubbery.

In an 1897 picture letter Beatrix writes next to a picture of a rare little Scottish fungus like holly-berries: 'I have been drawing funguses very hard, I think some day they will be put in a book but it will be a dull one to read.' No expert could be found to write the text, till in 1966 Dr W. P. K. Findlay, impressed with her paintings which he saw at the Centenary Exhibition in Ambleside, used fifty-nine of them for *Wayside and Woodland Fungi* (Warne, 1967). Nearly all her specimens

185 *Gomphidius glutinosus*, Hatchednize Wood, Coldstream, August 1894

186 *Lepiota friesii*, Wray Castle, September 1895

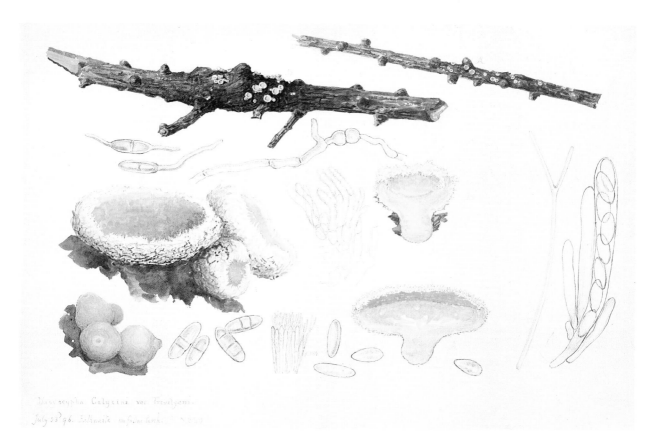

Dasyscypha Calycina var Woodyani...
July 23'96. Esthwaite in fir...tank.

187 *Lachnellula willkommii* (Larch Canker Fungus),
Esthwaite, July 1896

had been gathered between 1887 and 1901 in the woods of Perthshire and the Lake District, but she studied and photographed them most intensively from 1893 to 1898. The majority of the 'large fungus' drawings belong to the Armitt Library, Ambleside. Her wish for anonymity was respected by Henry Coates, who in his biography of Charlie McIntosh (1923) tactfully refers to her as a lady who afterwards made a name for herself as a student of fungi.

Beatrix's fungus experiments extended to dry rot (*Serpula lacrymans*); she sneaked out after dark with a paper bag and a sixpence to secure some rotten wood from a shop-front. One sample she buried in the garden: 'How I should catch it, my parents are not devoted to the cause of science. I think I will take it out after dark and grow it in the Boltons. I slept badly.' Forty years later, reminded of her interest in Pasteur and his experiments with *Penicillium*, she scribbled a note, which she automatically edited as if for publication, suggesting the use of dry rot or fungus growths on trees in cancer research. A birch tree fungus has, in fact, recently been tried out in Russia as a cure for human cancer.

Her observation of fungi such as *Lachnellula willkommii* (Larch Canker Fungus) anticipates our present understanding of the close association between certain trees and fungi. Trees are often the first major indicators of change, and agarics can absorb heavy metal ions toxic to man; lichenized fungi are nowadays used to gauge environmental conditions.

Beatrix realized that many fungi must survive the winter months in the form of a mould – a mycelium and propagated by spores. She succeeded – by what method is not known – in sprouting spores of over forty fungi, in at least one case taking records every six hours and drawing the spore germination x 600. Other workers had long been able to germinate other fungi, but she was the first to succeed with Basidiomycetes (in particular, agarics) in Britain. Before her, only Brefeld in Germany had recorded their germination. She was also one of the first to be aware of the symbiotic compound nature of lichens (alga and fungus in intimate association), preceded only by Schwendener – and even he thought that one organism was parasitic on the other. At any rate, in 1896 no one else was 'at it' in London.

The spores Beatrix grew were originally thought to be those of the 'winter fungus', *Collybia* or *Flammulina velutipes* (Velvet Shank), which McIntosh had sent her in 1893. It has now been established that she probably used *Aleurodiscus amorphus* (then known as *Corticium amorphum*), for which she asked in January 1897 – a rare and inconspicuous, lichen-like fungus. She had in fact already drawn the germinating spores without realizing it, possibly mistaking this fungus for a lichen because of a 'jelly fungus' parasitic on it. Sure of her ground and 'under the delusion no one has grown them except me and Dr Brefeld', she had already consulted the experts at Kew, which she first visited in 1896 under the protection of Sir Henry Roscoe 'in a sudden fit of kindness'.

At Kew she met the Assistant Director, George Massee, and another who appeared to have been dried in blotting-paper under a press, and then the Director himself, Sir William Thiselton-Dyer, 'wide awake and boastful', with a 'dry, cynical manner' but a healthy respect for Uncle Harry. Seeming surprised by the drawings, he wrote a letter which Roscoe would not show her – '*rude* and *stupid*'. Roscoe tried to discover 'what they knew, without saying I did' from Massee, of whom Beatrix writes ruefully: 'I opine that he has passed several stages of development into a fungus himself – I am occasionally conscious of a similar transformation'.

As an amateur and a woman Beatrix shocked the scientific establishment by making independent experiments and developing theories. But in December she was confident enough to 'have it up and down' with Thiselton-Dyer. 'I informed him that it would all be in the books in ten years, whether or no, and departed giggling.' Even Massee had come round.

On the basis of her research Beatrix prepared a paper (now lost): 'On the Germination of the Spores of *Agaricineae*'. Her father went through it with a pencil, making remarks upon the grammar, but her supervisor was Uncle Harry, annoyed by Thiselton-Dyer and determined to see it through. 'It will want a great deal more work in references and putting together, but no matter. I shall keep these pencil marks when I am an old woman.' Having written something out and got it typed she went by train to Kew – but was too shy to give it in person to the Director. The paper was read, possibly 'by title' only, by Massee on 1 April 1897. Beatrix was not allowed to present it in person. She informed Charlie McIntosh however that it had been 'well received', but 'they' say more work is needed on it. In any case, Beatrix was already preparing more advanced studies of spore development. Most of her mycological drawings made under the microscope still await scientific appraisal. Contemporary experts failed to realize the importance of her work, but time has proved that the 'shy person' was right.

Beatrix's expert knowledge of mycology spills over into her imaginative works, and she invests fungi with personality, possessed 'with the fancy that they laugh and clap their hands, especially the little ones that grow in troops and rings amongst dead leaves in the woods'. Fairy rings intrigued her: an unpublished rhyme, 'Nid nid noddy, We stand in a ring', was to be illustrated by three fungi with faces dancing 'in the merry moonlight' (339). The rhyme reappears in a chapter of the *Fairy Caravan* sequel entitled 'A Walk amongst the Funguses'. This whimsical but informative introduction to fungi is an instance of her talent for description.

> The first was like a very tall cream-coloured umbrella with brown spots on top, and a white fringe round its waist [The Parasol 425] . . . I know Mixomycetes [sic] walks about; I have seen him go from one end of a log to another . . . Look at that very big one, solitary, under the birch tree, with chestnut cap and speckled white gray stem; he too is a Boletus, his name is Scaber [Brown Birch Bolete]. And here is another Boletus, cousin Edulis [Ceps] . . . There is a beauty, but do not touch him, he is poisonous. Look at his velvet coat, all buff and crimson; but if a bit were broken off his edge it would turn verdigris blue [*Boletus luridus?*].

Xarifa curtseys to the Boletus, reprimanding her nervously aggressive pupil Tuppenny: 'It is injudicious to throw nuts at things which we do not understand.' 'The Boletus took no notice; it sat out in the sun, drying its sticky cap': typical behaviour for a *Boletus*.

Beatrix uses her mycology with wit. Paddy Pig in *The Fairy Caravan* suffers from the hallucinogenic effects of toadstool tartlets (Fly Agaric ?); and the toads at their tea-party (336) perch on paddock stools, or toadstools. Like Mrs Tittlemouse and her guests they drink honey-dew from acorn-cups: honey-dew refers to the exudate of the ergot fungus.

In the 1890s two subjects came close to usurping the fungi: palaeontology and geology. Fossils first became a passion at Dalguise, though finds are most often recorded between 1893 and 1897. During that last Scottish summer in 1894 at Coldstream she not only made 'about 40 careful drawings of fungi' but collected some interesting fossils, including one fine

188 Paddy Pig in hollow tree with bracket fungus, *The Fairy Caravan*, p. 90, 1929

189   Fossil studies, one done at Lennel, Berwickshire, October 1894

specimen at Berwick, on a cinder-walk just below the Goods Station. By October she had found out which stones to split and how to use a cold chisel. Near the end of the holiday she discovered yet more fungi and fossils: it was aggravating to leave with the district only half investigated, but she had done 'a good summer's work'.

Her tastes were catholic and she took fossils as she found them. Through her Gloucestershire cousins she met Mr Lucy, an amateur geologist who helped her to identify specimens, amusing her by putting them in his mouth. 'He seems to think it positively improper to collect fossils all over the country, but I do not feel under any obligation to confine my attention to a particular formation, viz., the various zones of the Inferior Oölite at Stroud, which I visit once a year for ten days. I beg to state I intend to pick up everything I find which is not too heavy.' Though heavy indeed was her father's discarded camera with which she photographed fossils and boulders. Back in London, she wondered 'whether geology names the fossils or the fossils geology' but at Swanage in the spring, 'scrabbling about the unsafe quarries', she concludes 'I find it better not to expect or worry much about geology'.

Quarries were an important source of fossils, though the quarrymen made her nervous. She disinterred ammonites from a quarry in the white Portland stone and corals, encrinites and shells in Denbighshire, and the stone walls of Cumbria produced more treasures. In August 1895 she climbed up Nanny Lane above Troutbeck, finding many shells and spying 'something sticking up grey on the top of a wall'. That something she recorded with other finds in a remarkably dense and photographic technique (32). She was naturally interested in the fossil types of fungi and in 1897 asked Dr Woodward at the Museum about the eozoon, Mr Massee having told her there were funguses in the Laurentian. 'It is a very beautiful green.'

Even after the 'Tales' were in full swing, Beatrix returned to fossils from time to time. She tells Norman that she has been 'very industriously drawing fossils at the museum upon the theory that a change of work is the best sort of rest!' In 1894 she mused philosophically: 'The funguses will come up again and the fossils will keep. I hope I may go back again some day when I am an old woman, unless I happen to become a fossil myself, which would save trouble.'

Nothing on or in the ground escaped investigation, whether the vestiges of plants and animals, the ravages of glaciers or the artefacts of man. Every movable object of interest would be taken home to copy, for one really observes an object only in the act of drawing it. On holiday she scoured museums not merely for fossils, and was much annoyed to find the Kelso Archaeological Museum locked up: the Curator had gone for her holiday and taken the key. Later during the Lennel stay she was recompensed by a find near Flodden Field (where she succeeded in pinpointing the exact location of the battle). 'To my great pleasure I picked up a very thin, rusted strip of iron about the size of the palm of my hand . . . It might indifferently be an old kettle or a fragment of armour, but I was quite satisfied.'

The Antiquarian Museum at Salisbury had both fossils and the Blackmore collection of antiquities, which contained an exceptionally fine collection of flints (and some forgeries too). Beatrix comments with characteristic modesty, 'The subject is beyond an ordinary person'. Otherwise the earlier antiquities are hardly mentioned in comparison with classical remains. The Salisbury collection was founded on Roman objects unearthed during the drainage after the cholera: small pieces of ironwork and Roman pottery.

Beatrix went twice to Burlington House to see the results of the Silchester excavations. Enthusiastic especially about the pottery, she admired the figured Samian ware but admitted that it was 'perhaps not the highest type of art'. Two of the pieces, a stag-pattern and a running scroll, were almost identical with ones found at Bucklersbury which she borrowed from 'the squire' to draw. She went again in April 1896 to see the Silchester finds at Swanage, intrigued by an object 'similar to the Bucklersbury drawn by me, which I took to be a weight off a steelyard'. She also remarks on the bad taste of Roman art. The pavements would be better seen in place: 'Reared on end their hideousness of pattern is so strongly reminiscent of the modern jerry-builders, that their antiquity fails to impress.'

The Bucklersbury pieces to which Beatrix refers were all drawn in 1894–5, when a certain Tom H. Squire lent her some Roman artefacts dug up twenty years earlier at Queen Victoria Street in the City of London – near the place where the celebrated mosaic pavement came to light in 1869. A characteristic collection of antiquities was found on this site in 1872–3 and again in 1954–5, when the Temple of Mithras was

190 Fragments of Samian potsherd, 1895

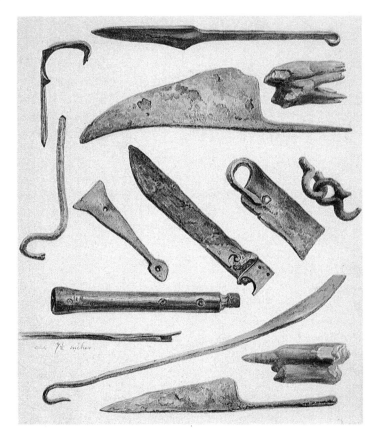

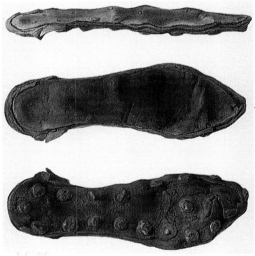

191 (left) Objects from the Bucklersbury excavations, including knives, ?1895

192 (above) Roman shoe leathers, probably from the Walbrook, 1895

discovered. During the first century of Roman occupation many small manufactured articles had been lost in the Walbrook stream: personal ornaments, shoes, domestic utensils, surgical or toilet instruments and small craftsmen's tools. Beatrix meticulously recorded the objects from every angle, supplying scale diagrams. Her drawings reflect the conventional antiquarian approach of her time, but they are much more than aids to identification. Superbly arranged on the page, they convey the texture of old leather and rusty iron to a positively tactile degree. In much the same way she also made experimental studies of a modern horseshoe.

Entomology, botany, mycology or geology were all possible fields of expertise for Beatrix: only astronomy failed to attract. 'I do not often consider the stars, they give me a *tissick*. It is more than enough that there should be forty thousand named and unclassified funguses.' Beatrix sometimes regretted the serious research she had abandoned in the belief that it was leading nowhere. The 'funguses' which originally raised her low spirits inspired some of her best watercolours – but if her discoveries had been taken seriously there might have been no Peter Rabbit books.

A.S.H.

5
THE TALE OF PETER RABBIT

For many people the names of Beatrix Potter and Peter Rabbit are synonymous. *The Tale of Peter Rabbit* was the first of her little books to be published and since its appearance in a privately printed edition in 1901 it has been read by countless children. As Frederick Warne took up publication, and as other books similar in size and format followed in quick succession, the series became known as 'The Peter Rabbit Books', thus perpetuating the linking of the author's name with that of her first hero.

Rabbits had been part of Beatrix's life from an early age. When she was just eight her father told her in a letter about 'a bunny on the lawn no bigger than your bear' and, a few years later, an old family friend, William Gaskell, sent greetings to her current pet: 'A rabbit lying among the heather reminded me of Tommy, who I hope is taking his food properly, and doing well. If you think he remembers me, please give him my kind regards.'

Beatrix started drawing rabbits early, too. In the sketchbook that she kept when she was 9, among the meticulously realistic drawings of flowers and birds, there are two pages of rabbit fantasies by the young artist (67). Although the fully-clothed figures are more human in their actions than rabbit-like, they clearly have rabbit heads and long rabbit ears protrude from under their hats.

Two delightful rabbit watercolours by Beatrix (75, 194), believed to have been done in 1880, are preserved in the

193 (below) Three heads of a rabbit, ?1904

194 (below right) A recumbent rabbit, probably Peter, c.1880

Victoria and Albert Museum collection of her work in London, and they are remarkable paintings for a 14-year-old. Happily, there are also a number of her early sketches and watercolours in other collections in Britain and America and although not many of them were dated by her it is known that they were done when she was in her teens and early twenties. They stand as valuable evidence of her increasing artistic skill and technical ability in this particular field.

For models Beatrix used her own pets, and it was Benjamin H. Bouncer (Bounce for short) who featured in her first published work. The name of Beatrix's next pet rabbit was Peter, 'bought at a very tender age, in the Uxbridge Road, Shepherds Bush, for the exorbitant sum of 4/6'. Like his predecessor, Peter became an important member of the Potter family, accompanying his mistress, who was now well into her late twenties, to Scotland and the Lake District on holiday. Peter featured often in her drawings and letters, for whenever

195 (left) A toy picture made for Walter Gaddum

196 (above) Design for a Christmas card, probably for Hildesheimer & Faulkner

197 Peter Rabbit lying by the fire at 2 Bolton Gardens, 1899

she went away Beatrix wrote enchantingly to young friends, illustrating her letters with quick sketches.

Many of her letters were written to Noel Moore, the oldest son of her former governess, Annie Carter, for Noel was a delicate child and often ill. One year, when Beatrix was on holiday in Scotland, she ran out of things to say to Noel and instead of her usual account of holiday activities she made up a story for him, a story about 'four little rabbits, whose names were Flopsy, Mopsy, Cottontail and Peter'. Her letter, from Eastwood, Dunkeld, written on 4 September 1893, became one of the most famous letters ever written.

The children who received Beatrix's letters prized them highly and kept them carefully, so when, in 1900, she asked the 13-year-old Noel if she could borrow that particular letter back he was able to produce it without difficulty. Beatrix had had an idea that her story might make a book. She copied it out carefully, adding little bits here, changing details there, until she was satisfied that it made a pleasing whole. She also

198   A study of a rabbit, believed to be Peter

199   The first page of an eight-page letter to Noel Moore, 1893

experimented with numerous sketches before she decided on her final forty-one black-and-white drawings, one for each page, and then she added a coloured frontispiece, a picture of Mrs Rabbit dosing Peter with camomile tea. *The Tale of Peter Rabbit and Mr. McGregor's Garden* by H. B. Potter was ready, but now Beatrix had to find a publisher.

For advice in this she turned to her old Lake District friend, Hardwicke Rawnsley, himself an author of children's verses, and after due consideration the book was submitted to – and rejected by – at least six publishers. It was generally thought at that time that a large format and a lot of colour were the essential ingredients of any book for children, and H. B. Potter's book was small, the only colour soon over. There was one publisher however, Frederick Warne, who showed a passing interest, but their enthusiasm waned when they discovered that the author was adamant that the size and form of the book must remain exactly as it had been conceived.

By the following year Beatrix was becoming frustrated and annoyed. She was determined to see her book in print and the one way to achieve this was to publish it herself. She had some knowledge about the mechanics of printing, she had the money to finance a small edition and she had an artist friend who could recommend a printer. Beatrix ordered 250 copies of '*The Tale of Peter Rabbit* by Beatrix Potter' (Mr McGregor had been discarded from the title) to be produced by Strangeways & Sons of Tower Street in London, with the coloured frontispieces printed in the recently introduced three-colour process, delivered to them from Hentschel of Fleet Street. Beatrix had asked for 500 copies of the frontispiece in case the book should need to be reprinted in a hurry.

While Beatrix was negotiating with printers, Hardwicke Rawnsley was persevering in his search for a commercial publisher, and in an effort to attract a sympathetic editor he had rewritten Beatrix's text in his own, unmistakable style:

> There were four little bunnies – no bunnies were sweeter,
> Mopsy and Cotton-tail, Flopsy and Peter.
> They lived in a sand-bank, as here you may see,
> At the foot of a fir – a magnificent tree . . .

And he ended her story with a touch of his own *Moral Rhymes for the Young*:

> Enough now of Peter but what of the others,
> Those good little pattern-obedient brothers?
> They sat down to tea, too good mannered to cram
> And ate bread & milk and sweet blackberry jam,
> And thought, as we all think, by far the best way
> Is to do what we're told and our mothers obey.

Hardwicke sent part of his manuscript and Beatrix's illustrations to Frederick Warne once again in September 1901, telling them about her private publication plans and, more

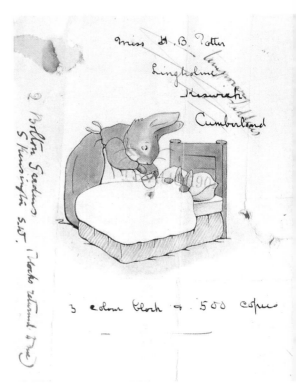

200 The printer's proof of the frontispiece for the privately-printed edition of *The Tale of Peter Rabbit*, 1901

importantly, about the existence of the plates with which to print the coloured frontispiece. This time Warne expressed serious interest, but only if Beatrix would colour all the pictures – and if the text could be in prose rather than in verse. There was no problem about the latter (except perhaps Hardwicke's wounded pride) but Beatrix was still reluctant about colour. 'I did not colour the book for two reasons – the great expense of good colour printing – and also the rather uninteresting colour of a good many of the subjects which are most of them rabbit-brown and green.'

Perhaps because she knew that, through her own publication, her little book would make its first appearance in exactly the way she wanted, Beatrix eventually agreed to Warne's proposals, not only to add colour to her pictures but also to reduce the length of the book so that there would be a total of thirty-one colour illustrations to print instead of the one colour and forty-one black-and-white of the original. The book could then be printed on one sheet of paper, which would help to keep the costs to a realistic level. In addition, as Warne could not publish until 1902, Beatrix's own edition, due for delivery in only two months, would have time to find its customers.

The privately-printed edition of *The Tale of Peter Rabbit* was ready on 16 December 1901. It was modestly produced, the light grey-green paper boards cut flush, the title and author printed in black and separated by a line drawing of four beribboned rabbits seated demurely in a semi-circle. The drawings throughout are very simple, with the minimum use of line and almost no shading, cross-hatching or highlighting. The text is set in the centre of each right-hand page, balancing the picture on the left. Often there is only a single sentence, starting with a large dropped capital, and a comparison of the printed book with Beatrix's original manuscript shows that it was she who dictated the design.

The story has a wonderful range of emotion and excitement and the pacing is superb. It is the classic tale of the naughty child, flying in the face of authority, deliberately disobeying

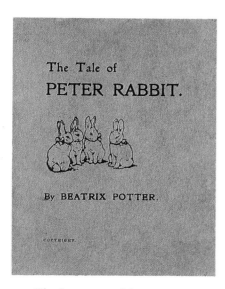

201 The front cover of the privately-printed edition of *The Tale of Peter Rabbit*, 1901

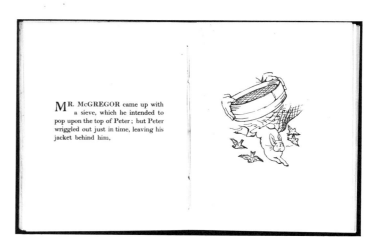

202 The privately-printed edition of *The Tale of Peter Rabbit*, pp. 40–1, 1901

instructions – and getting his just deserts. The adult is conveniently removed from the scene of action when old Mrs Rabbit goes off to the baker's and Peter is cleverly contrasted with his sisters 'who were good little bunnies'. Peter feels sick because he has overeaten, and the reader is given an old-fashioned remedy for the relief of indigestion. Peter is then frightened not only out of his wits but also out of his clothes when he is chased, but just as the tension gets almost too much to bear Mr McGregor gives up and resumes his gardening. Both Peter and the reader are given a quiet interlude in which to regain their breath while Peter is lost in the garden, although being lost is something all children dread and something no lost child ever forgets. Then the excitement of the chase starts again. As in all the best stories there is a happy ending in that Peter reaches home safely but, as in all true moral tales, he suffers for his disobedience.

Time and again people remember the ending as 'Peter was punished and sent to bed without any supper', but that is not at all how Beatrix Potter tells her story. Peter was put to bed by his mother because he was not very well, and for the same reason he was dosed with camomile tea. It was as a direct result of his own over-indulgence and not because of an imposed punishment that Peter was unable to share Flopsy, Mopsy and Cottontail's supper of bread and milk and blackberries.

One of the most interesting pictures in the book is the one of Peter standing by the locked door in the garden wall. It was Margaret Lane in *The Magic Years* who first drew attention to the similarity between this picture and American-born Anna Lea Merritt's *Love Locked Out*, and further research in this direction has been rewarding. The painting, inscribed 'ALM 1889', attracted particular attention when it was bought from the Royal Academy the following year for just £150 by the Chantrey Bequest. That the picture was of a nude and that it was the first painting by a woman to be bought by the Chantrey Bequest caused much comment, not least from the then President of the Royal Society of British Artists, Wyke Bayliss. 'One of the loveliest of the Landmarks in the realms of Art has been discovered within the lifetime of most of us. I mean the formal, authoritative recognition of the fact that women can paint pictures . . .' Such a comment might well have caught the amused eye of the 24-year-old Beatrix, who was a regular gallery visitor and who was just beginning to sell her own first drawings. It would also have been in character for her to remember it when she was preparing *Peter Rabbit* ten years later.

Within two weeks of Beatrix receiving the copies of her book she could see that she would be soon running out of stock and she ordered a reprint of 200. Her foresight in printing a double quantity of frontispieces had proved well justified. The reprint looked very similar to the first edition but there were a number of subtle changes. The book was given a stronger,

203, 204 *Love Locked Out*, Anna Lea Merritt, 1890, with 'Peter by the locked door', *The Tale of Peter Rabbit*, p. 44, 1902

round-backed binding in an olive-green paper and the title-page bore the date, 'February 1902', for Beatrix had omitted to date the first printing altogether. She also took the opportunity of the reprint to polish the text a little, inserting a word here, deleting one there, moving a phrase from one page to the next. Her book was now just as she wanted it to be.

In her negotiations with Frederick Warne over their edition Beatrix showed both determination and percipience. She insisted that the illustrations should be printed in the more expensive three-colour process of her original frontispiece, instead of in the wood-block process that Warne usually employed, though the price should be one 'that little rabbits could afford', and she made sure that her copyright would be well secured.

It was six months before Warne were satisfied with their costing and were able to prepare a contract for the author's signature, by which time Beatrix had not only reshaped the book but also finished all the new pictures. Her first task was to decide what to leave out, for she had to 'lose' eleven pictures. She eliminated only four from the first half, not such a difficult task for the text there was already brief and easily moved back to the previous page or forward to the next. The three she took from the middle of the story presented more problems, for the text there was already longer and could certainly not be fitted in to the remaining space. So Beatrix made some cuts to the story, the most important being her deletion of Mr McGregor singing 'Three Blind Mice' to himself as he hoed the onions. The final four pictures went from the last six spreads of the book, Beatrix deciding that the account of how Peter's widowed mother earned enough to keep her family clothed and fed could conveniently be removed. (Neither words nor pictures were lost altogether, however, for two years later Beatrix was to put them into *The Tale of Benjamin Bunny*, which was typical of her reluctance to waste anything.)

Once the length of the book had been reduced Beatrix turned her attention to the colouring of the pictures. She started by adding colour to her old black-and-white drawings but it soon became apparent that the result would be quite unsatisfactory and that she must start completely afresh. The task of redrawing was made more difficult for her by the death of the real Peter and with his replacement by a younger model who 'made the drawings look wrong'. She also had trouble with Mr and Mrs McGregor, commenting to Warne, 'I never learnt to draw figures'. They asked her to redo altogether the picture of Mrs McGregor serving up Peter's father in a pie, as they were concerned that the old woman might frighten some children. Into the redrawn picture, which shows a very much younger, prettier gardener's wife, Beatrix introduced the shadow of a junior member of the McGregor family, spoon raised in anticipation. In both versions, as Mrs McGregor has no protection for her hands one must assume that it was cold rabbit pie!

205, 206 The rejected (top) and redrawn (above) pictures for p. 14 of the first Warne edition of *The Tale of Peter Rabbit*, 1902

207 Mrs Rabbit sending her children out to gather blackberries, *The Tale of Peter Rabbit*, p. 11, 1902

For most of her new watercolour pictures Beatrix kept closely to the form and content of the original line drawings but with colour she was able to give depth and to add detail. She distinguished between the sexes of the rabbit children by using the age-old colours of sex difference – pink for the girls' cloaks and blue for Peter's jacket – and she solved the problem of how to frame her pictures by vignetting them. She kept her colours pale and offset her earlier fear of too much rabbit brown and green by introducing the red-breasted robin into two more of the pictures, red gooseberries into another and holly-berries into a third.

Edmund Evans printed the Frederick Warne edition. Beatrix was delighted with their reproduction of her artwork and made only a few suggestions for colour change to the first proofs. She selected brown and green as the colours for the binding and agreed that the prancing rabbit illustration should be repeated on the cover label. The endpapers were to be printed with a pale grey-blue leaf pattern.

The Tale of Peter Rabbit was published by Frederick Warne in October 1902 in an edition of 8,000 copies, 6,000 of which were paper-covered boards bound in grey or brown at 1/-, the rest bound in either a light-green or an olive-green cloth and priced at 1/6. By the end of the year Warne had gone back to press twice and 28,000 copies of the book were in print.

By the end of the following year there were two more books

208 A robin finds Peter's shoe, an unused illustration for the first Warne edition of *The Tale of Peter Rabbit*, 1902

209 (right) The front cover of the first Warne paper-covered boards edition of *The Tale of Peter Rabbit*, 1902

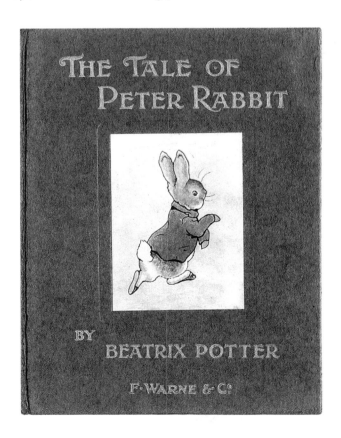

by Beatrix on the Warne list, *The Tale of Squirrel Nutkin* published in August 1903 and the trade edition of *The Tailor of Gloucester* which followed in October. For *Squirrel Nutkin* Beatrix had been persuaded to provide a full-colour endpaper, rather against her instincts. 'I always think that an endpaper ought to be something to rest the eye between the cover and the contents of the book; like a plain mount for a framed drawing.' Warne, however, felt strongly that the book needed full colour from the start and that it would greatly help the sales. Beatrix's portraits of her characters, linked by a delicate tracery and decorated here and there with flowers and small objects from the stories, were accompanied by a plea from her for the design to be 'kept rather small, or rather light coloured'.

Warne were delighted with the design and used it in both new books, and when yet another reprint (the fifth) of *Peter Rabbit* was needed in October 1903, they replaced the pale-blue leaf pattern with the new endpaper, repeated twice at the front and again at the back. In order to fit the four new pages of endpaper on to the single sheet of paper for colour printing, Beatrix was asked, once again, to reduce the length of *The Tale of Peter Rabbit*. She took the opportunity to remove the controversial picture of Mrs McGregor and the pie; the prancing rabbit also went (but was kept on the cover) and then she deleted two pictures from towards the end of the book – Peter going lippity-lippity and his return home to the big fir-tree. Beatrix did not cut the text; she moved the words from the 'lost' pages either to the page before or on to the next page, taking great care not to lose the flow of the book.

Only a month after the introduction of the new, single repeated endpaper Beatrix drew what appeared to be a mirror image design to face it, although close examination shows that it is not an exact mirror image and that there are one or two small detail differences. Over the next six years, as the series

210   One of the alternative endpaper designs intended but never used for the other language editions of the little books, 1913

211, 212   Two of the illustrations dropped from the fifth printing of *The Tale of Peter Rabbit* to make way for the coloured endpapers, 1903

grew, Beatrix added her new characters to the endpaper design, until in 1910 all the books in the series were carrying the endpapers with which we are so familiar today.

The binding of *Peter Rabbit* has changed, too, over the years. There have been editions bound in coloured paper boards, in cloth, in plain white laminated boards. There have been editions with thin tissue paper dust jackets, white laminated jackets, no jackets at all. But the feature that has remained constant for nearly a century has been the highlighting of the single rabbit figure on the front-cover board.

Since its first publication there has been speculation about the provenance of *The Tale of Peter Rabbit*, with definite claims for 'the actual Mr McGregor's garden' coming from locations as widely separated as Hertfordshire and Perthshire, while Mr McGregor himself has been positively identified by more than one person. There is no specific record but it is possible to glean a considerable amount of information from the rich collection of letters that Beatrix sent to friends and fans across the world. To a New Zealand friend in 1939 she wrote: 'Peter Rabbit's Garden – various. The most panoramic view with Peter in a wheelbarrow was done in a garden at Keswick which was completely altered afterwards. "Mr McGregor" gardened near Berwick – the only gardener I ever saw who weeded a gravel walk lying flat on his stomach! Mrs McG. imaginary. (Sorry for the lazy Mc's real wife!)'

The following year Beatrix answered an American en-quiry with: 'I never knew a gardener named "Mr McGregor". Several bearded horticulturalists have resented the nick-name; but I do not know how it came about, nor why "Peter" was called Peter . . . A few of the animals were harmless skits or caricatures, but Mr McGregor was not one of them and the backgrounds in Peter Rabbit were a mixture of locality.'

In a letter to her publisher written in 1942, Beatrix was a little more specific.

> If the vegetable garden and wicket gate were anywhere it was at Lingholm near Keswick; but it would be vain to look for it there, as a firm of landscape gardeners did away with it, and laid it out anew with paved walks etc . . . The lily pond in Peter was at Tenby, South Wales. The fir tree and some wood backgrounds were near Keswick. Mr McGregor was no special person; unless in the rheumatic way of planting cabbages . . . Peter Rabbit's potting shed and actual gera-niums were in Hertfordshire [at Bedwell Lodge, near Hatfield].

Peter Rabbit himself features in only two other Beatrix Potter books, *The Tale of Benjamin Bunny* and *The Tale of Mr. Tod*, though close study of the other books reveals that Peter's washing was done by Mrs Tiggy-winkle, that he shopped at 'Ginger & Pickles' and that he kept a nursery garden from which he 'lent' cabbages to the father of the Flopsy Bunnies.

213 'Whom should he meet but Mr. McGregor!', *The Tale of Peter Rabbit*, p. 24, 1902

214 'The first thing he saw was Mr. McGregor hoeing onions', *The Tale of Peter Rabbit*, p. 48, 1902

215　The frontispiece for *Peter Rabbit's Almanac for 1929*, 1928

He was also the main character in Beatrix's *Peter Rabbit's Painting Book*, published by Warne in 1911, and in *Peter Rabbit's Almanac for 1929*, a publication intended by Warne to be the first of a new series but which proved to be both the first and the last. The preparation of the illustrations interfered too much with Beatrix's involvement with her farm and the finished book was so much a disappointment to her that she declined to do another.

The image of the prancing rabbit, that dates back to the first trade edition of *The Tale of Peter Rabbit* in 1902, has come to stand for Beatrix Potter. Peter has always been the first choice for merchandisers and he can be found on products ranging from tea-cosies to jigsaw puzzles, from lampshades to bedroom slippers. The merchandise is by no means as recent a development as many believe. As long ago as 1903, Beatrix herself made a Peter Rabbit doll, tackling the problem of how to make him stand up in an unusual way. 'There is some shot in the body & coat tail, I don't think it will come out until the legs give way. Children sometimes expect comfits out of animals, so I give fair warning!'

The doll was followed the next year by wallpaper and then by 'The Game of Peter Rabbit', a board game devised by Beatrix and later developed by her publisher's wife. In 1924 Beatrix agreed to the use of Peter Rabbit's name in the campaign to raise money for the Invalid Children's Aid Association for which she was designing a collecting card, and from 1925 until her death in 1943 she provided drawings for the ICAA Christmas card, many of them featuring Peter Rabbit and his friends (455).

216　A selection of the current Peter Rabbit merchandise, 1986

217 The front cover of the Invalid Children's Aid Association (ICAA) Collecting Card, 1924

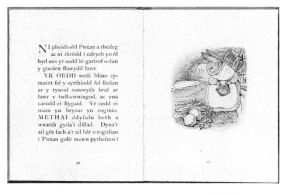

218 *Hanes Pwtan y Gwningen*, the Welsh-language edition of *The Tale of Peter Rabbit*, pp. 76–7, 1932

Beatrix supervised all the merchandise herself, looking after her 'side-shows', as she called them, with great care and attention. She had a good business sense and she enjoyed being involved in the negotiations, but what was of supreme importance to her was that any reproduction of her characters should be as faithful to the original as the medium would allow.

The Tale of Peter Rabbit has been translated into many languages and is a favourite of children across the world, whether they know the hero as Peter Rabbit, Peterchen Hase, Pierre Lapin, Pétur Kanínu or Pelle Kanin. The book has been set to music and dramatized for amateur production, and Peter is portrayed in the remarkable ballet film, *Tales of Beatrix Potter*. And he has had his imitators, too. The particular format of Beatrix Potter's books, the pattern of her words and pictures – especially those of *Peter Rabbit* – have been blatantly copied many times but nothing can destroy the magic of the original. *The Tale of Peter Rabbit* was Beatrix Potter's first book and it remains her most popular over eighty years after its first publication.

J.T.

6

THE LITTLE BOOKS

'It is much more satisfactory to address a real live child; I often think that that was the secret of the success of *Peter Rabbit*, it was written to a child – not made to order.' Infuriated only by adult criticism, Beatrix Potter tried out her tales on children, but she herself was the final judge. Like all the best children's authors she wrote – and drew – mainly for her own amusement, refusing to pander to popular demand. Popularity came however both easily and unexpectedly, at a time of well-known names and brightly-coloured toy books.

Beatrix Potter's most successful stories were published during a brief thirteen-year period; after her marriage in 1913 there were few books of the old calibre. The stories range from straightforward linear tales to more complicated minor epics – from domestic comedies to romances or more sinister dramas. The drama is increased by a matter-of-fact shrewdness – even toughness – and by a great economy in words: 'the shorter and plainer the better'. She took children seriously, believing that they deserved books written in simple, direct language. For the first time in literature for small children the words are as important as the illustrations. Beatrix laid the foundation for good reading – and writing: W. H. Auden and Graham Greene for instance acknowledge her influence. She rewrote and redrew indefatigably, taking great care over pacing and balance, suiting tone of voice to character and choosing the exact word and the right pictorial detail. Never slangy or verbose but elegant and understated, she was always aware of sound and rhythm. The complex resonances of her prose have their roots in rhyme and dialect, Shakespeare and the King James Bible – to which she returned when she felt her style needed chastening. She is part of the oral storytelling heritage, with its alliteration and repetition and its deceptive simplicity, in 'those brief, pregnant sentences which have slipped, like proverbs, into common speech' (Graham Greene).

Original in her writing, she was less able to draw from imagination: 'I can't invent, I only copy.' Like Caldecott she knew that the art of leaving out is a science: 'the fewer the lines, the less error committed', and her vivacious, flexible line is original in itself. Again like Caldecott, she joins the narrative tradition in English art. The picture draws us first – and sometimes says more than the words. Beatrix reacted with outrage to a comparison of her colour work with Constable, but no one is better at putting in his 'Dewy Freshness'.

219 'She sat there for *five hours*', while the invisible Peter and Benjamin cried in the onion-laden darkness beneath, *The Tale of Benjamin Bunny*, p. 47, 1904

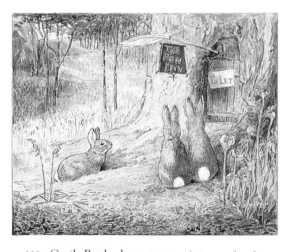

220 Cecily Parsley has run away, into a springtime sea of bluebells and uncurling bracken fronds, *Cecily Parsley's Nursery Rhymes*, p. 13, 1922

The settings, particularized yet ideal, are seen from an animal's perspective, and the creatures themselves are drawn large in relation to their backgrounds, with the precision of detail which children demand. The animal characters are usually young, inexperienced and irresponsible – and small, as are the books, made to fit a child's hands. Short enough to suit a brief attention span, the stories are never facile or trivial. Beatrix understood a child's need for the gravity concealed under the light relief. Her sense of comedy, subtle and ironic, is allied to a deep feeling for beauty.

There is also a sense of fair play. The stories are strongly moral, though that is not what leaves the most lasting impression; indeed, Beatrix more often than not is on the side of non-conformity and rebellion. The tables are turned on the aggressor – or else rash and foolish behaviour is met with the most effective punishments of all: ridicule or disgrace. Happy endings come in the nick of time, but an underlying melancholy remains. Beatrix never spares us from the truth, and out of the 'common objects of the countryside' she creates a microcosm of the world.

221 Jeremy Fisher in motion, sharply outlined against a soft backdrop of hills and trees, *The Tale of Mr. Jeremy Fisher*, cover, 1906

The Tailor of Gloucester was Beatrix Potter's own favourite among her 'little books' but, especially in its original form, it was one of her more complicated tales. It began life not as a picture letter like so many of her stories, but as the result of something she had heard about when staying with her cousin Caroline Hutton at Harescombe Grange in Gloucestershire. The strange story concerned a tailor who had to complete an elaborate waistcoat for a grand mayoral occasion, but at the end of the day he lacked the time to complete the commission and he also needed another packet of cherry-coloured silk. Beatrix's poor tailor was old and ill and could not get to work to complete the order; throughout his fever he murmured his concern about the task he was unable to do. But while his cat, Simpkin, was out doing the shopping, the tailor had let escape from under the tea cups all the mice that Simpkin had been saving for his supper. The cat was furious, but the mice were delighted with their freedom and rewarded the tailor by neatly finishing his work for him, except for one cherry-coloured buttonhole, where they left a message 'in little teeny weeny writing: "NO MORE TWIST"'. From then on the tailor grew quite prosperous and made wonderful waistcoats for all the rich gentlemen of Gloucestershire. (Later, Beatrix heard that in the 'real' tailor of Gloucester's case the work had been secretly completed by his two assistants.)

The story in itself was quite simple and, for Beatrix Potter, contained an unusual mixture of the human and the fantasy or magical elements. It was the second of her tales and was first published privately, at her own expense, which enabled her to put as much into the story as she wished, regardless of commercial considerations. When the book was ready she sent a copy

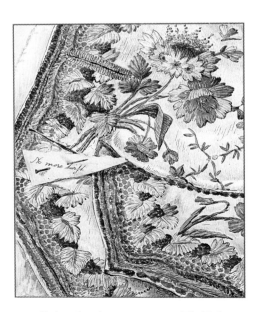

222 Embroidered satin waistcoat, *The Tailor of Gloucester*, p. 57, 1903

223, 224   Rough sketches for the mice on the dresser (*detail*), and an unpublished variant painting of the scene, *The Tailor of Gloucester*, p. 28, 1903

225   Mice making coats, from the privately-printed edition of *The Tailor of Gloucester*, 1902; only the mouse threading the needle was retained for Warne's edition (p. 35), 1903

to Warne, who decided to publish it themselves. Needless to say, when the commercial edition was being prepared, Beatrix was asked to make cuts – a considerable amount of text as well as illustration. She had once again displayed her interest in nursery rhymes by including a large number in the book (*see p. 59*), and some of these were among the first items to be eliminated. In *A History of the Writings of Beatrix Potter* Leslie Linder has given a detailed account of the differences between the privately-printed edition and the Warne version, which is the one that is still in print today.

First written and illustrated as a story for Freda Moore, and given as a Christmas present in 1901, it was then taken back and revised for the privately-printed version. The text was shortened and the pictures redrawn, two being omitted and some new ones added. Bound in pink paper boards, the privately-printed edition appeared in 1902. When Warne decided to print the book Beatrix began yet another revision of text and illustrations. Some of the pictures were retained and a further eighteen were added.

One of the interesting things about *The Tailor of Gloucester* is that we know so much about its origins, both as regards the text and the illustrations. Beatrix embellished the original story to suit her fancy, while the illustrations came from various sources and indicate the wide range of subjects from which she drew her inspiration. The story is given a period setting – 'in the time of swords and periwigs' – which is unusual since most of her tales have a timelessness which enables the reader to place them either in the 'here and now' or in the past. Human time is not relevant to the animal world. The frontispiece also sets the period, showing an eighteenth-century street scene. This is actually based on a Hogarth print, 'Noon' from *Times of the Day*, which she has adapted for the picture. Sketches show that she used her visit to Gloucester for various purposes as far as the book was concerned, wandering round

226, 227 (above left) Two studies of a boy posing as a tailor (*detail*), for use in *The Tailor of Gloucester* (pp. 8 and 20), and *The Tailor of Gloucester*, p. 8, 1903

the city to find suitable views, and drawing the son of her uncle's coachman posing as the tailor, sitting cross-legged or slumped in a chair.

Even more fascinating is the story attached to the main period costumes shown in the book: the mayor's waistcoat, the cherry-coloured coat, the dress worn by the lady mouse and other items of apparel. A few years ago a family visiting the Victoria and Albert Museum asked to see the costumes which Beatrix Potter drew for *The Tailor of Gloucester*. No one in the Textile Department knew anything about them, and the staff were surprised to learn that their existence had been fully documented by Leslie Linder in *A History of the Writings of Beatrix Potter*. So a member of the staff took a copy of the book in her hand and began a long search through the Department's reserve study collection of eighteenth-century costume. All the garments were identified, except the magical cherry-coloured coat. Perhaps Beatrix Potter changed its colour to suit the story. As a result we are able to see the original costumes which she drew, together with her sketches and the finished book pictures.

The young Beatrix was in the habit of sketching objects in both the Natural History Museum and the South Kensington Museum (as the Victoria and Albert Museum was then called). At that time she was just another student to whom the collections were made available for the purpose of study. Objects were brought out, sketched, and put away again – a daily occurrence for museum staff, but a source of great joy to Beatrix Potter. In a letter to Warne she wrote: 'I have been delighted to find I may draw some most beautiful 18th. century clothes at the South Kensington Museum. I had been looking at them for a long time in an inconvenient dark corner of the Goldsmith's Court, but had no idea they could be taken out of the case. The clerk says I could have any article put on a table in one of the offices, which will be most convenient.'

But there were still more strands to be gathered into this book, for later the same year she wrote to Norman Warne from

228 'Ribbons for mobs! for mice!': lady mouse in a mob cap, *The Tailor of Gloucester*, p. 12, 1903

the home of yet another cousin, at Melford Hall in Suffolk: 'I have been able to draw an old fashioned fireplace here, very suitable for the tailor's kitchen.'

Another interesting aspect of this book is the figure of the tailor himself. Beatrix was never very good at drawing the human figure – the more she tried, the more completely she failed – and only in rough sketches, as in the 1903 Derwentwater sketchbook, was she more successful. Despite her sketches of the coachman's son, she has used another method here, which has worked well: we never see the tailor in too much detail. It is as if we were spectators of the events she describes, peeping through a window at scenes happening further inside the room. The mice, however, need not keep their distance in the same way, for they and the evocative snowy street scenes together cast the magical spell that is the essence of *The Tailor of Gloucester* and of all the things that *may* happen when the rest of the world sleeps and the animals come into their own.

Warne eventually published *The Tailor of Gloucester* with the third book, *The Tale of Squirrel Nutkin*, for Christmas 1903.

229   Rats 'dancing the heys' in the mayor's cellar, only used in the privately-printed edition of *The Tailor of Gloucester*, 1902

230   Alternative cover picture for *The Tale of Squirrel Nutkin*, 1903

The Tale of Squirrel Nutkin is about the nursery arch-sins of rudeness and disobedience and the punishment for those who commit them. It is also very much a story of place, since it is set firmly on the shores of Derwentwater, the most northerly of the larger English Lakes. This was where the Potter family had spent a number of their summer holidays, all but one of them at Lingholm, whose extensive grounds sweep down to the lake amid groves and trees. In 1897 Beatrix Potter wrote a picture letter to Noel Moore from Lingholm in which she mentioned the American story of squirrels using their tails as sails, following an account of how they invaded an island in a lake to gather nuts in the autumn. But in September 1901 she rewrote the whole episode as a complete story in a letter to Norah Moore, again during a stay at Lingholm, where there were 'such numbers of squirrels in the woods'. This contained many of the sketches which were to be reworked and coloured for the book published in 1903.

The squirrels sail over to 'Owl Island', using their tails, to seek permission from 'Old Brown' the owl to gather nuts on his island. They make several journeys, each time taking a gift for the owner, who graciously gives permission for his nuts to be taken by the squirrels for their winter store. All except Nutkin.

They also carried with them an offering of 3 fat mice for old Brown, which they placed upon a stone opposite his door.

Then Twinkleberry and the other squirrels each made a low bow,

231   Part of the picture letter to Norah Moore, 25 September 1901

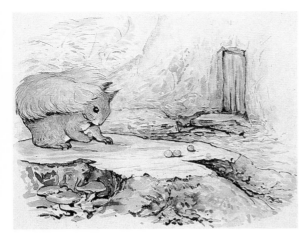

232 A preliminary study for Squirrel Nutkin playing marbles, *The Tale of Squirrel Nutkin*, p. 28, 1903

233 An early study of squirrels and mistletoe, possibly for use as a Christmas card (*detail*)

He is very rude to Old Brown, as every child would recognize, and takes no gift to his host; instead he runs around and dances in front of Old Brown singing riddles, not so much *to* him as *at* him. Old Brown puts up with Nutkin for so long, and then pounces, taking him back to his home in order to skin him. After a struggle Nutkin escapes – but without his tail. (Beatrix had seen a tailless squirrel in the woods, which must have been Nutkin.)

The story was complicated by the inclusion of some of Beatrix Potter's favourite riddles, of the kind which had been very popular when she was a child. But for the generation of children for whom she was writing – and for those to come – she included the clues to the riddles, which she had not done in Norah's picture-letter version.

Presently a little thread of blue *smoke* from a wood fire came up from the top of the tree, and Nutkin peeped through the key-hole and sang –
> 'A house full, a hole full!
> And you cannot gather a bowl-full!'

In addition to the drawings she had made for the two picture letters Beatrix made many other sketches during the time she was preparing the book for publication. There are sketchbooks containing a variety of squirrel poses where she tried to catch the essential squirrel movements and gestures in watercolour. But it is interesting to note that she obviously had no desire to paint squirrels in the same way that she painted mice: with the latter she usually made a meticulous, almost hair-by-hair painting, but when she came to the squirrels she used a much more flowing line, which conveys something of their light airy movement. She had frequently drawn and painted squirrels in the past, often in her imaginative sequences, but she did not clothe her squirrel subjects as she did so many of the other animals in her fantasy scenes, though she did show them in somewhat anthropomorphic activities (169). *Squirrel Nutkin* itself is full of examples of squirrels indulging in human-type behaviour without the benefit of clothes.

Then she needed background scenes. The squirrels set sail on their little rafts from Derwent Bay, a tree-lined inlet on the Lingholm estate, from which there is a view of St Herbert's Island ('Owl Island') and the fells on the opposite side of the lake. The bay is still there today – though rather more overgrown than in Beatrix Potter's time, but still recognizable from her sketches. The extreme accuracy of the paintings in the book can be seen when we compare her sketch of the shore and tree of Derwent Bay with the picture on page 20 of the book – all she has done is to add the squirrels to her original painting. In the scene which shows the squirrels setting out on their voyage (page 15 of the book), the background view of the island and fells would be quite recognizable to anyone standing on that spot today. It was obviously a view which attracted her,

234, 235 (right) Sketch from
the shore at Derwent Bay and
(below left) the same view on
p. 20 of *The Tale of Squirrel
Nutkin*, 1903

236, 237 (above right) The
squirrels sailing over to Owl
Island, *The Tale of Squirrel
Nutkin*, p. 15, 1903, and (right)
a sketch of the same view over
Derwentwater, showing St
Herbert's Island and the fells
beyond

for she made sketches in pen-and-ink as well as the watercolour renderings, and there are photographs of the same scenes, including Derwent Bay, taken by Rupert Potter.

It was not only the recognizable Lake District scenes that Beatrix Potter painted for this book. There are sketches, some of them merely hesitant marks on the paper, in which she tried out the effect of the rocks or the reeds which she needed for the more general scenes of the squirrels by the water. Then there are the various woodland scenes. The sketches for these are difficult to identify, since one woodland glade can look very much like another, and trees have grown up and been replaced since the Potter family walked among them, unlike the shapes of fells and lakes, which change little.

The owl too needed careful study, and various preliminary owl studies survive. Fortunately Bertram Potter had at one time kept a pet owl, which Beatrix mentions and sketches in a letter to Eric Moore in 1896, so she had a good chance to get an accurate picture of him in all his movements. Nevertheless, she was anxious about her owl drawings for this book. 'I thought my owls very bad when I went again to the Zoological Gardens,' she wrote to Norman Warne. But she was still not satisfied and wrote later: 'I am going to meet my brother at the Lakes . . . I think *he* could very likely improve that owl.' Norman Warne's comments were always constructive and well received and when it came to the book pictures she was quite diffident about her work and very open to suggestion. 'I will alter the squirrel, that is a good idea,' she wrote to him on another occasion.

In addition to the main pictures, there were also endpapers to be considered, and a special cloth binding, over whose design Beatrix spent a considerable amount of time and thought. The pictorial endpaper was to become a familiar part of the subsequent books, but the special binding which she chose appeared only on the *Tailor of Gloucester* and *Squirrel Nutkin*. The de luxe editions of these two books appeared with a pretty flower-pattern cloth, 'rather quaint . . . like pansies', chosen from samples sent from her grandfather's textile print-ing works. She had also revised the text, having noted in a letter to Warne 'the words of the squirrel book will need cutting down, to judge by the children here'. (She was writing from her cousin's home at Melford Hall.) Her attention to the text did not simply stop at the words, but it also took into account the position of those words on the page. It is typical of her sense of drama that when Nutkin is caught she changes to italics to emphasize the fact that '*Nutkin was in his waistcoat pocket!*', while on the next page are just a few words in a large white space: 'This looks like the end of the story; but it isn't.' The child eagerly turns over the page in the hope, fully justified, of a happy ending after all – though, quite rightly, Nutkin is punished for his naughtiness, as every child would know it was proper he should be.

238 Study for Old Brown (*detail*), *The Tale of Squirrel Nutkin*, 1903

239 A photograph of Old Brown's oak, possibly used by Beatrix Potter for *The Tale of Squirrel Nutkin*, 1903

No wonder that after all this loving care bestowed on the book by both Beatrix and Norman Warne she was able to write: 'I am *delighted* to hear such good account of Nutkin. I never thought when I was drawing it that it would be such a success.' And as if to prove how much she had enjoyed sketching the scenes for the book, her 1903 Derwentwater sketchbook contains yet more drawings of Derwent Bay and the woods around Lingholm – even though the book was already printed by then. She obviously continued to paint the views for the love of them, and this love is reflected in the whole book, text and paintings alike.

The summer of 1903 was once again spent on the shores of Derwentwater, but Lingholm was not available that year, so the family took the adjacent Fawe Park instead. It was during her stay at Fawe Park that Beatrix bought the Derwentwater sketchbook, on the front cover of which she wrote 'Benjamin Bunny Mrs Tiggy Winkle'.

The Tale of Benjamin Bunny is less complicated than *The Tailor of Gloucester* and *The Tale of Squirrel Nutkin*. After them Beatrix Potter felt that something more like *The Tale of Peter Rabbit* was needed. She had several possible stories in mind but the one she finally settled upon was the continued adventures of Peter Rabbit – and his cousin Benjamin. Beatrix was able to employ a large part of her summer holiday preparing the drawings for the proposed new book which, together with the text, she planned to work up during the winter months spent in London.

Peter and Benjamin set out to rescue Peter's clothes which

240 View over Derwentwater from the gardens at Fawe Park, from the 1903 sketchbook

are adorning the scarecrow in Mr McGregor's garden – he and his wife having conveniently gone off to market. They slide (or fall) down the pear tree into the garden, rescue the clothes, help themselves to some lettuces and onions, and then set off home – this time to go through the gate. They see a cat and take refuge under a basket – on which the cat promptly sits. They are finally rescued by Benjamin's father, old Mr Bunny, who 'had no opinion whatever of cats', and he marches both little rabbits out of the garden, but not before he has given them a hiding – and collected up the onions. On his return Mr McGregor finds several things to puzzle him, apart from the loss of the clothes on the scarecrow, while old Mrs Rabbit is so pleased to see Peter back that she quite forgives him – and keeps the onions. Everyone gets their just deserts.

Most of the scenes for this story are set in the gardens of Fawe Park, and in particular the kitchen gardens. They provided ideal sketching material for Beatrix, who found that she much preferred the unpretentious to the grandiose. As a result, and given the fine weather of that particular summer, there is a remarkable series of background sketches for this book. We get the feeling that Beatrix really enjoyed the homely articles she was sketching – the flower pots and basket, the onions and the wall on which old Mr Bunny pranced. Moreover, she used many of her sketches with very little alteration in the actual

241, 242 A rough sketch for Peter and Benjamin on the wall, and the painting of them looking down into Mr McGregor's garden, *The Tale of Benjamin Bunny*, p. 23, 1904

243 'They got amongst flower-pots, and frames and tubs': background sketch for p. 40 of *The Tale of Benjamin Bunny*, 12 September 1903

244, 245   A study of the wall on which old Mr Benjamin Bunny pranced (?1903) and its use on p. 48 of *The Tale of Benjamin Bunny*, 1904

book so that it is possible to put some of them side by side to compare them.

Fawe Park itself is not open to the public, but the gardens have not been greatly altered since the days when Peter and Benjamin made their illicit expedition. Even the gate, the potting shed, the cold frames – and of course the famous wall – are still recognizable, and similar plants and vegetables grow there. It is this extraordinary mixture of reality and fantasy which is part of the charm of Beatrix Potter's stories, aided by the competent drawing of the animals, which are always *real* animals and not men with animal heads on their shoulders (what Beatrix Potter once described as 'animal pictures').

As we know, Beatrix had had plenty of opportunity of drawing rabbits from her own pets, and when she was preparing her rabbit books she continued to try out a variety of postures and movements. This meticulous preparation before she commenced the final pictures is recorded by Beatrix in a letter to Norman Warne from Fawe Park: 'I think I have done every imaginable rabbit background and miscellaneous sketches as well – about seventy! I hope you will like them, though rather scribbled.' While there are indeed some 'scribbled' or rough sketches for this story, the quality of many of her backgrounds painted at Fawe Park is in fact remarkably high.

An interesting example is that of the onions, which feature

246   Rough sketch of old Mr Bunny (*detail*) as he appears on p. 55 of *The Tale of Benjamin Bunny*, 1904

247   Onions at Fawe Park: background study for p. 31
of *The Tale of Benjamin Bunny*, 1903

248, 249   (below) A study of carnations for a proposed
frontispiece and (bottom) the unfinished painting
for it; the carnations subsequently appeared on p. 39
of *The Tale of Benjamin Bunny*, 1904

quite largely in the story, but are still only incidental to it. In
the Linder Bequest at the Victoria and Albert Museum there
are no fewer than three beautifully painted studies of onions:
one showing onions actually growing, and two depicting
carefully painted groups of onions. There are also about five
sketches of carnations, some of them intended for a frontispiece which was not used, showing Peter and Benjamin
standing underneath the carnations – though the flowers were
subsequently incorporated in the book picture which shows
Peter letting go of the onions for the second time. All this
indicates the serious application which Beatrix Potter brought
to even the smallest detail in her books. She was also aware
that the type of story she was painting – like *Peter Rabbit* (*see
p. 95*) – was primarily set in colours of brown and fawn and soft
green, so that 'the handkerchief will make a good bit of colour
all through the book' she wrote in a note – the handkerchief, of
course, being red. It was equally characteristic of her that she
gave the same minute attention to the words of the story,
trying it out on children of her acquaintance.

The Tale of Benjamin Bunny was published in 1904, but not
with the Derwentwater sketchbook story about Mrs Tiggy-
winkle, because Beatrix had written a non-Lake District tale
about mice.

The Tale of Two Bad Mice began as 'The Tale of Hunca
Munca' – the last of three stories resulting from a '*very* wet
week' in Hastings at the end of 1903. The other two were 'The
Tale of Tuppenny' (*see p. 162*) and an early version of *The Pie
and the Patty-Pan*. Beatrix found this one the funniest, and it
was printed in the same small format as *Benjamin Bunny* to suit
its mouse subjects. By dummy stage the title had become 'The
Tale of the Doll's House and Hunca Munca', after one of two
mice rescued from the cook at Harescombe Grange, her
cousins' house. Beatrix tamed them and named them after

Fielding's equally satirical Hunca Munca and Tom Thumb. Watching the mice carry off small objects gave her the idea for a story about mice which live as humans, coupled with a doll story – always a popular genre. She was already using mice as models for nursery rhymes, and 'glad to get done with the rabbits'. 'Hunca Munca is very ready to play the game; I stopped her in the act of carrying a doll as large as herself up to the nest, she cannot resist anything with lace or ribbon.'

The two mice of the tale, infuriated by the discovery that the delectable doll's house dinner is inedible, smash the ham with tongs and shovel and break up 'the pudding, the lobster, the pears and the oranges'. 'As the fish would not come off the plate, they put it into the red-hot crinkly paper fire in the kitchen; but it would not burn either.' Then they began to vandalize the rest of the doll's house.

Norman Warne made the real doll's house for his niece Winifred M. L. Warne, to whom the book was dedicated (*see 38 and p. 24*). Winifred remembers it as a very good reproduction of an Edwardian villa of that period, described feelingly by Beatrix as 'the kind of house where one cannot sit down without upsetting something, I know the sort!' There were difficulties over the doll's house – Mrs Potter's rules of etiquette did not allow luncheon with tradesmen (and they included publishers). Beatrix had to rely on her memory and Norman's photographs. Mrs Potter's strictures were useless, however: Norman and Beatrix grew closer as they entered into the fun of inventing new ingredients for the story. Beatrix preferred the dolls bought by Norman at Seven Dials to the existing family. 'I will provide a print dress & a smile for Jane; her little stumpy feet are so funny.' The furniture and food from Hamleys inspired some exceptionally fine pictures, and an enchanting back view of Hunca Munca chopping at the ham – though 'its appearance was enough to cause indigestion.' The real Hunca Munca despised the dishes.

Beatrix called *The Two Bad Mice* a girl's book, like *Mrs. Tiggy-Winkle*, but it is particularly accessible to any small child. Who could forget the fascination of discovering the secret life behind a doll's house façade – even more alluring if the inhabitants are mice. In a picture letter sent from a cottage at Winchelsea Beatrix had already opened up just such a façade and peopled it with mice. Though the house in the story sits on a nursery carpet, it is part of Sawrey: 'Lucinda and Jane Doll-cook always bought their groceries at Ginger and Pickles.' A child might see emotion in their stolid doll-faces, but far more memorable are the invading and anarchic mice!

'Hunca Munca had a frugal mind' and remembered herself just in time, turning wilful waste into ingenious acquisitiveness. She hurriedly restuffed the mattress and secured various useful articles, making amends with a sixpence in the Christmas stocking and an offer of her services with dustpan and brush. Both mice were responsible parents, warning their

250   Study for *The Tale of Two Bad Mice*, p. 24, 1904

251, 252   (top) The fish consigned to the fire, and (above) the mouse-trap lesson, *The Tale of Two Bad Mice*, pp. 31 and 55, 1904

offspring about mousetraps (252) – but according to the miniature letters Hunca Munca was *not* a reliable housemaid.

The real Hunca Munca came to a melancholy end – Beatrix wrote to Norman Warne on 21 July 1905: 'I have made a little doll of poor Hunca Munca, I cannot forgive myself for letting her tumble. I do so miss her. She fell off the chandelier, she managed to stagger up the staircase into your little house, but she died in my hand about 10 minutes after. I think if I had broken my own neck it would have saved a deal of trouble.'

With *The Tale of Two Bad Mice* out of the way, Beatrix was free to start on *Mrs. Tiggy-Winkle*, but a greater tragedy than Hunca Munca's was in store for her. Norman Warne died in August 1905 and she had to continue writing without his help.

The Tale of Mrs. Tiggy-Winkle was one of the books in Beatrix Potter's 1903 Derwentwater sketchbook, though it was not published until 1905. Mrs Tiggy-winkle herself had been one of Beatrix's favourite pets – she had had several hedgehogs over the years – and she was used for the preliminary drawings for the book, though she proved a somewhat temperamental model. 'If she is propped up on end for half an hour, she first begins to yawn pathetically, and then she *does* bite,' wrote Beatrix to Norman Warne. Later she found it more convenient to dress up a cottonwool dummy figure for sketching.

A hedgehog was an unusual subject to choose for a children's book – rabbits, mice, cats and other more familiar animals had a long tradition behind them by the time Beatrix Potter began her books, but for many children a Mrs Tiggy-winkle must have been a relatively unfamiliar creature in spite of her presence in many of their gardens, owing to the nocturnal habits of hedgehogs. But the unfamiliar had long been resident in the Potter nursery, and there can be no doubt that Beatrix Potter's choice of animal protagonists has widened children's appreciation of the less familiar creatures of the wild.

In *The Tale of Mrs. Tiggy-Winkle* a little girl called Lucie has lost her handkerchiefs and her pinafore, and goes in search of

253 An unfinished sketch of Mrs Tiggy-winkle, a variant of the cover picture, *The Tale of Mrs. Tiggy-Winkle*, 1905

254 Study of a hedgehog's head (*detail*), assumed to be for use in *The Tale of Mrs. Tiggy-Winkle*, 1905

them. Seeing something white in the distance on a hillside path above her home, she sets off to see if it is the missing articles. Instead she finds a door in the hillside, and when she goes through it, 'Alice' fashion, she finds herself in Mrs Tiggy-winkle's kitchen, where Mrs Tiggy-winkle is finishing off the local washing. Lucie retrieves her belongings and the pair set off down the hill together to return the various items to their owners. As Lucie crosses the stile home and turns to thank Mrs Tiggy-winkle, all she can see is the little brown prickly figure of a hedgehog running away up the hill. That is all there is to the story, but Beatrix Potter embroiders it in such a way that the figure of Mrs Tiggy-winkle has become one of the most positive of her creations. She was based to some extent on an old Scottish washerwoman, Kitty McDonald, first employed by the Potters as early as 1871, but revisited by Beatrix on her later Tayside holiday in 1892, and described in her journal at that time. 'She is a comical, round little woman, as brown as a berry and wears a multitude of petticoats and a white mutch.'

But of course there is more to *Mrs. Tiggy-Winkle* than the story, which was originally written down for Beatrix Potter's cousin Stephanie Hyde Parker in 1902. It is another of the books firmly placed in a recognizable setting, here in the Newlands Valley, which lies west of Derwentwater and beyond the mass of Cat Bells. It was perfectly possible for Beatrix to drive herself out there from Fawe Park, where she was staying in 1903, or from Lingholm – which is next door. The valley is still remote and unpopulated, except for the cluster of cottages around Little Town, and the church, and a few other farmsteads. The 1903 sketchbook has many scenes from along the path on the side of Cat Bells, above Little Town, and into the narrowing valley itself, as well as fine views of the fells and Skiddaw beyond. Several of these sketchbook scenes were almost exactly reproduced in the published book, with the addition of the figures. Nevertheless, a detailed study of this particular sketchbook has thrown some light on the way in which Beatrix modified her drawings for the books, when it suited her. For example, on page 15 of the book Lucie is seen running along the path towards the Newlands Valley, while below her lie Little Town, the houses, the bridge and, hidden in a clump of trees, Newlands church, of which the real little Lucie Carr's father was vicar. In the sketchbook, we can look down on the same scene, but wherever you stand today it is quite impossible to see that grouping as Beatrix has shown it, although the individual details are correct – Beatrix knew a good composition when she saw one, and used artistic licence to portray it. The distant view of the valley also appears in the sketchbook, almost exactly as Beatrix has shown it in the book, and with just the same colours, except that it would not be possible to see round the bend and view both scenes from the same position.

255, 256   A view in the Newlands Valley from the Derwentwater sketchbook, 15 September 1903, and the painting of Lucie on the path above Little-town from *The Tale of Mrs. Tiggy-Winkle*, p. 15, 1905

In the same way, Beatrix Potter no doubt felt it would be a delightful spot for her heroine (if Lucie *is* the heroine rather than Mrs Tiggy-winkle, which many would doubt) to live in – a place which really *was* called Little Town – so that is where Beatrix puts her. But the painting of Lucie's house makes it quite clear that in fact Beatrix has sketched Skelgill, where Lucie *did* live, and which is still recognizable today.

The scenery of the Newlands Valley is delightful and Beatrix obviously enjoyed her sketching expeditions into its quiet stillness. She also took pleasure in using her own pet hedgehog as a model. There remained, however, two other important aspects of the story to be drawn – the interior of Mrs Tiggy-winkle's house, and Lucie. The interior scenes gave her little problem. She had been sketching all sorts of interiors since she was quite young, and for Mrs Tiggy-winkle's kitchen she used typical Lakeland kitchens of the kind she could see as she went about Sawrey and the other areas where she stayed. But Lucie was another matter, and she is still the weakest part of the tale. As Beatrix herself said later: 'I am not good – or trained – in drawing human figures (they are a terrible bother to me when I have perforce to bring them into the pictures for my own little stories).' Beatrix made a number of sketches to try and get Lucie right – perhaps she tried too hard for, as before, the same Derwentwater sketchbook shows that when she didn't try too hard she could manage figures quite well (*261*). She also had a problem with Lucie's cloak, changing the colour half way along, which fortunately Norman Warne noticed. 'I have been rather sorry about the little blue cloak. Shall I cut it out and make it red? . . . I know I have no taste in colour and would gladly alter it,' she wrote. In the end the cloak turned out 'a warm nut-brown' and both were satisfied. But if Lucie is poorly drawn and not a very sympathetic character, there can be no

257 A sketch for Lucie's 'farm called Little-town' – actually Skelgill near Gutherscale; for p. 8 of *The Tale of Mrs. Tiggy-Winkle*, 13 September 1904

258, 259 Sketch for Mrs Tiggy-winkle's kitchen, and the painting showing her there, *The Tale of Mrs. Tiggy-Winkle*, p. 44, 1905

260 (above) A rough sketch of Lucie entering Mrs Tiggy-winkle's kitchen, for p. 20 of *The Tale of Mrs. Tiggy-Winkle*, 1905

261 (above right) A sketch made in Keswick market, from the Derwentwater sketchbook, 19 September 1903

doubt about Mrs Tiggy-winkle. Her expressions, her postures, her speech – everything about her – make her one of the most delightful of Beatrix Potter's creations and, like Lucie, we are all reluctant to admit: 'Why! Mrs. Tiggy-winkle was nothing but a HEDGEHOG.'

Beatrix used a Lake District setting again for *The Pie and the Patty-Pan*, her next book, and it was published with *Mrs. Tiggy-Winkle*, despite Norman Warne's death before its completion.

The Pie and the Patty-Pan is one of the few books to mention Sawrey by name. During the third Sawrey holiday, in the summer of 1902, Beatrix sketched the interior of Mrs Lord's cottage, one of three at Lakefield – the stone-floored pantry, the carved oak furniture and the geraniums on the window ledge. In some sketches there were even rough outlines of a cat. A cat story using these backgrounds was planned for 1903 while she was still working on *Mrs. Tiggy-Winkle*, and Norman Warne discussed with her a new and larger format similar to that of *Johnny Crow's Garden* by Leslie Brooke, to do justice to the rich detail of her drawings. *The Tale of Two Bad Mice* was chosen instead and the cat book delayed until 1905, when Beatrix wrote to Warne: 'I don't think I have ever seriously considered the state of the *pie*, but I think the *book* runs some risk of being over-cooked if it goes on much longer!', and 'if the book prints well it will be my next favourite to the "Tailor"'. Not long after, Norman proposed by letter – but died suddenly on 25 August.

Beatrix battled on to finish the book they had begun

together. *The Pie and the Patty-Pan* was published in October, dedicated to the sixth Moore child, and also to her goddaughter Beatrix, last in the family: 'for Joan, to read to Baby'. The endpaper design had been forgotten, and the book appeared with plain white or mottled lavender papers. Not until several years later were the pie and patty-pan endpapers introduced and the cover picture changed – to Ribby by the fire. In 1930 *The Pie* was brought into line with the rest and printed in the small format, its title changed to *The Tale of the Pie and the Patty-Pan*.

The original version, 'Something very very NICE', was one of the three tales written out in stormy Hastings (*see p. 118*). This story is thinner but more amusing than the final version, and domestic details are lovingly itemized – not all survive in the published book. Preparing for the tea-party, Ribby polishes her silver spoons with a wash leather, takes out a blue dish and goes to Buckle Yeat for honey; then she puts on her best black net cap trimmed with beads and a black silk apron (in the book she wears lilac silk). Not till the very end is the respectable façade cracked – when we discover that both Ribby and Duchess have raided the hen house!

Sawrey characters and Sawrey village are remembered in *The Pie and the Patty-Pan*, rewritten with a new and rather complicated plot. Duchess, a 'genteel and elegant little dog', accepts Ribby's invitation to tea but is apprehensive about the promised pie: it is sure to be made of mouse. She pops into Ribby's oven her own pie (veal and ham), but there is no sign of the mouse pie. It is in the stiff-handled bottom oven. At the party Duchess gobbles up a most delicious pie, convinced that she is eating veal and ham – but where is her patty-pan? She begins to feel very ill. While Dr Maggotty *Pie* is being summoned, she discovers her own pie in the top oven. To avoid awkwardness, she puts it outside the back door, and submits to a bread pill when the doctor arrives. Slipping back to rescue the pie, she discovers three jackdaws eating piecrust – and Dr Maggotty drinking gravy out of a patty-pan!

The real Mrs Tabitha Twitchit lived at Hill Top, though in the book her shop is in Hawkshead (448), and her cousin Ribby was another Sawrey cat. Tabitha is snobbish about dogs: 'A little *dog* indeed! Just as if there were no CATS in Sawrey!' Duchess was an amalgamation of two pedigree Pomeranians belonging to Mrs Rogerson, wife of the Lakefield gardener, who lived in another of the Lakefield cottages; the real 'Duchess' was more handsome but less intelligent than 'Darkie'. Poms were larger in those days, and also less well-known. Beatrix had to send Warne a photograph of Duchess begging on a chair to prove that the fine mane she had drawn was not an exaggeration. Duchess brushing her mane is a parallel to the 'Amiable Guinea-Pig' of the *Appley Dapply* rhyme – brushing back his hair like a periwig in front of a different mirror.

262 Duchess brushing her coat, *The Pie and the Patty-Pan*, p. 29, 1905

263 The 'Amiable Guinea-Pig': alternative drawing for *Appley Dapply's Nursery Rhymes*, p. 33, ?1917

264   Background painting for 'The Invitation',
The Pie and the Patty-Pan, p. 13, ?1905

In the book it is Ribby and not Duchess who lives at
Lakefield cottage, and Duchess has moved to Buckle Yeat
(then the Post Office, opposite 'Ginger and Pickles'). A
background painting for one plate, 'The Invitation', shows
Buckle Yeat garden with its poppies and snapdragons; the
final picture moves closer, and the postman supplants Mrs
Rogerson. In 'The Veal and Ham Pie', another book picture,
Duchess stands outside the Post Office doorway, flanked by
tiger lilies from the 'Ginger and Pickles' garden (*176*). The
frontispiece has Ribby returning from the farm across the
meadow where later Aunt Pettitoes feeds her piglets, in *Pigling
Bland* (*39, 404*). In the background is Hill Top before the 1906
additions, with Coniston Old Man behind. Ribby's pink-and-
white dish is described as blue-and-white in the text, and on
another page she is looking at the wrong oven – even Beatrix
could be confused by the plot! The picture of Duchess in the
porch (*178*) was drawn in rather crude colours, from a different
angle and with more pots of flowers, for the 1930 cover; in
front are the pattens Mrs Rogerson slipped on for going to the
pump. Duchess on a sofa searching for the 'pie made of mouse'
parodies a Briton Rivière portrait of Beatrix's cousin Kate (*see
p. 40*) – just as in *Peter Rabbit* Beatrix had imitated with tongue
in cheek another popular painting, *Love Locked Out* by Anna
Lea Merritt (*203, 204*).

Many of the original sepia cottage interiors, which Norman
had hoped to reproduce in brown ink, were not used in the
book. The purely figure drawings remained: Duchess in the
pantry, Ribby shaking out mats. Not a detail is left out – the
trailing campanula and maidenhair fern, the hard horsehair
sofas spread with knitted shawls. Among the original 'roughs'
are back views of Ribby crossing the field and disappearing

265   'Where is the pie made of mouse?', *The Pie and
the Patty-Pan*, p. 27, 1905

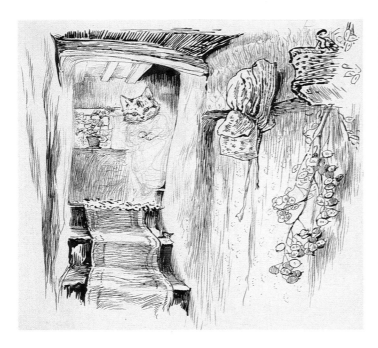

upstairs; here she descends a staircase hung with honesty, basket and bonnet. The coloured tea-table picture seemed a little unfinished to Warne – but Beatrix had intended a light background. Standing on the table is her Edward VII coronation tea-pot. 'Ready for the Party', a characteristic cosy fireside scene, shows a north-country open range with an unexpectedly large number of mouse-traps in the foreground, Just visible in the last picture is a scarecrow wearing Peter Rabbit's blue jacket!

With the death of Norman Beatrix Potter felt that she needed work to take her mind off her loss. Norman's brother Harold was now her contact at Warne and to him she wrote: 'I know some people don't like frogs but I think I had convinced him [Norman] that I could make a really pretty book.' So it was agreed she could go ahead with one.

The Tale of Mr. Jeremy Fisher was one of the last stories Beatrix Potter had discussed with Norman Warne before his death, but the origins of the tale go back as far as 1893. In September of that year she had sent a letter to Eric Moore beginning: 'Once upon a time there was a frog called Mr. Jeremy Fisher, and he lived in a little house on the bank of a river . . .' At that time the Potter family were spending their long summer holiday at Dunkeld, staying at a house on the banks of the Tay, so the location of Mr Jeremy Fisher's home was there. The following year she was again working on a frog theme. She produced a series of pen-and-ink sketches for the firm of Ernest Nister entitled 'A Frog he would a-fishing go' (*see p. 54*). However, they were less than enthusiastic – 'People do not want frogs now' – but they nevertheless continued to

266 (above left) Ribby comes downstairs: unused drawing for *The Pie and the Patty-Pan*, 1902

267 (above) 'Ready for the Party', *The Pie and the Patty-Pan*, p. 31, 1905

268 Studies of frogs (*detail*), probably drawn from life

haggle over the price for them. Beatrix stood her ground and got her own figure, and in due course the set of drawings appeared in one of Nister's children's annuals. Shortly after the publication of *The Tale of Peter Rabbit* Beatrix Potter decided to buy back both the drawings and the blocks from Nister, so she was obviously still anxious to follow up the tale. 'I think I could make something of him', she told Norman Warne.

Not everybody is as fond of frogs as Beatrix Potter was but she had kept frogs as pets when she was quite young, and mourned their deaths as much as she did her rabbits' demise. She and her brother also kept tortoises and newts, so she knew very well what she was about when she came to sketch all these creatures for *The Tale of Mr. Jeremy Fisher*.

Mr Jeremy Fisher (*always* called 'Mr') now lives in a little damp house at the edge of a pond – not a river. One nice wet day (just right for frogs) he decides to go fishing so that he can feast his friends. He takes his boat (which looks very much like a water-lily leaf and not at all like the wooden one of the picture letter) and punts out into the middle of the pond. But he is not lucky in his fishing (Beatrix must have remembered stories like that from her father and brother), so he decides to moor the 'boat' and have his lunch. At this point he attracts the attention of a large trout, which swallows him – only to spit him out again because of the taste of his mackintosh. So Mr Jeremy Fisher returns home in a bedraggled state and without his fish. But he still invites his friends, Alderman Ptolemy Tortoise and Sir Isaac Newton, to supper and feeds them on roast grasshopper with ladybird sauce – except that the Alderman brings his own salad meal with him.

Though the story is perfectly simple it is full of careful naturalistic observation. The creatures behave in every way as their real counterparts would – the frog thinks a rainy day is nice and a tortoise eats salad. Then there is the touch of humour in the names of Mr Jeremy Fisher's friends, while their depiction paints their respective characters all too well. Later on, when writing her miniature letters to children, Beatrix

269 (above left) 'The fishes are still laughing at him': a drawing from *A Frog he would a-fishing go*, 1894

270 (above) A rough sketch of Mr Jeremy Fisher in his larder, from the manuscript of *The Tale of Mr. Jeremy Fisher*, p. 11, 1906

271 Mr Jeremy Fisher greets his friends, *The Tale of Mr. Jeremy Fisher*, p. 52, 1906

127

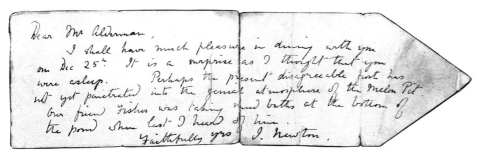

272 (left) An invitation, in miniature, from Mr Alderman Ptolemy Tortoise to Sir Isaac Newton, The Well

273 (below left) A miniature letter from I. Newton to Alderman Ptolemy Tortoise, The Melon Pit

Potter included the invitation and response which passed between Mr Jeremy Fisher and his friends, showing that she continued to enjoy the joke she had made.

Various claims have been made as to the location of Mr Jeremy Fisher's pond: the lake at Melford Hall, home of Beatrix Potter's cousin; the shores of Esthwaite Water, near to Hill Top; or, even more likely, Moss Eccles Tarn, hidden above Near Sawrey (450). Its position does not matter, for the pond is an immortal water on which the water-lilies are always

274 Water-lilies and reeds on Esthwaite Water: possibly a background painting for *The Tale of Mr. Jeremy Fisher*, 1906

green and where one can always hope to see some of Mr Jeremy Fisher's descendants.

Beatrix continued her fondness for frogs even after the publication of *The Tale of Mr. Jeremy Fisher*, since she included one of her finest frog paintings in her original scheme for the 1905 Book of Rhymes, which was eventually published in 1917 as *Appley Dapply's Nursery Rhymes* (*see p. 153*). Here, in the painting 'Fishes come bite' (*337*), we have a charming picture of Mr Jeremy Fisher and his friends sitting forever under large umbrellas in the rain, waiting, like all good fishermen, for the 'bite' that all too rarely comes.

It is in this work, perhaps more than in any other, that we are aware of the roots of Beatrix Potter's art, for in it she comes closer than ever before to the work of Randolph Caldecott, whom she so greatly admired. She herself admitted: 'I did try to copy Caldecott; but . . . I did not achieve much resemblance.' It was not so much the resemblance that mattered as the inspiration, and that she certainly had from the older artist. As a result we have two classics of frog life instead of one: Randolph Caldecott's *A Frog He Would A-Wooing Go* and *The Tale of Mr. Jeremy Fisher*.

Early in 1906, still occupied with *Jeremy Fisher*, Beatrix was planning three stories for very young children – to be in panoramic form in the style of Cruikshank's *Comic Alphabet*.

The Story of Miss Moppet and **The Story of A Fierce Bad Rabbit** were the only two panoramic stories published, both for Christmas 1906. The kitten for *Miss Moppet* proved to be an exasperating model, 'very young & pretty and a most fearful pickle'. Beatrix tried to avoid painful pictures, explaining on one: 'She should catch him by the tail/ less unpleasant.' Miss Moppet tricks a taunting mouse by tying her head in a duster to look ill, peeping out through a convenient

275 An early version of Jeremy Fisher on a water-lily leaf: a variant form of p. 32 in *The Tale of Mr. Jeremy Fisher*, 1906

276 (left) Sketch from the panoramic manuscript of *The Story of Miss Moppet*, for p. 29, 1906

277 (above) Miss Moppet looks through a hole in the duster, *The Story of Miss Moppet*, p. 26, 1906

hole. The mouse is too bold: Miss Moppet catches him, ties him up in the duster and tosses it about like a ball – but she has forgotten the hole. The mouse escapes and dances a triumphant jig on top of the cupboard.

The *Fierce Bad Rabbit* manuscript was given to Harold Warne's daughter Louie, who had thought Peter much too good and demanded a story about a really naughty rabbit.

In 1916 both titles were reprinted in book form, in a slightly smaller format than the rest of the series. After Beatrix's marriage she sent a new picture (never used) of the gun: 'My husband undertakes to hold a gun properly, which was a defect in the Bad rabbit pictures.' The fierce bad Rabbit steals the good Rabbit's carrot – and scratches him into the bargain – but a man with a gun sees something on a bench which looks like a very funny bird, and lets fly. All that remains on the bench is carrot, tail and whiskers.

278   The bad Rabbit, *The Story of A Fierce Bad Rabbit*, p. 26, 1906

The third story, **The Sly Old Cat**, specially bound for Louie's sister Nellie, was not sold in its concertina form because shopkeepers were reluctant – panoramic books were so easily damaged. Probably intended for early 1907, it was announced on a 1916 endpaper as 'The *Story* of the Sly Old Cat', but the watercolours were never prepared for printing. Only the draft sketches were eventually published, in 1971. The Cat invites the Rat to tea, but on her own terms – leaving only drops of milk and crumbs to her guest, whom she intends to eat for dessert. The Cat tips up the milk-jug to drain every drop, but her greed is her downfall. The Rat jumps on the table and pats the jug so that it traps the Cat's head. Then he drinks tea from a mug and goes away with a muffin in a paper bag. Beatrix did not relish the idea of redrawing the pictures: her eyes were weakening and the city background was no longer familiar. She preferred not to do a cat story – 'if any' – and in 1916 suggested commissioning Ernest Aris as illustrator: 'his plagiarisms are unblushing, and his drawing excellent'. Aris's cats were better than hers, however 'his mice have too large ears, he should be advised that rats have still smaller ears'. In the event, the finished rough is perfect in its fusion of word and picture, visually reminiscent of Caldecott in its rhythmic narrative flow. The story is told mainly through conversation and, with non-intrusive rhyming elements, in words of one syllable used with great economy.

279   From the panoramic manuscript of *The Sly Old Cat*, 1906

The Tale of Tom Kitten is 'dedicated to all Pickles, especially to those that get upon my garden wall'.

As a model for her next character, Tom Kitten, Beatrix returned to the drawings of the pickle from *Miss Moppet* – the mason's cat from Windermere – and the new book was ready for publication in 1907. Tom Kitten's mother, Tabitha Twitchit, was named after the new kitten at Belle Green, where Beatrix stayed during the Hill Top alterations; she became the farm cat. Tom is a hero in the *Squirrel Nutkin*

280 Variant cover illustration for *The Tale of Tom Kitten*, 1907

mould – inquisitive, adventurous and disobedient. He stares out at us from the cover, with bursting buttons and an expression of dumb insolence.

At least a quarter of the tales are set in Sawrey. This one grew out of Beatrix's first adventures with a cottage garden: the garden at Hill Top – seen clearly in the illustrations. It was modelled on her cousins' garden at Gwaynynog – 'very productive but not tidy, the prettiest kind of garden, where bright old fashioned flowers grow amongst the currant bushes'. The borders she crammed with snapdragons, pinks and pansies, old roses, lavender and lilies. 'I have had something out of nearly every garden in the village' – some of it taken surreptitiously, since 'stolen plants always grow'.

Tabitha Twitchit expects company to tea, so she fetches Tom and his sisters indoors to be washed and dressed. After a painful interlude of brushing and combing – painful also to

281 (below) Mrs Tabitha Twitchit fetches the kittens indoors, *The Tale of Tom Kitten*, frontispiece, 1907

282 (below right) Moppet's face is scrubbed, *The Tale of Tom Kitten*, p. 12, 1907

their mother – the kittens are seen processing down the long sloping path to the stone wall above the wicket gate. They are dressed in the sort of Fauntleroyish 'elegant uncomfortable clothes' most unsuited to pickles. On the way they trip, and Tom catches a butterfly. They climb on to the wall, Tom shedding buttons on the way up. Harold Warne disliked the words 'all the rest of Tom's clothes came off', but Beatrix pointed out that '*nearly* all' wouldn't do, as he had already been drawn with nothing. 'There are not many garments for Mr Drake to dress himself in; and it would give the story a new & criminal aspect if he forcibly took off & *stole* Tom's trousers!' Tom and his sisters fall prey to the advancing Puddle-Ducks; 'they had very small eyes and looked surprised'. Rebeccah and Jemima put on the hat and tucker dropped by Tom and Moppet. Mr Drake Puddle-Duck, instead of helping to dress Tom, appropriates the clothes himself; they are an even worse fit. The ducks set off in step: 'pit pat, paddle pat! pit pat, waddle pat!'. Tabitha Twitchit is affronted, and sends the kittens upstairs to bed. 'I am sorry to say she told her friends that they were in bed with the measles; which was not true': on the contrary, they create havoc and disturb the 'dignity and repose' of the tea-party (438). The dénouement turns into a myth-like explanation of the up-ending of ducks.

Beatrix felt that the duck pictures (43) – some done in London from her cousins' ducks at Putney Park – would lighten the book. Finishing touches had been added to other drawings during the family holiday at Derwentwater, in the stuffy but draughty Lingholm attics: she hated working indoors in the country. The story was written out in a penny exercise book.

283 (above left) The kittens are turned out into the garden, *The Tale of Tom Kitten*, p. 23, 1907

284 (above) The kittens forget themselves, *The Tale of Tom Kitten*, p. 24, 1907

285 The Puddle-Ducks lose their clothes, *The Tale of Tom Kitten*, p. 57, 1907

For children *Tom Kitten* is more approachable than *The Pie and the Patty-Pan*, and gratifyingly full of detail and naughty doings. Tom Kitten reappears in miniature and picture letters – and in painting books, talking to Jemima Puddle-Duck.

The Tale of Jemima Puddle-Duck, 'a Farmyard Tale for Ralph and Betsy [Cannon]' published in 1908, leaves Hill Top garden for Hill Top Farm, where Beatrix's agent John Cannon lived with his family in the newly-built wing. By 1908 the farm had ten cows and fourteen pigs, as well as ducks and hens, and over thirty Herdwick sheep. Mrs Cannon is seen feeding her poultry (406), with Betsy beyond the gate and Ralph finding Jemima's eggs among the rhubarb.

Ducks in general tend to be bad sitters, and Mrs Cannon had sometimes to substitute a hen as mother. The hen was Henny Penny – a wonderful layer of immense white eggs – but 'Jemima Puddleduck might have taken a lesson from her in the art of hiding nests'. That vain and foolish bird was a great trial – and delightfully dumb she looks as she confides in the fox or toils up the hill at his bidding with her doom in a carrier bag. Of all her dogs, Beatrix liked Kep the most (412); Jemima was in awe of him. The foxy gentleman, however, was Beatrix's favourite villain: a silver-tongued charmer who, laying a finger to his nose, invites Jemima to make free of his summer residence for her nest, plotting a vulpine version of *droit de seigneur*.

Jemima Puddle-Duck is not just a farmyard story, or even 'Red Riding Hood' retold, but a fable warning of the consequences of venturing into the unknown – and in *quite* unsuitable

286   (below left) Jemima complains to the gentleman with sandy whiskers, *The Tale of Jemima Puddle-Duck*, p. 27, 1908

287   (below) Sketch from the manuscript of *The Tale of Jemima Puddle-Duck*, for p. 31, ?1905

288 (above) Jemima nestling among the feathers, *The Tale of Jemima Puddle-Duck*, p. 32, 1908

289 (above right) The foxy gentleman counts Jemima's eggs, *The Tale of Jemima Puddle-Duck*, p. 36, 1908

clothes. Credulous, rash and untypically undomesticated for a Potter heroine, Jemima (though dramatically rescued in the best romantic tradition – by Kep and two foxhound puppies) meets an untypically unjust fate: she loses her eggs. Ambiguities such as the feathers in which Jemima makes her nest, or the sage and onion which she dutifully gathers for her own stuffing, teach children about irony. Another challenge, here and in *The Roly-Poly Pudding*, is the coexistence of two time-sequences – or rather, the story is told from two different points of view. It is an achievement for a child to grasp that, while Kep is marshalling aid for Jemima, an increasingly nervous 'Tod' back at the woodshed is awaiting Jemima's arrival with the sage and onion. *The Roly-Poly Pudding* is more complicated and much longer. The first third of the story is seen through the eyes of Mrs Tabitha Twitchit and Cousin Ribby, Moppet and Mittens; the central section tells of Tom and the rats – and the curious 'roly-poly noise' is at last explained when the two narratives come together in the activities of John Joiner.

'No birds look well in clothes', and when the animals revert to the wild all clothes are shed: the fox inspecting duck eggs or the duck at home, proud mother of a brood at last (401); while the fatherly Kep, like most Potter dogs, has no clothes at all. A bonneted duck on the wing in her father's sketchbook (64) may have fuelled Beatrix's imagination for the picture of Jemima skimming over the tree-tops in search of a nesting place away from 'superfluous' hens.

This book also contains some of Beatrix's most memorable and idyllic landscapes (454). The view across Esthwaite Water from Jemima's Wood remains virtually unchanged today; it

was her favourite among the Lakes. Unfortunately few background studies survive apart from a number of farmyard scenes, some fine paintings of (aptly) foxgloves (*175*) and a coy-looking Jemima for the painting book. One manuscript contains evidence of the great care with which Beatrix prepared her books. The corrections are revealing: punctuation for instance had to be exact. 'There are too many exclamations, the fox is not meant to be excited in manner.' Beatrix was fond of the *mot juste*, yet at the start of *Jemima* she altered 'aggrieved' to 'provoked' for the sake of child readers. Warne seem to have intervened with a blander choice ('annoyed') but 'provoked' is back again in the Puddle-Duck *Painting Book*. She wrote two versions of the opening paragraph, the first slightly cynical: 'What a gratifying thing it is in these days to meet with a female devoted to family life!' This was abandoned for the simpler 'What a funny sight it is to see a brood of ducklings with a hen!'

Against Warne's advice Beatrix insisted in all her books on expressive or fine-sounding adjectives ('fatterer') and piled up adjectives ('little small'). Never boring or monosyllabic, she chose unconventional, incantatory words for children to listen to or guess at rather than understand. She liked complementary pairs of characters – Peter and Benjamin, Miss Moppet and the mouse – or rhythmic pairs of words – 'vindictive and sandy whiskered', 'dignity and repose'. Speech is matched to speaker, and the fox's personality-change betrayed by an abrupt descent from circumlocution to a snappish brevity. The names too are just right: Farmer Potatoes, Alderman Ptolemy Tortoise, Mrs Tiggy-winkle.

Her publishers sometimes found Beatrix a little outrageous. They censored the rollicking rats from *The Tailor of Gloucester*

290 (above left) Jemima skims along over the tree-tops, *The Tale of Jemima Puddle-Duck*, p. 20, 1908

291 (above) 'She set off on a fine spring afternoon', *The Tale of Jemima Puddle-Duck*, p. 15, 1908

292 *Jemima Puddle-Duck's Painting Book*: sketch for the title-page, 1925

(229) but not Cecily Parsley's gentlemen (354), apparently sober enough citizens. She delighted in ribbing them and wrote about *Jemima*: 'If you want to pick holes – has anybody noticed the embarrassing fact that the foxywhiskered gentleman appears *without his knickerbockers* on p. 38 . . .?'

Only one endpaper includes Jemima (210), but she stars again in an unpublished painting book which describes the Hill Top livestock, and in an ICAA Christmas card – and she makes an entrance in both *Peter Rabbit's Painting Book* and *Tom Kitten's Painting Book*. *Jemima Puddle-Duck's* came last of all, in 1925, done rather grudgingly in response to public demand for yet another book. Beatrix found she could still draw, but waited in vain for ducklings to hatch – they had not been made enough of in the original pictures – but after three weeks the eggs were addled. The colouring instructions are as for *Tom Kitten*, but the kittens with crayons are replaced by six ducklings dabbling in paint water. Inside the back cover is a Hill Top ewe with her lambs. A new design was made for 'They took Jemima home': in the painting book Kep and the foxhound pups, first seen outside the Tower Bank Arms, escort Jemima weeping over her broken (but uneaten) eggs. Incongruously, the same sad theme was chosen for chocolate Easter eggs made by Crabtree & Evelyn.

Jemima appears in other merchandising: silk or linen table mats painted by Beatrix for her friends include a Jemima set, with an abridged text but only twelve of the pictures. Amused at a rather swollen-headed Jemima toy, Beatrix patented a 'new and original design for stuffed imitation ducks' in 1910. She had already made her own Jemima doll for a model, dressed in bonnet and Paisley handkerchief.

Jemima Puddle-Duck is a much-loved book, almost as successful as *Peter Rabbit*. Beatrix once found a group of children playing the Jemima story and gave the heroine an inscribed copy, on her own last birthday.

The other book published in 1908 was also set at Hill Top, and Tom Kitten makes another appearance.

The Roly-Poly Pudding, later renamed *The Tale of Samuel Whiskers*, was the second of Beatrix Potter's books to be issued in the larger format. This not only gave Beatrix more space for her paintings, which she preferred, but it also allowed for black-and-white sketches, which the earlier small books did not. This story was very much a celebration of Hill Top. The book is set for the most part in the interior of the farmhouse, much of which has remained unchanged to this day. In letters to Millie Warne in 1906, Beatrix had commented on the war she was waging against the rats which infested the property, and how bold they had become – not to mention their intramural scutterings. All this is most faithfully reproduced in the tale of poor Tom Kitten, who was so nearly made into a roly-poly pudding by the aggressive rats.

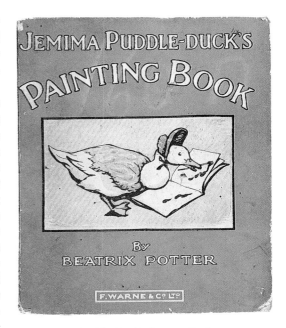

293   *Jemima Puddle-Duck's Painting Book*, cover, 1925

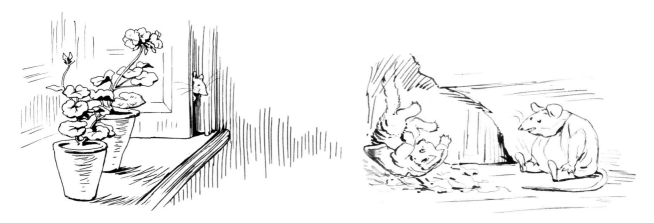

294 (above) A study for Anna Maria on her way to steal dough, *The Roly-Poly Pudding*, p. 58, 1908

295 (above right) Tom Kitten landing on a heap of dirty rags: a sketch for p. 48; from the manuscript of *The Roly-Poly Pudding*, Christmas 1906

296 Samuel Whiskers and Anna Maria on the run, with Beatrix herself looking on, *The Roly-Poly Pudding*, p. 73, 1908

The Roly-Poly Pudding once again features the great childhood sin of disobedience – and the retribution which follows. The story concerns the kittens Moppet and Mittens and their brother Tom, whose adventures had appeared in *The Tale of Tom Kitten*. He escapes from his mother's supervision by climbing out of the kitchen by way of the chimney – and it is not a pleasant experience. Poor Tom Kitten gets lost, and he gets dirty, and the chimney is dark and frightening – and then he falls straight into the hands of Samuel Whiskers and his wife Anna Maria who decide to make a roly-poly pudding out of him. He is only saved at the last minute by the intervention of the dog John Joiner, and when rescued and returned to his mother Tabitha Twitchit he has to face yet another ordeal, in the shape of a hot bath!

Rats of course are different from mice and give rise to less agreeable associations. However, at one time Beatrix Potter had had a tame white rat as a pet, whom she called 'Sammy' and to whose memory *The Roly-Poly Pudding* was dedicated. She had therefore had considerable experience in drawing rats and, of course, she had drawn a number of cats and kittens in her earlier books. But two things make this particular work stand out: one is the Hill Top backgrounds; the other is the character of Samuel Whiskers himself. The story too has just that *frisson* of fear which children enjoy when they know everything will be all right in the end.

Beatrix Potter endowed Samuel Whiskers, who eventually took over the title of the story, with a very definite personality. Whenever he appears in the book, either in colour or in black-and-white, he dominates the scene, with his poor wife Anna Maria coming a bad second in the rat race. Fat, self-satisfied and domineering, no wonder he was puffing as he turned in at the gate of Farmer Potatoes' barn. One gets the feeling that Beatrix Potter had a sneaking fondness for the old rogue, and on page 73, in her own drawing of herself, she stands there watching – with some amusement one suspects – the rats about to transfer their attention away from Hill Top to Farmer Potatoes.

297, 298 A photograph of the original 'Farmer Potatoes' with his daughters Ruth and Mary Postlethwaite, and the painting of him in *The Roly-Poly Pudding*, p. 76, 1908

299 A duplicate illustration of Tabitha Twitchit standing on the staircase at Hill Top, looking for her son, *The Roly-Poly Pudding*, p. 15, 1908

Earlier in this quite lengthy book it is definitely Hill Top which dominates the scenes. We see the kitchen range, which Beatrix admitted she was reluctant to change because she wanted it for a book, the staircase, still unchanged today, the front door, the dresser – all the things that bring out the 'oohs' and 'aahs' of the visiting children (of all ages). What we cannot hope to see, at least in the same way, is the view Tom Kitten enjoyed over Sawrey from the chimney top, but from the higher parts of the village the scene can still be recognized.

One of the interesting things about this book is that we have an example of Beatrix Potter's use of photography for her work. There exists a photograph of Farmer Postlethwaite, a near neighbour in Sawrey, and this she has used for the painting of Farmer Potatoes on page 76 – he is quite recognizable. Beatrix had seen how Millais frequently made use of photography in this way – often seeking photographs from her own father. She makes it quite clear that she found it more and more difficult to work at her books during her holidays or her visits to her Lakeland property, so that they tended to be worked up from sketches – or photographs – during the winter months and her sojourns in her London home. Another curious fact is that one of the sketches in the Linder Bequest at the Victoria and Albert Museum, showing Mrs Tabitha Twitchit looking for her son Tom Kitten and standing on the staircase at Hill Top, has the head of the cat cut out and pasted on. Was this because the first painting was wrong, or was it because it gave a dimensional effect?

We have seen how the influence of Randolph Caldecott could be traced in the figure of Mr Jeremy Fisher, and the same Caldecott toy book, *A Frog He Would A-Wooing Go*, also

300 (above) An illustration from *A Frog He Would A-Wooing Go*, by Randolph Caldecott, 1883

301 (above right) Samuel Whiskers running off with a pat of butter, *The Roly-Poly Pudding*, p. 32, 1908

302 (below right) A study for the frightened Tom Kitten confronting a rat, *The Roly-Poly Pudding*, p. 81, 1908

provides a close relative of Samuel Whiskers. But Caldecott's painting of his rat is quite bland in comparison with the wickedness that radiates from Beatrix Potter's character. No wonder poor Tom Kitten never durst face anything bigger than a mouse after his traumatic experience of actually becoming a Roly-Poly Pudding.

For some children it was probably a relief to get back to the less frightening rabbit world of Beatrix Potter's next book.

The Tale of the Flopsy Bunnies reintroduces some of the characters who would already have been known to young readers. The arch-villain is Mr McGregor again, but Benjamin Bunny is now grown up and married to Peter Rabbit's sister, Flopsy – hence the Flopsy Bunnies of the title, who are the children of Benjamin and Flopsy. There is something greatly satisfying about the very sound of 'Flopsy Bunnies' and in this book Beatrix used the sound of words to great effect, as witness her famous inclusion of the word 'soporific' in the opening lines of the book. To some extent this story is another version of the Peter Rabbit or Benjamin Bunny tales. By eating too many (soporific) lettuces the little rabbits fall victim to Mr McGregor and a prey to his fondness for them – even as

Peter's father had done. The second half of the tale recounts how, thanks to the efforts of Mrs Tittlemouse, the Flopsy Bunnies are eventually restored to their anxious parents.

Various locations have been suggested for *The Tale of Peter Rabbit*, and *Benjamin Bunny* we know was given backgrounds from the gardens at Fawe Park, in the Lake District. *The Flopsy Bunnies*, however, is set in the gardens of Gwaynynog, the home of Beatrix Potter's uncle and aunt in Wales. This was – and indeed still is – a delightful old house, set in a rambling country garden. The descendants of Beatrix Potter's aunt and uncle still live at Gwaynynog – and so do the descendants of the Flopsy Bunnies – although neither house nor garden is normally open to the public. The grounds have changed little since poor Flopsy went searching for her missing babies, who were securely tied up in a sack which had been placed on the wall. It is still possible to stand where Flopsy stood and see the same wall, though trees and shrubs have grown considerably since Beatrix Potter's day.

The backgrounds to this book – and indeed the rabbits themselves – offered Beatrix just the kind of painting she enjoyed. She was always at her best with rabbits, and when painting flowers and gardens. A number of her preliminary sketches for the garden scenes have survived – not all of which were used – indicating the care which Beatrix took to get just the right setting for each part of her tale. Among the more delightful associations of this particular book is the series of miniature letters which purport to come from various members of the Flopsy Bunny family. The letters decrease in size and competence of execution according to the position of each rabbit within the family, until the letters from '5th (Miss) F. Bunny' and '6th Master F. B.' are minute miniatures, consisting of scribble and a few kisses.

The Flopsy Bunnies was published in 1909, but the Welsh connection was abandoned for the other book published that year, when Beatrix chose a Lake District setting again.

Ginger and Pickles is the story of the village shop: *any* village shop, but more especially the one owned by Mr John Taylor of Sawrey at the time when Beatrix Potter first bought Hill Top. The original story was written for Louie, the daughter of Harold Warne, the member of the firm with whom Beatrix dealt after Norman died. She said that her best stories were always those written for specific children. In this one she introduced a number of the characters from the earlier books.

The shop is kept by a tom-cat called Ginger and his terrier friend Pickles. They run into trouble because they always give credit and therefore have no money for Pickles to buy his dog licence with, so he is afraid to go out in case he meets a policeman. The word 'credit' is carefully explained to the young readers: 'When a customer buys a bar of soap, instead of the customer pulling out a purse and paying for it – she says she

303 'She looked suspiciously at the sack and wondered where everybody was?': Mrs Flopsy Bunny searching for her babies, *The Tale of the Flopsy Bunnies*, p. 35, 1909

304 (above) Ginger and Pickles serving Samuel Whiskers and the rabbits, *Ginger and Pickles*, p. 13, 1909

305 (above right) Pickles giving credit to Mrs Tiggy-winkle for her bar of soap, *Ginger and Pickles*, p. 18, 1909

306 Ginger watching the departing mice, who made his mouth water, *Ginger and Pickles*, p. 14, 1909

will pay another time. And Pickles makes a low bow and says "With pleasure, Madam," and it is written down in a book.' Needless to say, with such a system the shop eventually has to close down and Ginger and Pickles take up alternative, and rather dubious, occupations. The other shopkeepers are delighted, of course, but the customers are less so, until Sally Henny Penny decides to reopen the shop, which she fills with an assortment of bargains – 'there is something to please everybody'.

The story is certainly quite simple, but there are very subtle touches in it which the older child might deduce for himself and smaller children would enjoy when they have been explained. For example, the rabbits were always a bit afraid of Pickles, while Ginger couldn't bear to serve the mice because it made his mouth water.

Pickles says: 'It would never do to eat our own customers; they would leave us and go to Tabitha Twitchit's.'

'On the contrary, they would go nowhere,' replied Ginger gloomily.

Children love jokes in a story, and there are plenty for them in this one. There is also the joy of recognition as they see the various familiar animals appearing in the pictures: Jeremy Fisher trying on a pair of galoshes, Mrs Tiggy-winkle buying a bar of soap, and so on.

The book was issued in the large format used for *The Pie and the Patty-Pan* and *The Roly-Poly Pudding*, which enabled Beatrix Potter to make both black-and-white and coloured

illustrations. The larger scale of the pages also encouraged the kind of painting which Beatrix preferred, and the interior of the shop is shown in all its detail. From the very first picture, where we see Tom Kitten, Moppet and Mittens peering through the window, to the last coloured illustration of Sally Henny Penny and her customers, the detailing is done with obvious enjoyment and drawn from the existing shop and its surroundings. In November 1909 Beatrix wrote to Millie Warne: 'The "Ginger & Pickle" book has been causing

307, 308   Background sketch of the interior of John Taylor's shop in Sawrey, and the same scene as it appeared in *Ginger and Pickles*, p. 37, 1909

309, 310   (left) A sketch of Sally Henny Penny from the manuscript of *Ginger and Pickles*, Christmas 1906; and (above) a study of the mice round the bending candle, for *Ginger and Pickles*, p. 52, 1909

amusement, it has got a good many views which can be recognized in the village which is what they like, they are all quite jealous of each others houses & cats getting into a book.'

Strangely, few background studies seem to have survived from the preparation of this book, though it is obvious from the letter quoted above that Beatrix must have gone about the village in her usual way, collecting pictures for her book. She remarked that when she copied a picture from her original sketch, she often failed to recapture the charm and spontaneity of her first attempt, and sometimes she suggested that as the original sketch could not be improved upon it should be used in place of the new one. That certainly happened in this book, where she wrote: 'I think the drawing of "Lucinda and Jane" [the dolls from *The Two Bad Mice*] had better be used as I don't believe I can hit it off again. It is rather spotty, but could be scraped out in the block. Also the sketch of the till might do. They are easily slipped off with a knife.' The former painting was removed, the latter still remains in Louie's manuscript – so perhaps she did 'hit it off again' to her final satisfaction.

The next book was published in 1910, and it started life as a New Year's gift for the other little daughter of Harold Warne, and was known in the family as 'Nellie's little book'. This is how it appears in the dedication to the present day.

The Tale of Mrs. Tittlemouse is one of the stories in which humans play no part at all, and the whole tale is treated as though the events described were continuing endlessly below the level of human observation. The book has the simplest of stories, such as would appeal to a very young child – a day in the life of a little wood mouse who is ultra-houseproud. The drawings for *Mrs. Tittlemouse* are quite delightful – but it is not only the more elaborate watercolour scenes which make this such a charming book, but the black-and-white sketch of Mrs Tittlemouse addressing the butterfly, which appears on the title-page, is equally attractive and memorable. Once again Beatrix shows her knowledge of natural history, for there is no concession here to any demands that the story might make. The little creatures that invade or visit Mrs Tittlemouse's house behave in a characteristic way, and are described with the eye of a naturalist.

It was about this very aspect of the book, which we find so delightful today, that Beatrix Potter and her publishers had a difference of opinion. Always sensitive to the reactions of the buying public – as they interpreted them – Frederick Warne had doubts about some parts of this book. They had by now become more or less accustomed to Beatrix Potter's strange choice of animal subjects, but this book seemed to go too far. Beatrix herself saw the natural world quite unsentimentally, and there were no 'good' or 'bad' creatures for her. Hence, without a second thought, she described an earwig losing its way in Mrs Tittlemouse's house, or woodlice haunting the

311   Lucinda and Jane Doll-cook looking in the window of the shop, *Ginger and Pickles*, p. 11, 1909

312   Sketch for the title-page drawing of Mrs Tittlemouse talking to a butter-fly, *The Tale of Mrs. Tittlemouse*, 1910

pantry. Mice and rabbits were all right, ladybirds and toads were – well, not *too* bad – but earwigs and woodlice! This went beyond anything the publishers could allow, so in the published version the earwig becomes a beetle and the woodlice become 'creepy-crawly people' (how Beatrix must have hated that). But it remains a charming tale where, for the young at least, today, tomorrow and last year are indistinguishable, and there is nothing surprising in having Mr Jackson to supper – provided you do not mind having thistle seeds in your room.

In contrast to *Mrs. Tittlemouse* the next book is quite different from the others in the series, featuring animals that are not indigenous to the Lake District or indeed to Britain. The grey squirrel came into the country from North America (though as a result of its being far more adaptable than the native red squirrel, it is now the dominant of the two species). The chipmunk is a North American ground squirrel of which there are none in Britain outside zoos. Neither are there bears – and certainly not the American black bear.

The Tale of Timmy Tiptoes was intended to please her American readers, of which, after publishing sixteen books, she had a great many. Her original intention had been to follow *Mrs. Tittlemouse* with 'a pig book . . . upon the same plan and size as the *Ginger & Pickles*', but the farm at Hill Top was increasingly absorbing her attention and now that her parents were in their seventies their demands on her time were considerable.

Beatrix shelved the pig book after a number of false starts and spent the winter supervising the production of *Peter Rabbit's Painting Book*, before turning her attention to the surprising new story, featuring animals for which she had no models outside reference books. 'The book obtained from Rowland Ward will be very useful, & I am sure I can find out any botanical point at Kew.' Her story was about a grey squirrel who is chased by other squirrels into the bottom of a hollow tree. Plied with nuts by a friendly chipmunk who is staying there, Timmy Tiptoes becomes so fat that he has to wait until the tree is blown down before he can be reunited with his wife.

The text for *Timmy Tiptoes* gave Beatrix trouble, for she had made it too long and she was also uncertain about how to convey certain bird calls (is one of them a yellowhammer?). 'I have compressed the words in the earlier pages; but it seems unavoidable to have a good deal of *nuts*. The songs of the little birds will be easier to judge as to spelling when one sees it in type.'

The text and most of the illustrations were ready at last and at the end of July Beatrix sent them to London from the Potters' holiday home, Lindeth How, in Windermere. Harold Warne was embarrassed when he had to ask for some alterations but Beatrix took it well. 'There is no need to apologize for criticism. But there is no doubt the animals strongly resemble

313 '"Tiddly, widdly, widdly! Pouff, pouff, puff!" said Mr. Jackson': painting from the manuscript of *The Tale of Mrs. Tittlemouse*, 1 January 1910

314 The cover picture for *The Tale of Timmy Tiptoes*, 1911

rabbits, the head which you question was copied from a photograph in the book.'

It would be interesting to know what was in Beatrix's mind when she was preparing *Timmy Tiptoes*. Did she clothe Timmy and Goody (but not the other grey squirrels) because she was unsure of how to draw her other main characters, Mr and Mrs Chippy Hackee the chipmunks, and had to start by clothing them? Or were the Tiptoes dressed because they collected their nuts in sacks, an unnatural way for squirrels to behave and a ruse that Beatrix had used before (Peter Rabbit only walks on his hind legs when he is wearing his jacket)? Certainly her idea to make Timmy eat so much that he couldn't get out through the woodpecker's hole is an amusing one and has been copied by other authors since, notably by A. A. Milne when Pooh ate so much that he could not get out of Rabbit's hole. Whatever was Beatrix's intention the fact remains that *Timmy Tiptoes*, published in 1911, is an uneasy book, the only one in the series where not all the animals fit naturally into the background. However exciting it would be to see a pair of chipmunks and a black bear in the Sawrey woods it is an unlikely fantasy. Badgers and foxes were much more likely animals to find.

The Tale of Mr. Tod returns to Sawrey and to a wider setting beyond the garden wall. 'In winter and early spring he might generally be found in an earth amongst the rocks at the top of Bull Banks, under Oatmeal Crag.' Bull Banks was a pasture on Castle Farm which Beatrix allowed villagers to use for the 1911 Coronation celebrations; she draws Mr Tod at the lake edge (Esthwaite), and Brock looking down on him from Bull Banks. The story, sketched out some time before, is a forbidding one with little light relief except in the landscapes. Graham Greene contended that Beatrix had been suffering from emotional disturbance at the time of writing – but she would have none of it. Nothing had disturbed her save the after-effects of 'flu, and she deprecated sharply the 'Freudian school of criticism'.

Tommy Brock is pressed to taste a glass of Flopsy's cowslip wine by old Mr Benjamin Bouncer, who falls asleep – so Tommy removes the rabbit babies in a sack ('"seven, . . . and all of them twins"'). Benjamin, aided and advised by Peter, tracks Brock to Mr Tod's house at the top of Bull Banks. No

315 'Who's – been – digging-up *my*-nuts?', *The Tale of Timmy Tiptoes*, p. 58, 1911

316 Mr Tod by Esthwaite Water: preliminary drawing for *The Tale of Mr. Tod*, p. 12, 1912

young rabbits are to be seen, but 'the moonbeams twinkled on the carving knife and the pie dish'. Benjamin and Peter burrow under the kitchen floor, and hide there in panic as Mr Tod approaches in a testy mood which turns to fury at the discovery of Brock in his bed. Tommy Brock is too lazy and comfortable to move, but Mr Tod – no hero, and disconcerted by the sight of Tommy's teeth – devises a trap which can be operated at a safe distance. The plan involves a bucket of water and a rope, but it misfires: Tommy escapes and is discovered by Mr Tod, alive and calmly drinking tea. The ensuing battle rages round the kitchen and over the rocks ('"What dreadful bad language! I think they have fallen down the stone quarry"'). At home, Flopsy Bunny relieves her feelings with a therapeutic spring-cleaning. Old Mr Bunny is in disgrace – till the babies' safe return.

Mr. Tod deals with undesirable elements of society. The manuscript begins: 'I am quite tired of making goody goody books about nice people. I will make a story about two disagreeable people, called Tommy Brock and Mr Tod.' Warne disapproved, and changed the opening to 'many books about well-behaved people'. Beatrix retorts: 'If it were not impertinent to lecture one's publisher – you are a great deal too much afraid of the public, for whom I have never cared one tuppenny-button.' She knew the importance of beginnings and endings – 'I have always thought the opening paragraph distinctly *good*, because it gets away from "once upon a time"' – an opening which she had abandoned also in *The Flopsy Bunnies*, that other tale of kidnapping. She teases Harold Warne about the name Bull Banks and his sensitivity to ungenteel expressions: 'One thinks nothing about bulls and

317 (above left) The rope gives way, *The Tale of Mr. Tod*, p. 67, 1912

318 (above) Tommy Brock triumphant, *The Tale of Mr. Tod*, p. 72, 1912

319 Tommy Brock climbs into Mr. Tod's bed: unused drawing for *The Tale of Mr. Tod*, 1912

tups in the farming world; but after you objected to cigars it occurred to me to wonder.' To her surprise Warne questioned the term 'Tod' – surely everyone knew the Saxon word for fox, just as badgers were 'brocks' or 'grays'.

One detects a sneaking sympathy with the hero, less urbane than in *Jemima Puddle-Duck* – is he the same fox? Crestfallen, he sits chewing on a broken rope; then with a zeal worthy of Mrs Tittlemouse he tries to obliterate the last traces of his unwelcome visitor, Mr Brock. 'I will get soft soap, and monkey soap, and all kinds of soap . . . I must have a disinfecting. Perhaps I may have to burn sulphur.' Mr Brock is drawn with frightening irony, hobnobbing hypocritically with old Mr Bouncer.

Mr. Tod's novelty lies partly in the type of illustration used: only sixteen watercolours but forty-two line drawings – almost enough for each page to have its picture. Emphatic frames give the impression of woodcuts; Beatrix believed that a black frame pulls a picture together and sends back the distance. One unused design in sepia is drawn in an uncharacteristic manner. There are some charming studies: Cottontail with her family above Esthwaite – the view drawn for 'Kitty-in-Boots' (*see p. 153*); and the particularly well-composed picture of Benjamin and Peter climbing up Bull Banks. Sometimes the roughest sketches have the greatest vitality, as in the scene of attempted murder by a victimized Mr Tod, tying a rope above the usurper

320 Cottontail sitting in her doorway, *The Tale of Mr. Tod*, p. 30, 1912

321 (left) The rabbits creep up to Mr Tod's house, *The Tale of Mr. Tod*, p. 32, 1912

322 (below) Mr Tod sets a trap: sketch for *The Tale of Mr. Tod*, p. 58, 1912

of his bed. Illustrating the nightmarish passage 'The sun had set; an owl began to hoot in the wood', the rabbits peer into the kitchen, Peter's blue coat shining through the dusk. The interiors are gloomy. Mr Tod's kitchen, unexpectedly neat and stocked with good china, sports a chopper on the table. The brick oven, drawn from the Sun Inn at Hawkshead, is converted into a prison for baby rabbits, the rabbit pie destined for a more up-to-date oven in cast iron (409). Beatrix made the kitchen even darker to help with the difficult detail of the duel, a scene of horror and confusion – the culmination of a gathering tension, carefully worked out in somewhat puzzling and complicated detail.

The end of *Mr. Tod* is left a question-mark, and children complained that there was no sequel – but the characters lived on in Beatrix's mind, and she supplied news of their doings in letters. Cottontail was put in by special request (*Mr. Tod* is the fourth book about the extended family of rabbits, the highly-strung Peter and his unflappable, worldly-wise cousin Benjamin). In reply to one child Beatrix wrote: 'I have inquired about Mr Tod & Tommy Brock, and I am sorry to tell you they are still quarrelling.' Brock had lost a boot, but found it in the quarry. 'There was a beetle in the boot & several slugs. Tommy Brock ate them. He is a nasty person.'

The Tale of Mr. Tod was published in 1912, and dedicated to her cousin Caroline's new baby – 'someday'! It was to be the first of a 'New Series' of Peter Rabbit books, thicker and with a more elaborate binding. Warne had wanted an entirely new series, but in Beatrix's opinion children would expect as little change as possible. By now she was less inclined to produce short stories or large quantities of coloured pictures. She disliked the new endpaper, too, on which Samuel Whiskers sticks up a giant poster, watched by other animal characters: it was too like railway advertisements. Both *Mr. Tod* and the next book, *Pigling Bland*, were published as 'Series II, New Style', but this title was abandoned and Warne soon reverted to the ordinary binding.

The Tale of Pigling Bland, last of the Sawrey books, was also the last before Beatrix's marriage. Nineteen-thirteen had been a difficult year. Ill herself, she had to supervise improvements to Castle Cottage, her future home, and attend to her parents. It was always 'absolutely hopeless and impossible to finish books in summer', but after 'an awful hurry and scramble' this one was done at last, in September. With its intimate fireside scenes and shared adventures, *Pigling Bland* is almost a love story. However 'the portrait of two pigs arm in arm – looking at the sunrise – is *not* a portrait of me & Mr Heelis, though it is a view of where we used to walk on Sunday afternoons! When I want to put William in a book – it will have to be as some very tall thin animal.'

The story wanders further from Hill Top than before –

323 Peter and Benjamin peer through the bedroom window: preliminary painting for *The Tale of Mr. Tod*, p. 37, 1912

324 'A perfectly lovely little black Berkshire pig', *The Tale of Pigling Bland*, p. 56, 1913

325 'The sun rose while they were crossing the moor', *The Tale of Pigling Bland*, p. 69, 1913

though Pigling merely crosses Brathay Bridge into Lancashire on his way to market and then returns to Westmorland via Colwith Bridge to live in Little Langdale (434). Pigling Bland is an unusually virtuous hero, in fact almost the only good little pig of the litter apart from Spot. The others end up in the vegetable patch or the laundry basket; the piglet in a tub is another favourite motif. Pigling is a sedate little pig and old for his years, but interestingly brave and resourceful – and far from bland.

He is sent off with his more frivolous brother Alexander, with 'licences permitting two pigs to go to market in Lancashire' and eight conversation peppermints each, 'with appropriate moral sentiments in screws of paper'. Alexander eats his straight away, and when he scraps with Pigling the papers get mixed up. They encounter a policeman: Alexander's licence is missing and he has to be escorted home. The dejected Pigling goes on alone in the rain – and suddenly finds the missing paper. Rushing back after Alexander, he gets lost and cries 'Wee, wee, wee! I can't find my way home'. The moon reveals a new country and a hen house where he shelters for the night, only to be discovered by the owner, Mr Piperson. Pigling is given porridge to eat by the fire, and sleeps on the rug. Next night the cupboard with its mysterious occupant is left open – and the ebullient Pig-wig (recipient of Pigling's peppermints) introduces herself. She sings little rhymes and falls asleep, still singing. Just before dawn they creep out of the house and make for the county boundary. Narrowly escaping a ploughman and a suspicious grocer, they race downhill and cross the bridge hand in hand (434).

Already in 1910 a letter from 'Peter Rabbit' hints at a new book: 'Miss Potter is drawing pigs & mice. She says she has drawn enough rabbits. But I am to be put into one picture at the end of the pig book' – and on the last page rabbits watch

326 Alexander stuck in the pig trough, *The Tale of Pigling Bland*, p. 11, 1913

327 Little black pig in a tub, 1899

Pigling and Pig-wig as they dance 'over the hills and far away'. Beatrix wrote 'I think I shall put *myself* in the next book, it will be about pigs', and she longed to write a story about her 'six pink cherubs'. 'I have done a little sketching when it does not rain, and I spent a very wet hour *inside* the pig stye drawing the pig. It tries to nibble my boots, which is interrupting.'

Beatrix had a great affection for pigs, pink or black. They sit in chairs (330) or prop up the fence with a genial expression, as in the pig/Potter caricature of 1924 (166). This was precipitated by a confusion in the *Sunday Herald* over Beatrix Potter and Mrs Sidney Webb (née Beatrice Potter). Beatrix was affronted: 'I do not think that nice oldfashioned people who like my books would like them quite so much if they believed them to be of socialist origin,' and she complained to the editor that her sales might be affected. The best remedy was to be photographed with a favourite pig or cow: the resulting drawing reveals pig and owner as equally jovial and amazingly alike (*see 166*). The pig in question was 'hanging up, unphotographed & cured now.'

Beatrix had the farmer's unsentimental approach, and sent baby pork to her publishers at Christmas – though, working on sketches for the heads (41) she writes: 'The poor little cherub had such a sweet smile . . . It is rather a shame to kill them so young.' In 1905 the whole district was 'planted out' with her pigs, which managed to devour most of the potatoes before their departure. In 1909 two Hill Top pigs had to be sold, though it took away from the completeness of the family group, because 'their appetites were fearful – 5 meals a day and not satisfied' (404). To the book she adds at proof stage 'And they drink bucketfuls of milk; I shall have to get another cow!' But Beatrix's feelings overcame her better judgement in the matter of Pig-wig, 'a perfectly lovely little black Berkshire pig', whom she first met at Hard Cragg when fetching pigs for John Cannon from Farmer Townley. Cannon would countenance

328 'Over the hills and far away', *The Tale of Pigling Bland*, p. 84, 1913

329 'Come dance a jig, to my Granny's pig', for the 1905 Book of Rhymes, 1891

330   Pig-wig on a Hill Top chair, *The Tale of Pigling Bland*, p. 61, 1913

331   The pigs at the crossroads, *The Tale of Pigling Bland*, alternative frontispiece, ?1913

only pedigree pigs and refused to take the 'tiny black girl-pig' – so Pig-wig became a household pet, bottle-fed and kept in a basket by the bed.

With Pig-wig the feminine pig makes her first appearance in literature, and captivates but embarrasses the very English Pigling. 'Inquisitive, unromantic, demanding to be amused, fond of confectionery and admirably unselfconscious' (Graham Greene again), she is equally charming bolt upright on a chair – *without* the conversation peppermint (Beatrix confessed to Willie 'Peppermint accidentally omitted from p.67'), or dancing with joy – as elegant as the pigs at Putney Park (*see p. 79*). Alexander danced all the time – inspiring a famous dance critic to take the name 'Alexander Bland'.

Other pig pictures commemorate earlier Hill Top pigs. Aunt Susan, 'very fat and black with a very turned up nose and the fattest cheeks I ever saw', loved being tickled under the chin. Aunt Dorcas was smaller and less tame. Both in *Pigling Bland* and in *Pig Robinson*, where the serene Aunts Dorcas and Porcas lead 'prosperous uneventful lives' (but end as '"Bacon, hams"' – as Pig-wig laconically remarks), Beatrix intervenes as narrator. Glimpsed till now only in *The Roly-Poly Pudding*, she appears featureless in several scenes (2, 47), two unpublished, one the pinning on of Alexander's licence, and another in two coloured versions. The real proprietor of the farm in *Pigling Bland* is Aunt Pettitoes, a much-loved character; Beatrix thought she would make a good doll. In a dignified and epic speech to her departing sons she exhorts Pigling always to walk on his hind-legs: once on all fours animals become vulnerable to danger, all etiquette forgotten.

Pursuer and pursued, eating and being eaten – these were realities which Beatrix could not hide but softened with humour, keeping the violence off-stage. In other tales the pictures are benign and sunny, but *Pigling Bland* and its darker predecessor *Mr. Tod* convey an atmosphere of nocturnal loneliness, unease and fear. The sad farewells are barely masked by the comedy and even the happy ending is a close-run thing.

Pigling Bland was intended for smaller children than *Mr. Tod*, and accordingly made shorter though again written as a continuous narrative. The black-and-white pictures are freer, without the heavy frames of *Tod*: 'I do not intend to put lines round them as they are mostly light subjects.' For the frontispiece she first sketched the crossroads behind Hill Top (405), then added the two lively boy-pigs in green coats, commenting on the back 'This is much better than the one in the book'. The book picture shows Pigling in brown and Alexander in green. Peter Thomas Piperson is a believable villain in the style of Mr Tod – gardenless, and with a kitchen just as barren and plantless. His fireplace was drawn from one in Spout House, Far Sawrey. Contrast comes with the rich bright colours of the hen house (50) and the Hill Top scenes. The pen

332 (above) Pigling shakes hands with the cock Charles, *The Tale of Pigling Bland*, p. 22, 1913

333 (above right) Pig-wig dancing and singing, *The Tale of Pigling Bland*, p. 71, 1913

334 'Kitty-in-Boots': unused study for the frontispiece, 1914

drawing of Charles the cock was inspired by a child's suggestion that he should stand on a dish to shake hands. Most lyrical of all is the scene where Pig-wig dances and sings at the sight of distant hills.

'Over the hills and far away!' seemed to symbolize Beatrix's own escape into a new life: a recurring theme and the refrain of her last major book, *The Fairy Caravan*, though several more works intervene, some well-known like *Johnny Town-Mouse*, others hardly known at all.

By 1910 it was already proving impossible to produce more than one book a year, and by the start of the First World War there was hardly time even for one, what with failing eyesight and farming responsibilities, more onerous in wartime. Searching for wandering sheep and lambs drove Beatrix to remark: 'Somehow when one is up to the eyes in work with real live animals it makes one despise paper-book-animals.' In the years just before and after her marriage Beatrix wrote a number of articles and leaflets on farming and country affairs, and four **'Tales of Country Life'** in north-country dialect, composed during Sunday evenings at Hill Top. 'Carrier's Bob' is a sad story founded on a true one, and 'The Mole Catcher's Burying' a prose poem chanted by the moles in honour of their dead. Local field names are celebrated in this tale, and a local Easter custom in 'Pace Eggers'. 'The Fairy Clogs' tells the story of two children miraculously saved from the Windermere ice; it was printed in *Country Life* (25 October 1913).

'Kitty-in-Boots' was planned for 1914, but Warne were discouraging and so it remained unpublished; only the frontispiece illustration was finished. It told of a 'well-behaved prim black Kitty cat' who led a Jekyll and Hyde existence, going out 'on moonlight nights, dressed up like puss in boots', but happily armed only with a pop gun. Next came 'The Oakmen', a story-letter written in 1916 for her niece Nancy. Beatrix had commissioned Ernest Aris to carry out her designs, providing him with detailed instructions. It was never published, owing to some doubts as to the originality of the plot – perhaps fortunately in view of Aris's garish colours and conventional style. His work did *not* meet with her approval. *Johnny Town-Mouse* replaced 'The Oakmen' as the book for 1918.

Appley Dapply's Nursery Rhymes was published before *Johnny Town-Mouse*, in 1917. It is not one book but two. Beatrix Potter began to plan a book of rhymes soon after the publication of *The Tale of Peter Rabbit*, but in its final version – when it was eventually published – it was a rather different book from the one she had originally planned. Like many children, Beatrix had been brought up on the traditional nursery rhymes, and in her case their influence was even further emphasized by the fact that many of them had been illustrated by two of the most popular artists of the day, Walter Crane and Randolph Caldecott.

We know that she possessed at least one book by Walter Crane – *The Baby's Opera* – which was a collection of nursery rhymes (*see p. 45*). After he had produced a number of toy books, whose subjects were mainly fairy tales ('The Sleeping Beauty', 'The Frog Prince' and others) Crane issued several compilations: *The Baby's Own Aesop, The Baby's Opera, The Baby's Bouquet*. For these he provided not only the illustrations but also the page decorations. These books undoubtedly

335, 336 (below) A decorative border of acorns and twigs intended for 'The Toads' Tea Party' (right), a painting made for the 1905 Book of Rhymes

impressed Beatrix as her original intention was to decorate and illustrate *Appley Dapply* in a style similar to the Crane volumes. Randolph Caldecott's subjects were nursery rhymes (such as *A Frog He Would A-Wooing go*) and well-known ballads (such as *The Babes in the Wood*). As we know, both Beatrix and her father greatly admired the work of Caldecott, so it would not be surprising to find her wishful to emulate him too. In a letter to Warne in 1902 she directly linked her thoughts of a book of rhymes with Caldecott's work. 'It may sound odd to talk about mine and Caldecott's at the same time,' she says modestly. 'I think I could at least try to do better than *Peter Rabbit*, and if you did not care to risk another book I could pay for it. I have sometimes thought of trying some of the nursery rhymes about animals, which he did not do.'

Warne expressed some interest, so Beatrix Potter went on thinking about her nursery rhyme book even while other works were in hand. She discussed the layout and the number of pages, the type of decoration and other details. 'I had thought it might be in a style between Caldecott's and *The Baby's Opera*: I cannot design pattern borders, but I like drawing flowers.' It was definitely a work in which she was personally much involved and she repeated from time to time her decision to publish it herself if Warne were not interested. During 1904 she got as far as obtaining a large-size dummy in which to sort out her ideas, and letters were going backwards and forwards between her and Norman Warne about the rhymes and the pictures for the proposed book. One of the last letters she wrote to Norman before he died was on the subject of *Appley Dapply*, but with his death the whole project was put aside.

In 1917 Fruing Warne was pressing Beatrix for yet another book, but her marriage had led to other interests and she was not anxious to devote herself to the intense work involved in preparing a new one. She remembered the nearly-completed

337 'The Rain it Raineth Every Day': an illustration to verses beginning 'Fishes come bite', painted for the 1905 Book of Rhymes

338, 339 Pages from the 1905 dummy Book of Rhymes, illustrating the verses 'Diggory Diggory Delvet' and 'Nid nid noddy'

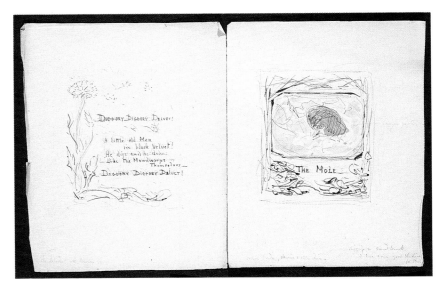

340, 341 'Old Mister Prickly Pin' painted for the 1905 Book of Rhymes (above), and 'Old Mr. Pricklepin' as he actually appeared in *Appley Dapply's Nursery Rhymes* (above right), p. 23, 1917

Appley Dapply – 'Would it be too shabby to put Appley Dapply into a booklet the size of Miss Moppet?' she wrote. 'I could scrape together sufficient old drawings to fill one.' The original idea, she pointed out, had been for a large book with borders, but this she could no longer cope with and so in 1917 the much less ambitious *Appley Dapply's Nursery Rhymes* appeared, with fewer rhymes and pictures and no decoration. Indeed, some of the pictures display her earlier style and show how many of the drawings had been in her portfolio for some time, even if they had been reworked for publication.

Appley Dapply is therefore a very uneven book and shows signs that it was a compilation rather than an original work. The Appley Dapply rhyme ('Appley Dapply, a little brown mouse') at the beginning is illustrated with framed pictures and there is evidence that the sequence was originally done as a small booklet on its own. The pig, too, sits in a frame, and her painting is much more fluid than that of the mouse knitting (117) or the mice in the shoe, which again are rather in the earlier dry-brush technique. It is interesting that both the dummies survive: the large-format one and the *Miss Moppet* one, so that we can actually see Beatrix adjusting her ideas.

As for the little rhymes, which, following Kate Greenaway's

342, 343 Two paintings done in 1891 illustrating verses beginning 'Appley Dapply, a little brown mouse' (left) and 'Appley Dapply has little sharp eyes' (right): these pictures were subsequently used in *Appley Dapply's Nursery Rhymes*, pp. 10 and 14, 1917

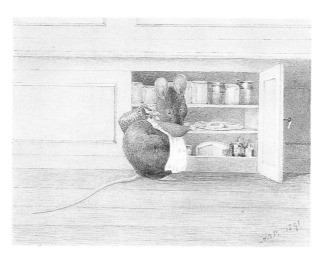

example, she composed herself, these are very simple. Several of them contain definite echoes of the traditional nursery rhymes which had undoubtedly influenced her style of composition, as in 'You know the old woman who lived in a shoe?'. She has certainly caught something of the jog-trot rhythm of such verses, but they are none of them especially memorable. The book is more like the last squeezings of an almost dry sponge, but it is a tribute to the genius' of the younger Beatrix Potter that the picture chosen for the delightful frontispiece was none other than that of the two gentlemen rabbits walking through the snow, originally done for Hildesheimer & Faulkner as long ago as 1894 (110).

The Tale of Johnny Town-Mouse was the last book in the old style, the only late one to be a unity rather than a patchwork. Beatrix dedicated it to 'Aesop in the shadows'. She had proposed a second rhyme book for 1918, but Fruing Warne asked for a story and *Cecily Parsley's Nursery Rhymes* had to wait until 1922. Odd scraps of text and pictures done years before came to light in portfolios. Beatrix asked: 'Do you think this mouse story would do? It makes pretty pictures, but not an indefinite number as there is not a great deal of variety.' She sent off the drawings in desperation: 'I simply *cannot* see to put colour in them – the coal cellar [130], which I tried to work up, is the least satisfactory,' but 'it would have made a good book, with sight & cheerfulness to do it.' The text came out well, however, and was well received.

The title was changed three times – 'Timmy Willie' would not do, because of Timmy Tiptoes, and nor would 'A Tale of a Country Mouse'. The final choice of title necessitated a change in the opening: 'Timmy Willie went to town by mistake in a hamper' becomes 'Johnny Town-Mouse was born in a cupboard. Timmy Willie was born in a garden' – immediately underlining the contrast between town and country mouse. 'One place suits one person, another place suits another person.' Beatrix preferred to live in the country like Timmy Willie, who went to town by mistake in a hamper with the vegetables. Escaping from the cook, he lands in the middle of Johnny Town-Mouse's dinner party. Town life disagrees with Timmy Willie, though Johnny endeavours to entertain him, and he soon goes back with the hamper. In the spring Johnny returns his visit – but finds the country too quiet.

One early picture shows Timmy Willie, ill-at-ease, dining in style with Johnny, who tips back his wine with an air of unconcern; its counterpart has Timmy Willie in a relaxed attitude, framed in foliage. Johnny arrives 'with bag in hand, all spick and span'; the curve of his tail completes the harmony of the composition. An obvious precursor of the bank vole Timmy Willie with ears of corn is Tommy Tittle-mouse who 'lived in a tiny little house'.

In spite of some delightful scenes of mice at table, it is the

344   The elegant dinner, *The Tale of Johnny Town-Mouse*, p. 24, 1918

345 (above) 'The Town Mouse and the Country Mouse'

346 (above right) 'The Country Mouse and the Town Mouse'

347 (right) 'Tommy Tittle-mouse': unfinished design for the 1905 Book of Rhymes

348 (above left) Timmy Willie at home,
The Tale of Johnny Town-Mouse, p. 32, 1918

349 (above) Timmy Willie and the hamper,
The Tale of Johnny Town-Mouse, p. 43, 1918

rural episodes which inspire the best designs (55, *173*). Occasionally Timmy hankers after the wide world beyond the garden gate. Other poignant pictures are reminders that different worlds cannot meet. The town mice lived in Hawkshead, in the house of a Mr Bolton, who received vegetables from Sawrey each week and sent back laundry. The arch was drawn from life, and so was the carrier's cart-horse (*163*): 'Old Dimond [sic] our farm horse is my favourite of the pictures.' The housemaid with the hamper was Mrs Rogerson of Sawrey, and Johnny was Dr Parsons with his long bag of golf clubs – he and Willie Heelis had a private course made at Sawrey.

The story is packed with pictures and told in just the right tone for a child's ear. There are subtler touches for adults: Johnny's courtesy to the gauche intruder, whom he places on his right, and his polite enquiry about Timmy's garden. 'It sounds rather a dull place? What do you do when it rains?' *Johnny Town-Mouse* is a warning about the danger and extravagance of town life. It is a satire on human society – but Beatrix was as interested in different varieties of mice as of men.

Cecily Parsley's Nursery Rhymes, the promised rhyme book, supplanted a planned fable book, and it was the last in the Peter Rabbit format. Seven of the eight rhymes were the 'hoary favourites' Beatrix had always wanted to publish. She worked on the drawings whenever time could be stolen from other distractions: a plague of visitors, poultry problems and a bad drought. Dedicated to the orphaned 'little Peter of New Zealand', the book was finished just in time for Christmas 1922, in spite of the last-minute delay to restore an omitted line about the carving knife in the 'Three Blind Mice' rhyme ('Three Blind Mice' had already been cut from the Warne *Peter Rabbit* (*see p. 101*)). This particular rhyme, also sung as a round, is probably better known than 'Bow, wow, wow! Whose dog art thou?'

Though a sequel to *Appley Dapply*, the rhymes and pictures have even earlier associations. The only completely original rhyme is 'The Guinea-Pigs' Garden', which dates back to 1893 when Beatrix borrowed several long-haired guinea pigs for models from Miss Paget, a friend and neighbour. The 'very particular guinea-pig with a long white ruff' – known as Queen Elizabeth, and descended from the Sultan of Zanzibar – 'took to eating blotting paper, pasteboard, string and other curious substances, and expired in the night'. Beatrix returned to its owner a damp and disagreeable body, followed promptly by the drawings. Guinea pigs nestle in their basket on a Christmas card (*161*), and feature in several versions of the 'Amiable Guinea-Pig' (*263*). Two of the pictures were redrawn with garden backgrounds for *Cecily Parsley*.

Also in her portfolio were three versions of the ancient riddle about a candle:

> Ninny Nanny Netticoat,
> In a white petticoat,
> With a red nose, –
> The longer she stands,
> The shorter she grows.

Beatrix's old nurse, 'that little old lady with white woollen stockings, black velvet slippers and a mob-cap', was apparently also called 'Nanny Netticoat', perhaps after the candle which presided over the table at Camfield, 'guttering, homely, lop-sided with fascinating snuffers in a tin dish'. The central candle (or Bunsen burner!), provides a focal point in the strangely behaved seven-inch candle of *Ginger and Pickles* and in 'A Dream of Toasted Cheese' (*310, 182*).

'This little pig went to market', shouts Pig Robinson's cousin as his milk float leaves Robinson standing in the road. Beatrix made no fewer than four pictures for the popular toe-rhyme. The adventurous pig is transported by Dolly, the Hill Top pony; the stay-at-home knitting pig and the pig cooking 'a bit

350 'We have a little garden', *Cecily Parsley's Nursery Rhymes*, p. 33, 1922

351 'Ninny Nanny Netticoat': preliminary painting for *Cecily Parsley's Nursery Rhymes*, p. 36, ?1897

of meat' are both 'Old Sallie', who used to open the garden gate and follow her mistress about. The cheerful pink pig peeling potatoes – who 'had none' – is at least the third so occupied in Beatrix's drawings. The little pig lost at the crossroads (who 'cried Wee! wee! wee! I can't find my way home') recalls Pigling Bland, just as an unused *Pigling Bland* picture (47) of Cross-patch in bed with measles (ministered to by Beatrix herself) recalls the 'Goosey, goosey, gander' illustration of geese peering into a pig-sty at 'my lady', the pig.

There are chestnuts at the fire and ale to drink in the frontispiece, which illustrates the title rhyme with Cecily Parsley's 'gentlemen' who 'came every day' (Peter and Benjamin grown up?). The original watercolour was drawn for Noel Moore and intended for the 1905 rhyme book; in *Cecily Parsley* the second gentleman's pipe becomes a newspaper. Two more homely interiors, with echoes of nursery tea, illustrate 'Pussy-cat sits by the fire', quoted also on the title-page of *The Pie and the Patty-Pan*. 'Pussy-cat' toasting muffins in a second-best lilac gown – without the embroidered apron – is surely Ribby preparing for another tea-party?

Apparently ignorant of the effects of cowslip wine, Warne insisted that Cecily's rosy apples must be changed to cowslips and the barrels of cider to cowslip wine. The deserted Pen Inn illustration, after Cecily Parsley 'ran away', shows rabbits in a state of nature among bluebells: 'I don't know why – but I have never been able to imagine the dressed up rabbits coming to the inn door; it comes to my mind's eye deserted!' The original cover picture, a rabbit carrying a tray, was converted into a line drawing for the title-page, being too like the *Appley Dapply* cover. It was replaced by a vignette of Cecily Parsley with a wheelbarrow piled with her belongings. Like Elsie Marley,

352 'This little pig cried Wee! wee! wee!', *Cecily Parsley's Nursery Rhymes*, p. 23, 1922

353 (above) 'Goosey, goosey, gander', *Cecily Parsley's Nursery Rhymes*, p. 14, 1922

354 (left) 'Gentlemen came every day', given to Noel Moore (and later redrawn for the frontispiece of *Cecily Parsley's Nursery Rhymes*), 1902

355 (above) 'Pussy-cat sits by the fire', *Cecily Parsley's Nursery Rhymes*, p. 24, 1922

356 (above right) Cecily Parsley brewing cider: banned illustration for *Cecily Parsley's Nursery Rhymes*, p. 10, c. 1905?

another notorious nursery rhyme figure, Cecily was no better than she should be – and had to run away. The 'Cecily Parsley' rhyme, like 'Ninny Nanny Netticoat', dates back to an 1897 booklet; it is included in an earlier fragment of code writing (70). Even in later years Beatrix occasionally lapsed into code, as in a passage about the collie Kep, by Beatrix Heelis – Miss Potter no longer. It was as Mrs Heelis that she produced one of her last major works, **The Fairy Caravan**.

Only the persuasiveness of a Philadelphia publisher, Alexander McKay, convinced Beatrix that she should publish again; Warne were put out, and wrote 'rather an unpleasant letter'. Always irritated by the fact that her favourite *Tailor of Gloucester* was the least successful '*because* it was less *comic*', she complained that her English publishers regarded her as an investment rather than a cultural property. Impressed by the New Englanders who had 'drifted over' to Hill Top, she felt that they understood an aspect of her writings not appreciated by the British shopkeeper – and no one else had complimented her on her prose. She wrote this to Bertha Mahony (later Miller), founder of the pioneering Bookshop for Boys and Girls in Boston and of the *Horn Book*, a magazine dedicated to children's literature – neither had an English counterpart.

She felt the *Fairy Caravan* stories were too personal to publish in England, and too local to the Lake District for the general public. Unsure of her own judgement and feeling she had written herself out, she did not relish the break with Warne but was grateful to Miss Mahony for her encouragement, and it seemed that she could still write.

To secure copyright one hundred unbound sets of the American edition (1929) were sent to Ambleside. The first eighteen pages were reset to give English title and copyright pages and then hand-bound with the American sheets. Beatrix had to redraw the five black-and-white illustrations, and added a sixth. Though an offer was made for the half-dozen original paintings in the book, she prudently kept them in case of an

English edition – it came only in 1952. A privately-bound copy for McKay's daughter Margery (Mrs Cridland) had 'explains' in the margins: pencilled notes about local terms and places. For American consumption only, she wrote in the preface: 'Through many changing seasons these tales have walked and talked with me. They were not meant for printing; I have left them in the homely idiom of our old north country speech. I send them on the insistence of friends beyond the sea.'

Early in the 1920s Beatrix had been planning a new book – a sheep book or a guinea pig book (her new pets were long-haired guinea pigs). *The Fairy Caravan* was both, and much more besides, a 'wandering, interminable adventure' reconstituted from unused fragments: rhymes, fairy tales, notes on farm animals and letters to children. 'The Tale of Tuppenny' the guinea pig, rewritten as Chapter 1, was one of the three Hastings stories (*see p. 118*). Like the lamb 'Tale of Daisy and Dumpling' (retitled for Chapter 9), it was originally intended for the Peter Rabbit series. Advertised on endpapers but never illustrated, 'The Tale of Tuppenny' was published in the *Horn Book* for February 1929 as 'Over the Hills and Far Away'. It tells of the depressed guinea pig with toothache and thin, patchy hair, obviously 'a suitable subject for experiment' (and subject too of the 'Picture story about a guinea pig'), who is overpersuaded by his friends and treated with Messrs Ratton and Scratch's elixir (359). Tuppenny's hair grew and grew, although Mrs T. cut it and cut it, and 'stuffed pin-cushions with it, and pillow cases and bolsters'. Tuppenny escapes and falls in with the 'Fairy Caravan' – Alexander and William's circus troupe who, made invisible to humans by fern seed, travel the countryside performing to other animals. A circus was the only kind of entertainment Beatrix cared for. In 1885 and again ten years later she visited Ginnet's Travelling Circus at Ambleside, and 'had a good laugh': 'I would go any distance to see a Caravan (barring lion-taming).' The guinea pig story was discovered by a visiting American boy, Henry P. Coolidge, soon a favoured correspondent. To him *The Fairy Caravan* was dedicated, and in his honour she named one guinea pig 'Henry P.'.

Tuppenny's travels with the Caravan and descriptions of its diverse characters weave a continuous thread which links nearly a dozen self-contained tales. After the guinea pig 'Tale of Tuppenny', sheep stories are clustered in Chapters 9 to 11 (*see pp. 163–4*). The last is a traditional spinning tale told by one of the ewes, namesake of the Habbitrot who spares 'Bonny Annot' the hardships of spinning. '"That story," said Pony Billy, "has no moral".' Chapter 17, ostensibly a tale of Mistress Heelis's runaway clog, dancing shoes and horseshoes, is really a celebration of the horse. 'The Veterinary Retriever' (Chapter 21) includes a fable (*see p. 66*), as does Chapter 9. Meanwhile, Paddy Pig has a terrifying experience in Pringle Wood and is rescued by Pony Billy with his shoes reversed. The Caravan

357, 358, 359 The ailing Tuppenny (above centre), descendant of the picture story guinea pig with toothache (top), as he appeared on p. 14 of the American edition of *The Fairy Caravan*. For the privately bound English edition, the first sixteen pages were reset and Beatrix Potter drew five 'duplicate' pictures, including this one (above) for p. 14, 1929

360 Mary Ellen by the fire, *The Fairy Caravan*,
p. 142, 1929

361 Sketches of Scotch Fly, *c.* 1929

puts on a performance at Codlin Croft Farm; the cats gossip
and attempt to cure Paddy Pig. By the end he is well again,
and the Caravan moves up to Cuckoo Brow Lane. Xarifa is
rewarded with a mouse party, and the final chapter (23) is her
tale of 'The Fairy in the Oak' (*see p.* 64).

Numbered and inscribed copies of the English edition were
given to relations and friends, farmhands and shepherds – one
'to John Mackereth in remembrance of Hill Top and the
Sheep' and one to Tom Storey (*see p.* 191). 'It is very comical
how seriously the village has taken it': the children kept
looking up references to favourite animals, and it was 'received
with acclamation by the men – only they are all claiming bits
and disputing whose who [sic]'. It evoked the same competitive
spirit in Sawrey as *Ginger and Pickles* twenty years earlier. Her
most exacting critics were the blacksmith and her own
shepherds: she did not care tuppence about anybody else's
opinion. 'I am sure the average Londoner would care nothing
about Herdwick sheep! That chapter made my old shepherd
cry with pleasure; that is appreciation worth having.'

Although local children loved it, and the separate stories
read aloud well, there is no *Fairy Caravan* tradition in England.
Even in America it was in less demand than her shorter stories
– 'mostly illustration' – but Beatrix decided that like *The Tailor*
it was not everybody's book. She compared it to the curate's
egg, excellent in parts but too rambling and indigestible. The
smudgy colour displeased her, but she liked the small pen-and-
inks which at last she was allowed to put at top and bottom of
the pages, where they looked better. Similar dark little tail-
pieces decorate the American *Pig Robinson*.

The setting gave her an excuse to write once more about
local animals (164): her pet guinea pig, the dog next door
(Sandy), Pony Dolly who loved water (Pony Billy crossing the
ford). In a favourite drawing her own cat Tomasine stares at
the fire; a seventeenth family arrived next day. In the book she
is Mary Ellen, a 'fat, tabby cat with . . . an unnecessarily purry
manner' whose ministrations increase the sufferings of Paddy
Pig. Paddy Pig was a portrait not of any special pig but of young
pigs in general. One of Henny Penny's 'large white shiny eggs'
had hatched into 'that remarkable bird Charles', a Silver
Campine with 'handsome white neck hackles, finely barred
and spotted breast, and a magnificent tail'. The turkey spars
with Charles – who died still fighting, soon after *The Fairy
Caravan* was published. Beatrix also celebrates the collies:
Roy, Bobs and Matt lying lazily in the sun at Troutbeck Park
Farm ('This picture is considered the best in the book'), and the
dogs at the forge (424), nostalgically recalling the good old days
before asphalt and lorries. Among them are Nip and her pup
Scotch Fly, 'extremely good, . . . only very nervous', recorded
in a sheet of sketches. A fly-leaf of dog drawings was added for
the Ambleside edition, to replace the discarded preface.

Herdwick sheep are always woven into the background,

hardy threads of a hardy breed. 'They are beggars to ramble, these hill sheep' but, 'heft' to their native 'heaf', they always return. We first meet the ewes – Cribby Woolstockit, Habbi-trot and Hill Top Queenie – by the beck at Eller-Tree Camp. They tell the fable of a fox in sheep's clothing (*129*), and stories of crag-fast sheep. The Walla Crag view Beatrix had drawn 'all *wrong*! because on a ledge like that one – the sheep could turn.' (*421*) At the head of Troutbeck stands a ram much like her favourite 'Saddleback Wedgwood' who died in 1929, 'the perfect type of hard, big boned, Herdwick tup, with strong clean legs, springy fetlocks, broad scope, fine horns, a grand jacket and mane. He had strength without coarseness. A noble animal.' Beatrix honours the proud, ancient Herdwick lineage in a stirring passage which begins 'Cool is the air above the craggy summit . . .'

Nearly all the places in the book are real, but some she did not identify: the Caravan creeping through the early morning April meadows, or the final tailpiece of the caravan at rest, 'over the hills and far away'. Mice escape from Louisa Pussy-cat's mouse seminary, alias Thimble Hall in Hawkshead, 'a little steep, three-storied house with diamond panes in the windows'. The frontispiece, 'Louisa Pussy-cat Sleeps Late', shows mice calling her 'punctually at 8.30 – I should say 7.30 – I sit up late, you know, trimming bonnets.' Redrawn and coloured in 1929, it originally illustrated Beatrix's version of the Elsie Marley rhyme: 'Tabitha Twitchit is grown so fine, She lies in bed until half past nine!' The bed with green curtains came from Camfield; Beatrix used to sit up in it listening to the nightingales.

The Caravan roamed round Sawrey, which is drawn with hens in the snow and Coniston Old Man behind (*430*). Pony Billy trudges with Sandy down a lane banked up with snow drifts. In Troutbeck he trots over Ing Bridge (*427*) and earlier (in Chapter 4), unprotected by fern seed, he is seen, caught and impounded in the Pinfold (*410*). The setting for the vixen curled up asleep above her playing cubs was copied from an etching by Bertram, possibly done at Newlands but very like Broad How in Troutbeck (*365, 78*). The farmhouse, snugly set at the foot of Troutbeck Tongue, acquires some beehives and a parrot (*419*). Beatrix loved Troutbeck most of all. 'Many a hunt I have seen there' – but John Peel was at another

362 (above left) Herdwick ram at the head of Troutbeck, *The Fairy Caravan*, p. 82, 1929

363 (above) 'Louisa Pussy-cat Sleeps Late', *The Fairy Caravan*, frontispiece, 1929

364 Pony Billy and Sandy go down to Eesbridge, *The Fairy Caravan*, p. 33, 1929

365 (above) 'The vixen was curled up asleep' above Woundale in Troutbeck, *The Fairy Caravan*, p. 79, 1929

366 (above right) 'Many a hunt I have seen there': hounds by Tongue Ghyll near Troutbeck Tongue, *The Fairy Caravan*, p. 136, 1929

Troutbeck. It was here that she first saw the ponies 'dance the heys in the lonely wilderness behind the table land of Troutbeck Tongue', cantering round a stunted thorn. 'Round and round, then checked and turned; round and round reversed; arched necks, tossing manes, tails streaming . . . Who had taught them? . . . These half wild youngsters had never been handled by man.' The shepherds thought the Tongue was haunted.

The 'haunted' picture of Pony Billy trotting over the shadows (122) was her other favourite. The fairy pictures however are less successful than the locally inspired ones – even the Mouse dancing with the Fair Maids of France, 'little prim white flowers with white double ruffs and green stockings', evidence of Beatrix's enthusiasm for country dancing. Individual tales inspire a diversity of illustrations: the pony wading through a sea of bluebells in Pringle Wood, or springing forward in panic through the serried ranks of tree trunks as three roe-deer suddenly canter by; Paddy Pig, terrified and huddled inside a fungus-bracketed tree, his fore-trotters pressed against his tummy (188). Beatrix's spring episodes for the 'Little Mouse' tale (Chapter 6) are delightful: the nest of dormice at Birds' Place, Camfield, and the great cedar, glory of the garden she adored (10).

'Demerara Sugar' (Chapter 14) tells of the chickens' Christmas Eve adventure, ruined by John Stoat Ferret. The hens are ingloriously rescued by two boy carollers, but not before they have witnessed a magical scene: the animals treading a circle in the snow round 'a very small spruce, a little Christmas tree some four foot high', its branches 'wreathed with icicles and chains of frost' and shining with a clear white incandescent light. Beatrix drew this dance for a Christmas card (455), describing it again in a letter sent to a child subscriber to the ICAA from 'Peter Rabbit'.

The Fairy Caravan 'took well' in America, which pleased Beatrix – better than the plainer *Pig Robinson* (published the following year), which sold better in England.

The Tale of Little Pig Robinson was published in 1930, and was the last of the Peter Rabbit books to appear, but the story itself was one of the earliest to be written by Beatrix Potter and the idea for it went back to 1883, when she was staying at Ilfracombe. It is quite a long and adventurous story. Originally much shorter, it was even divided into chapters, which was an unusual feature in her books. There are a few framed water-colour illustrations, but the majority of the illustrations are in black-and-white. Beatrix had in fact planned quite a lot of black-and-white illustrations for the story, which was offered both to Warne and to her American publisher, Alexander McKay. In July 1930 Beatrix wrote to McKay to say that Warne planned to leave out quite a number of the illustrations she had prepared for the book, and she wondered if McKay would include them in the American edition – he agreed – so there is quite a discrepancy between the English and American editions.

The Tale of Little Pig Robinson differs in many ways from the other books, both in its length and its character. In the first instance the story is set within a story, since the implication is that perhaps the tale was really the dream of Susan the cat, who had been so mystified to see a pig on board the *Pound of Candles* that she even dreamed about it. The story therefore begins with Chapter II when Little Pig Robinson is sent shopping by his aunts Dorcas and Porcas. His long walk to the town is described in detail and accompanied by a series of black-and-white sketches. After the confusion of the town and the shopping, Robinson is more or less kidnapped, and enticed on board the *Pound of Candles*, which then sets sail. Robinson discovers that he is meant to end up as the Captain's birthday dinner, which terrifies him. He is saved by the ingenuity of the ship's cat, who helps him to escape 'To the land where the Bong Tree grows'. And there in the wood, with a ring at the end of his nose, he is subsequently visited by the Owl and the Pussy Cat and 'for anything I know he may be living there still upon the island. He grew fatter and fatter and more fatterer; and the ship's cook never found him.'

Like most of Beatrix Potter's tales, *Little Pig Robinson* is firmly set in a definite location – or locations. Beatrix Potter's family used to go for spring or autumn holidays to various coastal towns in the south of England, and her memories of several of them are included in the backgrounds for this book. Most of the towns are in Devon – Sidmouth and Teignmouth for example. We can read about her stay in these places in the journal. The steep street scene is taken from Lyme Regis, in the neighbouring county of Dorset, while the old fishermen's huts are still to be seen, just as she drew them, on the shore at Hastings in Sussex. But it was not only memories of places that Beatrix incorporated into this book. There are also echoes of Edward Lear's poem 'The Owl and the Pussy Cat', and the land where the Bong Tree grew (see p. 70).

This book is a real story, not just a slight tale, and the meshing together of the various strands which compose the whole shows Beatrix Potter's skill as a sustained storyteller. The pictures may lack something of the charm of the earliest of the Peter Rabbit books, but we are certainly left wondering

367 Little Pig Robinson on his way to shop in 'Stymouth' (Sidmouth, Devon), *The Tale of Little Pig Robinson*, p. 36, 1930

368 Sketch for Robinson and the sailor on the quay, with the 'Pound of Candles' in the background, *The Tale of Little Pig Robinson*, p. 86, 1930

whether we did not lose a very competent storyteller to the fells and sheep-walks of the Lake District when Beatrix Potter put up her pen for good – at least as far as the tales were concerned.

The six short kernel-stories of *The Fairy Caravan* are set in a frame-story, a traditional device for linking a collection of tales. A good many others existed – 'some wanderings further of the *Caravan*' – and Beatrix planned a sequel for the summer of 1931. She tried to construct a framework to hold some rather long surplus tales, regretting that she had used up all the prettiest and easiest in one volume. She thought of making it a spring story, called 'Cherry Tree Camp', but only parts of it were ever published. Several 'rather pretty' ideas never hatched out – mainly narrations by the characters rather than their own adventures: the mouse's tale of Hill Top farmhouse, and 'A Walk amongst the Funguses' (*see p. 91*). 'The Solitary Mouse' is set at High Buildings, the lonely barn above Troutbeck Park used by Mrs Heelis and her shepherds. Here the Caravan too sheltered in a wild rainstorm, and Xarifa met the melancholy mouse Joseph. Beatrix thought the story too silly to print, and that it might offend the original of Joseph, her shepherd Joe Moscrop.

Nearly all Beatrix's last works were *Fairy Caravan* offshoots: two were published only in the United States (**Sister Anne** and **Wag-by-Wall**), and none has her illustrations. Two were adaptations of Perrault tales – her retelling of the 'Little Red Riding Hood' story was intended to be part of *The Fairy Caravan*; her grisly version of 'Bluebeard', told by the Second Cousin Mouse, was overlong. The mice were supposed to provide comic relief at a critical stage of the plot, where the First and Third Cousin Mice 'with nerves and fur on end' fall upon the narrator and bite him. Beatrix meant to publish it separately, without the mouse narrators, as *Sister Anne* – 'only if the mice are "eliminated" the tale becomes deadly serious . . . It certainly is not food for babes!' *Sister Anne* (1932) – the mouse narrators almost expunged – was offered to McKay, who was responsible for her last five books, and whom she had promised another book after *Pig Robinson*. Beatrix approved of Katharine Sturges's illustrations and thought their 'bizarre distortions' rather suited her story. She liked their sense of 'giddy heights' conveyed, though 'she cannot draw dogs – but no more can I. I should have sent a photograph of a wolf hound; they have *not* flap ears.' Surprisingly, Beatrix disagreed with the unfavourable opinion of Anne Carroll Moore – for this is an artificial tale, full of tushery and 'nameless horror', and far removed from her usual style.

Wag-by-Wall originates in an unfinished story of 'The Little Black Kettle' (1909). Its heroine was old Sally Scales of Stott Farm near Graythwaite, where Beatrix bought pigs for Hill Top. By 1929, when it was rewritten as part of *The Fairy*

369 'Anne, laughing and looking down fearlessly, threw bits of mortar at the birds', drawn by Katharine Sturges, *Sister Anne*, p. 57, 1932

370 'She had eight of a family', *The Tale of Pigling Bland*, p. 9, 1913

Caravan, the story was called 'Wag-by-the-Wall' – after the clock rather than the kettle. In 1940 Bertha Mahony Miller suggested making it into a Christmas story. Beatrix rewrote it, pruning out the *Fairy Caravan* characters and the longer verses. Publication was held back for the Twentieth Anniversary Number of the *Horn Book Magazine* (1944) and it was published in book form soon after, illustrated by J. J. Lankes. Beatrix never saw the final version. It is a human story, full of pathos, in which animals play only an indirect part but bring about the discovery of a stocking full of gold in the chimney. Beatrix writes: 'I thought of it years ago as a pendant to *The Tailor of Gloucester* – the old lonely man and the lonely old woman, but I could never finish it.'

The Faithful Dove too she compares with *The Tailor*, being 'older and sentimental', and featuring a courtly mouse. It was her last work, printed posthumously in 1955 (1956 in America, with illustrations by an unknown artist). Marie Angel's exquisite watercolours enhance the later English edition, published by Warne in 1970. 'Founded on fact', the plot came from Folkestone or Dover and the backgrounds from Winchelsea and Rye (*see p. 62*). It tells of a pigeon who, escaping from a predatory peregrine, falls into a chimney and is kept company by dancing mice dressed in smuggled lace. At the end she is saved – with her newly-hatched son – by the devotion of her husband, Mr Tidler. Beatrix wrote the story in Hastings in 1907 for the Warne children; it was one of two manuscripts sent to Harold Warne in late 1908. No more was heard till December 1918, when Fruing Warne discovered it, and pressed for the pigeon story rather than her preferred 'Tale of Jenny Crow' (*see p. 65*). Beatrix jibbed at the 'rather namby pamby' pigeons, since they left little scope for pictorial variety – 'it is *too much pigeon*, over & over' – and she had never been good at birds. She even suggested approaching the eminent Thorburn for pictures of doves. Hoping to deter Warne, she warned them that the story was sentimental and not comic. Like Uncle Remus, and especially in her later years, she occasionally felt the need to make the point.

These last crumbs from the store-cupboard are only sporadically typical of Beatrix Potter's best work, often imitated but still inimitable. They are the exceptions which prove the rule. Her stories began as picture letters for real children; they ended as tributes to real animals. In the years between she painted and wrote to please herself. 'The more spontaneous the pleasure – the more happy the result. I cannot work to order; and when I had nothing to say I had the sense to stop.'

A.S.H.   J.I.W.   J.T.

371   The pigeons with their nest on the Ypres Tower, *The Faithful Dove*, drawn by Marie Angel, title-page and p. 9, 1970

7
CREATIVE YEARS AND THE LAKE DISTRICT

Long before Beatrix Potter started to write her books, and before she bought Hill Top Farm, she loved the Lake District, but the idea that she would one day live there as a landowner and respected sheep farmer seemed unlikely.

It might so easily have been Perthshire that captured Beatrix's heart. The summers of her formative years were spent at Dalguise House near Dunkeld and it was not until 1882 when she was 16 that the Potters first stayed in the Lake District. The house chosen by her father, Wray Castle on Windermere, at what was known locally as 't'back o'lake', might have marred her first impression of the countryside. Built by Dr Dawson from Liverpool with his wife's money, which came from the manufacture of gin, the house was craggy gothic in style. Mrs Dawson had taken one look at the place and then gone back to Liverpool. The battlements were coldly forbidding and the mock ruins spoilt the view of the lake.

None of these drawbacks affected Beatrix. She took an immediate liking to the small scale of the countryside, the changing light on the fells and the way the whitewashed farms were so naturally a part of the landscape. 'The most pleasant countryside in all the world.'

372 *Hill Top by Night*

373 *Wray Castle with Beatrix and Bertram*, R. Potter, 1882

374 *Rev. H. D. Rawnsley* (1854–1919), F. Yates, 1915

375 *Portrait of Millais standing with gun* (at Dalguise), R. Potter, September 1880

In 1882 Wray Castle belonged to Mr Rawnsley. Three years earlier he had exercised his right of advowson and offered his newly-ordained cousin, Hardwicke Rawnsley, the living of Wray, a tiny village with a handful of parishioners. The church was by the entrance to Wray Castle grounds, the vicarage just up the road, and the vicar a cheerful, outgoing type of man. He was reputed to lecture his parishioners on diet and hygiene, to have literary leanings and be able to write verse at the drop of a hat. Rupert Potter, who at that time had the idea of collecting signed letters of the Lake Poets, invited Hardwicke Rawnsley up to the Castle to discuss literary matters. He soon became a regular and welcome visitor.

The charm of this genial and handsome man, whose portrait by Frederick Yates catches the twinkle in his eyes, even melted Beatrix's habitual reserve. For one thing Hardwicke admired her paintings as having real artistic merit, not because painting was a suitable occupation for a young lady. The two of them were able to discuss some of the painters of whom Beatrix approved as Hardwicke also had links with the world of art. His wife Edith had just shown one of her watercolours at the Royal Academy and during his Oxford days many of his friends had been artists. Ruskin, whom Hardwicke admired but about whom Beatrix had her reservations, was one of them, as was her father's friend, Sir John Millais. In one entry in Beatrix's journal Sir John is described as a great painter whose work was 'careful and minute'. She also liked Walter Crane's work and admired Holman Hunt. Both artists were known to Hardwicke and later supported him in the establishing of the Keswick School of Industrial Art. Hardwicke also encouraged her archaeological interests, which he shared, and approved of her animals. This was the start of a lifelong friendship.

In return Hardwicke was not reticent about his own interests. The Rawnsleys were a Norfolk family but Hardwicke had loved the Lake District from his first visit, a walking tour with his headmaster, Edward Thring of Uppingham. He had married Edith Fletcher from The Croft, Ambleside and been delighted by his cousin's offer of Wray parish, which gave him the opportunity to live in such a beautiful part of the country. He considered this beauty extremely vulnerable and was prepared to defend it against all those who sought to exploit it in any way. He explained his fears to the Potters, intent on making them understand the priceless charm of the Lake District. He so impressed them that when the National Trust was formed Rupert Potter became one of the first life members.

As early as 1844, Wordsworth had protested that the growth of the railways would bring destruction in their wake. The early Victorians had considered this mere sentimental interference with the current spirit of improvement and railways had been allowed to spread. By 1876, however, the opening of the Oxenholme–Windermere railway line had resulted in a crop of boarding houses in Windermere, examples of prickly

376 *Our English Coasts* (Strayed
Sheep), W. Holman Hunt

Swiss gothic architecture, growing up round the station; a
whole new village. The trains also brought hundreds of day
trippers, able for the first time to travel cheaply and in comfort,
who got under the residents' feet, while the wealthy industrial-
ists from Lancashire, now able to commute to work, were
buying up lakeshore land to build handsome summer villas and
the east shore of Windermere was becoming privately owned.
The 'Defend the Lake District' party began to recruit indignant
local residents.

This first organized opposition to the 'spirit of improvement'
was led by Robert Somerville, a Kendal industrialist who lived
in Windermere and was against a proposal to extend the
Windermere line as far as Ambleside, and perhaps Keswick.
He was supported by a powerful blast from John Ruskin, now
painting and writing at Brantwood in Coniston, in a preface to

377 *Ice Clouds over Coniston Old Man*, John Ruskin

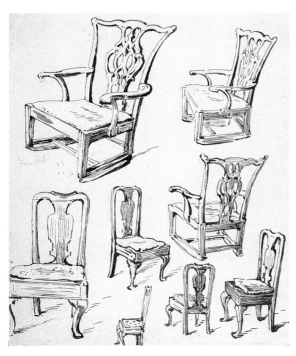

378 *Furniture at Fawe Park*, 1903

a pamphlet called 'A protest against the extension of railways in the Lake District'.

Ruskin had first been attracted to the Lake District on a family visit at the age of 5, when he had been taken to Friar's Crag on Derwentwater by his nurse. As an artist he filled his sketchbooks with studies from nature, which was his first love. On his move to Coniston in 1871 he had agreed to be a figure-head in the fight to prevent the exploitation of the Lake District, occasionally writing or speaking against the destruction of natural beauty. To the delight of the opposition, the railway-extension scheme was laid aside, though partly because the estimated building costs were extremely high.

Hardwicke Rawnsley, an advocate of Ruskin's teachings since he had listened to his Oxford lectures, was involved with this group. He told the Potters about the 'Defence Association' which was being organized to oppose Manchester Corporation's intention to turn Thirlmere into a reservoir, and he confided his own fears on the harmful effect this sort of development would have on the traditional life of the Lake District dales.

The next few summers saw the Potters staying on the shores of Derwentwater, either at Fawe Park or Lingholm. The family friendship with the Rawnsleys was easily maintained as Hardwicke had been inducted to the living of Crosthwaite near Keswick in 1883. Beatrix enjoyed Borrowdale, the lake and the views, and she had a particular fondness for Lingholm, which she sketched several times. She was delighted, therefore, when the result of the battle with 'the Steam Dragon of Honister' was also a win for the conservationists.

This fight was against a syndicate of quarry owners who had brought a bill before Parliament to enable them to run a railway, nicknamed by Hardwicke 'the Steam Dragon', down the side of Derwentwater past Lingholm, bringing slate from Honister to meet the Cockermouth, Keswick and Penrith Railway at Braithwaite. The intention was to take advantage of the textile boom in Lancashire and the need for slate for workers' houses. Opposition to the project had been well organized. With his usual energy Hardwicke had set himself to write to Members of Parliament, American Senators and people of influence in the academic and ecclesiastical world and to speak to meetings all over the country. He also asked the Commons Preservation Society, formed to defend common land in and around London from enclosure, for advice. J. B. Baddeley, the guidebook writer, had pointed out that Keswick's hoteliers' stage-coach traffic would be threatened if the railway line took passengers. *Punch*, and even the *Westmorland Gazette*, in spite of jeopardizing possible increased advertising revenue, took up the cause in the interests of preventing the destruction of an area of acknowledged beauty. The promoters of the Railway Bill had not liked the look of the lines formed against them and withdrew it.

379 (above) *Stairway at Lingholm, c.*1908

380 (above right) *Rain: Lingholm,* 1898

A Permanent Lake District Defence Society had also been formed and the committee members included Alfred, Lord Tennyson, Robert Browning, John Ruskin and the Duke of Westminster. In Hardwicke's opinion it came just in time. He was beginning to question the defensive attitude and was considering ways of ensuring long-term preservation of beautiful countryside. 'There will', he said, 'in the near future be more invasions and desecrations of Lakeland to be withstood.'

Though Hardwicke may not have realized it, the coming of the railways was changing more than the countryside; it was changing the viewpoint of Lake District landscape artists. The early landscapes had been mere backgrounds for paintings of expanding towns or impressive new buildings, commissioned by those responsible for their building. Then by the mid-eighteenth century the first landscapes for the mass market were drawn, painted and reproduced, though it was not until the early nineteenth century that the Lake District could be said to be really 'discovered'. Artists of note made 'artistic tours' through the Lakes, each with his own interpretation of the dramatic landscape.

John Constable stayed in the Lake District for two months in 1806 at Brathay Hall, the home of the amateur artists John

381 *Sty Head Tarn,
Borrowdale*, John Constable,
noon, 12 October 1806

382 *Ullswater Lake from
Gowbarrow Park,*
J. M. W. Turner, *c.* 1818

Harden and his wife Jessy. Beatrix was particularly interested in Constable's work, once copying his sketch of Sty Head Tarn, and she had boundless admiration for Turner, who visited the Lake District twice.

This enthusiasm for artistic tours was deflated by the publication of a satire by Thomas Rowlandson called *The Tour of Dr. Syntax* (1809). The parody of the bizarre enthusiasm displayed in the search for the picturesque, particularly as outlined by William Gilpin in his *Picturesque Tours*, indicated that the popularity of this pursuit was over. In fact the coming of the railways made change inevitable. The existing romantic style did not give a realistic picture of what the new tourists were discovering with their own eyes. One of the first landscape painters to cash in on this demand for something more realistic was William Longmire, who was reputed to work on

383 *Dr Syntax Sketching the Lake*, Thomas Rowlandson, 1812

up to twenty pictures at once, painting one colour at a time. His pictures were sold in the new souvenir shops – another development to worry those opposed to 'improvement'.

By 1893 Hardwicke had decided that the only way to withstand the 'invasions and desecrations of Lakeland' was to form a Holding Company to preserve beautiful countryside for the nation, not just for the Lake District but for the whole of England, Wales and Northern Ireland. In conjunction with Octavia Hill and Robert Hunter of the Commons Preservation Society, and with the support of the Duke of Westminster, who agreed to be President and to lend Grosvenor House for meetings, The National Trust for Places of Historic Interest and Natural Beauty came into being in January 1895. It was registered as a Limited Company under the Companies' Act, a statutory body or corporation – the first vested with such power – 'to promote the permanent preservation for the benefit of the Nation of lands and tenements (including buildings) of beauty or historic interest'. Hardwicke Rawnsley was made Honorary Secretary.

The Press reaction was encouraging, reflecting the general opinion that the time was ripe for such a movement. *Punch* called it 'The Grand National Trust' as though it were a new steeplechase, and warmly commended 'so patriotic a scheme'.

At first the Trust was a small, struggling organization and was almost submerged by the immediate flood of applications for help that descended on the new Company. These were from groups and individuals trying to save a local beauty spot or building. Almost before the ink was dry on the Articles of Association, Hardwicke Rawnsley was writing to the Inverness County Council calling on them to save the Falls of Foyers from the disastrous intention of the British Aluminium Co. to withdraw water above the Falls. This was the first of an avalanche of letters from his pen.

The first report was brought out in April 1895 and the new members learnt that their Council included the names of Lord Tennyson and G. F. Watts. Also that there had been several offers of properties, some very unsuitable, and that the Trust

had been asked to intervene in many disputes between owners of properties and protest groups trying to preserve them. By 1899 several properties had been acquired and the Trust was becoming established, beginning to provide, as Hardwicke Rawnsley described it, 'open green spaces in which working people were able to breathe'.

The Potters finally abandoned Scotland and always took their holidays in the Lake District, generally staying at Lingholm on Derwentwater or Eeswyke (then called Lakefield) in Near Sawrey. During the holidays Beatrix drove or walked round the countryside, collecting flowers and sketching. She explored the little market town of Hawkshead, once a centre of the wool trade and now exploiting its association with Wordsworth. She drove past the patches of oats grown for oatmeal to

384 (above left) *Lakefield, a walled garden*, mountains in background, 1900

385 (above) *Lakefield, at Evening Close, c.*1896

386 *Harvest scene, Esthwaite Water*

make 'clap bread', still the staple in rural areas. Corn and oats were cut with a scythe and stooked in the fields and bracken for bedding and peat for fuel were brought down the fells on sledges. Herdwicks were the commonest breed of sheep. Farm lads were paid £16 a year and their keep. Tom Storey, who was later to be Beatrix Potter's shepherd, described his own time as a farm lad as: 'A blooming hard life but we were a lot happier in them days than they are today.'

Though she was still an outsider, almost a spectator, it was a world in which Beatrix felt more at home than she did in London. It satisfied her sense of realism and practicality, she was able to see how things worked. The many sketches she made of the Borrowdale valley and the countryside around Sawrey and Hawkshead were the expression of her need to try to capture in paint or pencil the heart and the spirit of what Wordsworth called 'This Natural Commonwealth', with which she felt such an affinity.

388, 389 *Hill Top kitchen*, photographed before alteration (top) by Beatrix Potter, c. 1908 and after alteration (above) by R. Potter

Even during the years when Beatrix was absorbed in the work on her early books and enjoying the growing friendship with Norman Warne, she never lost interest in the Lake District. In 1903, when her increasing royalties allowed it, she bought a field in Near Sawrey. In 1905 a working farm called Hill Top, where Beckett, the Potters' coachman, his wife and two boys had always stayed when the Potters were in Near Sawrey, came up for sale and a further accumulation of royalties, with the addition of a small legacy from an aunt, made it possible for Beatrix to buy it.

Hill Top, a traditional eighteenth-century farm, was bought with the minimum of fuss. It represented an investment of earnings, a sensible move which had the approval of both Beatrix Potter's parents. It had been decided that the tenant farmer at Hill Top, John Cannon, should stay on, but that an extension should be built for him and his wife so that Beatrix could keep the old seventeenth-century house for her own use whenever she was able to visit it. Quite soon after Norman Warne's funeral in August she went up to the Lake District to supervise the alterations. The work of planning the extension, re-roofing the dairy, getting rid of the rats and decorating the

390 (above) 'They . . . hid the key under the door-sill', *The Tale of Mrs. Tiggy-Winkle*, p. 48, 1905

391 (above centre) 'Mrs. Tittlemouse . . . slept in a little box bed', *The Tale of Mrs. Tittlemouse*, p. 12, 1910

392 (above right) ' "I am affronted", said Mrs. Tabitha Twitchit', *The Tale of Tom Kitten*, p. 48, 1907

393 'She . . . polished her little tin spoons', *The Tale of Mrs. Tittlemouse*, p. 55, 1910

house was something different with which to occupy her mind in a dark winter.

The next eight years were ones of considerable achievement. Beatrix wrote and illustrated thirteen successful books whilst remaining the dutiful daughter of the house. For a large part of the year she was either in London or paying a round of visits with a mother yearly more querulous and a father whose health was steadily failing. Even when her parents were safely established in a house within reach of Sawrey for the long summer holiday, Beatrix could only get to Hill Top for a day or two each week, and though she usually managed to catch the Coniston coach to get there, she often had a long walk back.

However short the visits, it was at Hill Top that Beatrix found her real world. When there she was always sketching the house, garden, countryside and animals for illustrations for new books. She copied the way of life she gave her animals from what she saw around her. Mrs Tiggy-winkle, that admirable laundress, made up her kitchen fire with turf and hid the key under the doorsill, as did nearly every housewife in the Newlands valley. Mrs Tittlemouse slept in a little box bed, traditional in the old cottages. When in trying situations the animals behaved like the people of Sawrey. Mrs Twitchit, when she found her kitten with no clothes on, was 'affronted'. Mrs Tittlemouse relieved her feeling with a prolonged spring-cleaning when she had got rid of her unwanted visitors, the bees. The books and the life and landscape of the Lake District merged together.

Beatrix was part of a trend towards realism – what she called 'copying what she saw'. She painted the countryside exactly as she saw it. One painter of this school was Alfred Heaton Cooper, a Lancashire artist who moved to Hawkshead in 1900 and whose work explored the effects of light on landscape. He began a trend for painting country people in their natural surroundings.

The number of other artists working in the Lake District during those early years of the twentieth century was increasing all the time. Local painters were being reinforced by those who came to settle in the area. W. G. Collingwood was one of

394, 395, 396, 397 *Hillside with stormy sky*, 1913
(above), *Scene in village with snow*, 1909 (right),
Footprints in snow, Near Sawrey, 1909 (below),
Hillside under snow with sheep, 1909 (below right)

179

398 *Brantwood from the Lake,*
W. G. Collingwood, *c.* 1890

them. He came to Coniston to act as secretary to John Ruskin
and was another friend of Canon Rawnsley's from his Oxford
days – Hardwicke had been made an Honorary Canon of Carlisle in 1901. W.G.'s father, William Collingwood RWS,
had introduced his son to the Lake District, where he had a
particular interest in drawing the rich diversity of cottage
interiors.

Once living in the Lake District, W.G. found his vocation
as a painter, showing his views of Coniston at the Royal
Academy. He was a founder member of the Lake Artists'
Society in 1904, a society with the aims of bringing together
the many talented artists in the area and helping to maintain
high standards of quality and style. As well as being an artist,
W.G. was also a writer and historian and a founder member of
the Cumberland and Westmorland Antiquarian and Archaeological Society. He contributed several papers to the society's
transactions on his archaeological discoveries in the Lake
District, in which Beatrix took great interest.

Another founder member of the Lake Artists' Society was
J. H. Crossland, who also exhibited at the Royal Academy.
Like John Ruskin, who was fascinated by the cloud formations
over the Coniston Fells as well as by the vernacular architecture of the area, both Crossland and Collingwood would have
said they drew straight from nature. Each had his own interpretation of the landscape, but they shared an interest in streaming clouds, changing colours, sudden vistas and the winter side
of the fells.

Ruskin's ideals and style had exerted much influence on
Lake District artists; after Ruskin's death in 1900, Canon
Rawnsley organized a fund which resulted in a single block of
Borrowdale stone with a medallion portrait of Ruskin being
erected on Friar's Crag, Derwentwater.

399 *View overlooking Derwentwater,* 1903

Ruskin's memorial was also the first property owned by the Trust in the Lake District, but in 1902 the Honorary Secretary was writing with some excitement in the yearly report. The owner of Brandelhow Park Estate had consented to sell it to the Trust rather than for building development if the money could be raised within six months. 'At present the Derwentwater shores are entirely in the hands of private owners,' he told members, 'and the existence of an estate, on which visitors can land without trespass and where they may wander at will, would be a fine thing for the nation.' The price was £7,000, almost £70 an acre, at a time when land was being sold for as little as £20 an acre, but to save an area of such beauty for the enjoyment of those hitherto deprived no effort was too great. Local committees were formed in Manchester, Liverpool, Leeds, Birmingham and Keswick, and many individuals, including Beatrix, were asked to contribute. The money was subscribed within five months.

In 1906, the year after Beatrix had bought Hill Top, another successful appeal allowed the National Trust to buy Gowbarrow Park. Once a Norman deer park, this lovely area of woodland and fell on the shore of Ullswater had been threatened with building development. Many persuasive scrawls asking for subscriptions were sent out by Canon Rawnsley, including one to Beatrix again. When the Hon. J. W. Lowther, Speaker of the House, declared Gowbarrow open to the public in August 1906 he congratulated the 'sixteen hundred persons who had fallen victims to the solicitations of Canon Rawnsley and Miss Octavia Hill and who had so generously planked down the money'. Quoting a Greek text he went on to say, 'We have all heard of the mountain in labour that brought forth a mouse, this time the mice have been in labour and brought forth a mountain.'

By the close of 1906 the Trust was the owner of twenty-four properties in various parts of England, amounting to 1,700 acres. The Council felt it time to dispense with the title of 'Limited Company' and obtain greater powers, not only to preserve order in the management of their properties, but also to protect them. Under the skilled guidance of Robert Hunter a National Trust Act was passed by Parliament in 1907 giving it powers of management, including the authority to make by-laws for the preservation of order and declaring all present and future properties owned by the Trust to be inalienable. Canon Rawnsley viewed the Act with great satisfaction, seeing it as a bridge between the early experiments and the 'wide sphere of usefulness' the Trust could now encompass. The early work, he said, had 'served to partly lift the veil from the future and disclose the enormous mass of work within the scope of the National Trust'.

A letter written in 1913 by Canon Rawnsley, asking Beatrix for a subscription to the appeal for the purchase of Queen Adelaide's Hill on the shores of Windermere, brought him a

400 *Beatrix Potter and Canon Rawnsley*, R. Potter, ?1900–10

401 (above) Jemima with her four ducklings,
The Tale of Jemima Puddle-Duck, p. 58, 1908

402 (right) *Sawrey, sheaves of corn in field*

403 *Beatrix Potter with sheepdog*, ?R. Potter

letter of apology. 'I will send a small subscription for Queen Adelaide as soon as I am paid for a ham', she wrote. 'I had intended to do so and overlooked it.' The Canon had also inquired about her father. 'My father is much better since we had the nurse,' she told him. 'I am able to stay here sometimes [at Hill Top] for a night, but it has been a trying summer.' To a further inquiry about a right of way being closed because the farmer could no longer put up with gates being left open, Beatrix had quite a lot to say.

> Speaking for myself, it is always a pity to hear of visitors being turned back from *fell land*; I speak with feeling as a farmer as I have not forgotten the exasperation of seeing a party of large young women steeple chasing over a succession of newly 'cammed' walls in pursuit of mushrooms. I like to see them enjoy themselves and they are least in the way on the fells – if only they would shut the gates when they come down again. Ask the Footpath Association about automatic gates – I have seen a pretty good one in Wales, worked with a log, but it won't stay open for a cart, unfortunately.

This was a good idea later adopted by the National Trust at Gowbarrow Park and in several other locations where carts, and later tractors, did not require access.

The letter makes it clear that Beatrix thought and looked on herself as a farmer, even though, at the age of 47 and when she had owned Hill Top for eight years, she still found it difficult to leave her parents and stay there for any great length of time.

Certainly sketching was not her only occupation: Beatrix was also learning to be a farmer. She worked the straw-chopping machine, lent a hand in the hay field, and began to take an interest in sheep, both in management and breeding. Compulsory dipping had just replaced salving with tar and

404 '"And they drink bucketfuls of milk"', alternative picture for *The Tale of Pigling Bland*, p. 16, 1913

grease to protect sheep from blowflies and ticks: the animals were manually heaved in – and out – of barrels of dip by the farmer. Dipping was quicker than salving, where a good salver could only treat a dozen sheep in a day, but it was not as long-lasting, requiring shepherds to make regular visits to the fell to be sure the sheep were not being eaten alive by blowflies. Liver fluke was also a widespread scourge, and at lambing time so was a condition known locally as 'the drop'. Beatrix began to study diseases of sheep and Dr Milne, of Newcastle Agricultural College, was very surprised, after a technical correspondence on sheep diseases, to find that his informed sheep-breeder correspondent was a sturdy little lady known to the world as Beatrix Potter.

Castle Farm, a cottager's smallholding in Near Sawrey, was bought in 1909. Royalties had to be invested somewhere and the habit of buying property was growing on Beatrix. It had started with the need to increase the Hill Top holding to improve the farm, then a nice little cottage in Sawrey had to be saved from demolition, and a neighbouring farm, which was very run down, was going at a tempting price. Castle Farm was bought for its land, which ran with Hill Top, so the farms could be put together. The solicitor dealing with the sale, William Heelis of W. Heelis & Co., continued to take an interest in this lady farmer even after the Castle Farm sale was completed. He noted that she spent much of her time elsewhere, and he kept an eye on this farm and her other properties.

William Heelis, considered by Sawrey to be a quiet man and a good shot over rough ground, was tall and distinguished-looking. He had not only kept an eye on Beatrix's property but he had also pursued their acquaintance with deliberation and came to call when she was at Hill Top. In 1912 he asked her to marry him. The village was not surprised by the announcement of the engagement. Beatrix's parents, however, were dismayed at the thought of losing their invaluable daughter, and told her that to marry a country solicitor was much beneath her and they opposed the match. Beatrix, already exhausted by a trying summer, found this opposition to the achievement of her modest ambitions more than she could surmount. She fell ill.

Fortunately her brother came to her rescue, announcing on one of his infrequent visits to London that he had married a Scottish farmer's daughter seven years ago, a fact he had previously omitted to mention, and that Beatrix had every right, at 47, to marry whom she pleased. The opposition did not entirely disappear, going underground and threatening to break out every so often, but the marriage took place in Kensington in October 1913.

The short honeymoon was spent in London and then Mr and Mrs Heelis lived at Eeswyke in Sawrey whilst Castle Farm was altered and extended. According to Beatrix's shepherd, Tom Storey, it had only been a small farmhouse: 'A little

405 The crossroads at Sawrey, background painting for *The Tale of Pigling Bland*, frontispiece, 1909

406 (above) Mrs Cannon feeding poultry, *The Tale of Jemima Puddle-Duck*, p. 8, 1908

407 (right) *Moorland Scene*, Bertram Potter

cottage, you know, was Castle – the end by the yard, you'll be able to see the old part with flag floors. You go through and there's the dairy where the beer barrel used to be kept.'

Hill Top remained unaltered. It was too small and primitive for the married couple and Beatrix wished to keep it as it was, though she continued to look after the garden. Mrs Cannon was to come through the connecting door from the farmhouse to open windows and do the dusting there.

The next four years were in no way easy: Rupert Potter died in May 1914 and Beatrix brought her mother up to Sawrey just as war was declared. Farming became complicated by lack of labour and much red tape. These were sad, hard-working years, culminating in the quite unexpected death of Bertram in 1918 at the age of 46, a great grief both to his mother and to Beatrix.

It was 1919, after Beatrix had settled her mother permanently at Lindeth How in Windermere, near the ferry, before she was able to take stock of her life. Since her last book, *The Tale of Johnny Town-Mouse*, she no longer painted as her eyes were not up to it. The room she had made at Hill Top for writing and painting, and where she had hung pictures by Bertram, was hardly used. Her thoughts turned from her books to farming.

E.M.B.

8

LAKE DISTRICT FARMER

408 'The pie made of mouse': a traditional cottage kitchen, *The Pie and the Patty-Pan*, p. 19, 1905

409 (below) Mr Tod's kitchen, *The Tale of Mr. Tod*, a proof for p. 34, 1912

410 (below right) Pony Billy in the Pinfold at Troutbeck, *The Fairy Caravan*, p. 44, 1929

Willie and Beatrix were devoted to each other and their late marriage, which had brought Beatrix's life round to its new course, began to give her wider horizons and interests once the war was over. Willie liked dancing, and during the folk-dancing revival of the twenties he danced with the village team, transporting members to different villages, packed into the new Morris Cowley that had taken the place of his Bradbury motorbicycle. Beatrix watched the dancing in stone-flagged farm kitchens – dances called The Boatman or Black Nog – to the sound of morris bells and the taste of plum cake. The long drives home under the cold stars were a revelation in distance and time, after a life of travel limited, except for train journeys, to the capability of the horse.

Beatrix continued to drive herself in the pony-trap until the pony died in 1925; then she bought her own car. She enjoyed motoring, buying George Abraham's book *Motorways in Lakeland*, which later she gave to the Armitt Library in Ambleside, and she took pleasure in going about inspecting her farms and stock in this dashing manner. She had a chauffeur, Walter Stevens, who had been her mother's coachman and never really came to terms with the change from horse to internal combustion engine. He was very thin and wrinkled and rather old, so that Josephine Banner, a young artist friend, was to wonder if he could once have been a lizard transformed by Beatrix, the fairy Godmother.

411 *Stone wall with hogg hole,* 1910

Beatrix's interest in acquiring new property had increased after the war. Her love for the Lake District had become a steadfast attachment, strengthened by living and working in her adopted county, which brought with it a sense of responsibility, perhaps fostered by Canon Rawnsley's exhortations.

This sense of responsibility was not directed towards awe-inspiring scenery, nor the admired and elegant nineteenth-century lakeside villas with their landscaped gardens, of the type leased by the Potters for family holidays. Long before they were considered anything but unimportant relics of the past, Beatrix wished to protect the small farmhouses with their patchwork fields and stone walls, and the cottages, field barns and locally-named hogg houses – stone shelters for the over-wintering of year-old sheep – scattered across the valley sides. She saw clearly that these traditional homes and the people who lived and worked there were the heart of the Lake District.

The only sure way to protect the traditional homes and the way of life of the valleys was, Beatrix considered, to buy them herself and look after them, at least for the moment. Willie had every opportunity as a solicitor to know in advance when cottages or land were to be put up for sale – and there were many large estates being broken up in the aftermath of the war, apprehensive cottagers wondering who was to buy. Beatrix bought where and when she could, always with an eye to preventing jerry-built bungalows swamping the villages and traditional cottages being demolished. Would-be makers of a quick profit sometimes found themselves unexpectedly de-feated. These acquisitions were made with discretion, so few knew the total sum of her holdings; certainly not the village.

Beatrix, though, knew about Sawrey life and its ups and downs. Any social aspirations she left to her husband, who went shooting with members of the county set and met them in the course of his work. She preferred a quiet, almost secret,

412 Outside the Tower Bank Arms (Kep in the foreground), *The Tale of Jemima Puddle-Duck*, p. 44, 1908

life, taking occasional visitors to tea at Hill Top and letting it be thought she lived there, rather than having strangers invade Castle Cottage, the name she had given Castle Farm, where she had made a wildflower garden and put apples on the kitchen sill for blackbirds to peck.

She only met her neighbours by leaning over the fence – at Hill Top to talk to Margaret Burns, wife of the landlord of the Tower Bank Arms – and chatting to people in the post office whilst waiting to buy stamps. She learnt that doctors were scarce and cost money, and the village worried through the usual epidemics of measles, mumps, whooping cough and scarlet fever as best it could. Almost single-handed she created the Hawkshead and District Nursing Association, happening to have a cottage just outside Hawkshead for the nurse to live in and at the handing-over ceremony cheerfully planting a magnolia tree in the garden, which flourished with the nursing service. Village gossip, too, gave her news of furniture sales.

413 *Corner of room, Jacobean cupboard and doorway,* ?Hill Top

When she was only 18 years old, soon after her first visit to Wray Castle, Beatrix had written in her journal that if she ever had a house she would have oak furniture and that she wished to possess a cupboard like the one at Wray. After the war there were many such cupboards for sale, seventeenth- and eighteenth-century carved press cupboards from the stone-built farmhouses 'riven out', as Beatrix described it, to sell to dealers. She bought these, and other pieces of carved oak furniture being thrown out as 'old fashioned', to put in her cottages, as well as in Castle Cottage, preserving them from the saleroom and keeping them in the Lake District.

The National Trust had not neglected the Lake District either. Land threatened by building projects at the head of Windermere had been saved, as had lakeside land at Queen Adelaide Hill, and more and more of Borrowdale was coming under the Trust's protection. Edith Rawnsley, though, had died early in the war and Canon Rawnsley had resigned his work at Crosthwaite to retire to Allan Bank in Grasmere. Here, in 1918, he married again. Eleanor Simpson was an old family friend and for the remaining two years of Hardwicke's life was able to help him with his work for the National Trust and to continue it after his death in 1920.

414 *Room with dresser and grandfather clock*

Beatrix never had quite the same outlook as Canon Rawnsley on the protection of Lake District countryside. He was an idealist who, in common with Octavia Hill and Sir Robert Hunter, had been inspired by John Ruskin to improve the lot of the common man. Open countryside to be enjoyed by the general public was the first aim of the National Trust. Beatrix was a realist who saw clearly that open countryside does not look after itself, the Lake District landscape in particular being almost entirely man-made, and she did not agree that the general public should be allowed to roam at will. She saw the preservation of her small farms and cottages as being essential for the protection of the way of life and, as a

415 *Penny Hill Farm*, Robert Thrift

416 *In a Cumberland barn, Penny Hill*, Judith Ackland, 1934

417 *The Peat Cart*, Mary Stella Edwards, 1934

418 *Troutbeck Park Farm*, Robert Thrift

result, the landscape of the valleys, but was not yet altogether sure that the Trust, with its idealistic outlook, would be the best guardian. Farms needed a knowledgeable owner and responsible tenants who kept hikers to the footpaths.

Penny Hill Farm in Eskdale was now added to her estate. At one time it had been an inn beside the original packhorse track through the valley, now it was a strategic valley farm with its own flock of Herdwick sheep, attached by custom, or 'heafed', to one particular area of fellside. It had a traditional eighteenth-century farmhouse and barns of the same age, merging satisfactorily into the landscape. The barn interiors, painted in the early thirties by two artist friends, Judith Ackland and Mary Stella Edwards, were equally traditional.

In 1924 Beatrix made her biggest purchase yet, Troutbeck Park Farm in the Troutbeck valley near Windermere. One of the large Lake District sheep farms, its 2,000 acres stretched right round the valley head and had once been a part of a Norman deer forest belonging to the Lords of Kendal. There was considerable archaeological interest in it, too: a Roman road could be traced coming down the steep flank of Froswick from the summit of High Street; and there were ancient hut circles at the base of the Tongue, itself a remarkable ridge rising behind the farm. Ownership would protect the head of the valley from development and it had a heafed flock of 1,000 Herdwick sheep. This local breed, small, sure-footed as chamois and hardy above the average, was beginning to

419 Troutbeck Park farmhouse, *The Fairy Caravan*, p. 102, 1929

interest Beatrix very much. The sheep and the farm, however, were in a poor state. In the year she bought Troutbeck Park Farm Beatrix told a neighbour that when she followed the Coniston Hunt over Troutbeck Park land, she had had to take off her shoes and stockings and wade through a swollen beck and that she thought that to be the only clean place on the farm. Something had to be done to improve matters.

The first action she took was to engage Tom Storey as her shepherd. At that time he was working for the Greggs at Townend Farm in Troutbeck. 'We'd just finished milking and my boss, he said "There's a lady wants to see you,"' related Tom, 'and she came through the shippon door – Mrs Heelis – she looked, well, a bonny looking woman to tell you the truth. "I've come to see you about working for me," she said. "Will you come to Troutbeck Park to be my shepherd?" I said yes if the money was right and she offered me double what I was getting from the Greggs so that's how I got my start.'

Tom worked that winter with the sheep and lambed them in the spring. According to Tom, when he took them over the sheep were rotten with liver fluke, but a new remedy against this – 'the finest thing that ever came out in those days' – which Tom asked Mrs Heelis to send for – 'she thought nothing was too good for the sheep' – did the trick and he successfully lambed over 900 ewes. After that Tom was asked to take over the management of Hill Top and breed Herdwicks for showing. Mrs Storey was to make the butter.

Tom found a ram among the Hill Top Herdwicks, 'Old Colley', which he recognized as one he had himself picked out as a winner when it was a lamb at Eskdale Show, and with which he could make a start on the breeding programme. Two of its lambs were put into Hawkshead Show in the autumn of that year, 1927. They both won prizes. Hill Top Herdwicks won prizes at all the big shows, Keswick, Ennerdale, Loweswater and Eskdale as well as the smaller local ones, every year until 1939. Mrs Heelis won silver tea-sets, salvers, vases, and tankards – and she always gave the tankards to Tom.

420 *Beatrix Potter and Tom Storey with prize ewe*

421 Crag-fast sheep at Walla Crag, Skiddaw, *The Fairy Caravan*, p. 72, 1929

422 *Two studies of a sheep's head, c.* 1929

423 Tommy Brock looks down at Mr Tod from Bull Banks: preliminary drawing for *The Tale of Mr. Tod*, p. 14, 1912

As farmer and shepherd the relationship between Mrs Heelis and Tom was well balanced. Tom found her good to work for: 'I wouldn't have stayed twenty years if I didn't. It was her love was Herdwick sheep. They were my favourites as well.' She found Tom not only a skilled shepherd but also someone she could talk to about the Herdwick sheep.

The origin of Herdwick sheep is not known, the most popular theory being that they were brought to this country with the Norse invaders in the ninth century. It is certain that Herdwicks formed the monastic flocks that began the long process of ecological change to bring the high fells to their present form. Canon Rawnsley had realized that these exceptionally hardy animals, able to live on the high fells where the rainfall can reach 200 inches a year and survive the winter blizzards, were the basis for the present ecological structure of the fragile Lake District landscape. Herdwick mutton was still popular as having an exceptional flavour, but the demand for Herdwick wool was restricted to a dwindling carpet trade and farmers were beginning to question the point of keeping them.

Concern for the welfare of these animals was always at its peak in the winter when pasture was scarce. In one of her letters she wrote:

> This is such a bad time for the sheep. The snow storm that was so severe in the south missed us – or delayed – till last Sunday, when there was the heaviest fall for twenty years; and it thaws so very slowly; freezing under the bright moon again. Perhaps it is a superstition that the moon causes frost: effect, not cause. Also one may say of muttons as well as men 'they should have died hereafter', but it's ghastly to think about the carrion crows. We feed them [the sheep] here, but they don't thrive on hay, and it's impossible to feed a big fell flock. Old customs become disused. I have just been telling the men to cut some 'croppit ash'. That is why you see the surviving croppit ashes near fell farm-houses. It used to be the custom to crop ashes and hollies for the sheep.

Fond of the sheep as she was, Beatrix did not find them easy to draw. One spring she asked Tom to cut off the head of the next lamb that died and skin it back to the shoulder. 'I've such a job sketching a lamb's head,' she said. Tom did this, 'and next day I came down the lane to look at sheep and she had it pinned against the wall, inside the paddock, and was sitting on a stone sketching it. It was really a grand job when she'd finished it.'

The drawing was made when she was working on *The Fairy Caravan*. She wrote it either on the top of Bull Banks above Hill Top or, in bad weather, in the house. When it was published twelve copies were sent from America and Tom received the first one. 'She came over from Castle Cottage and said "Here, Storey, this is a copy of *The Fairy Caravan* I've written, sent from America and I'm giving you the first one."

424 Pony Billy with Nip, Scotch Fly and the rest at the smithy forge, *The Fairy Caravan*, p. 129, 1929

It's signed and the dogs sketched in it at the back and the inscription is "To Tom Storey in memory of Queeny and the sheep dogs".'

It was perhaps inevitable that Mrs Heelis should be made President of the Herdwick Sheepbreeders' Association, the first and only time a woman has been elected to the office. The Association had been formed by Canon Rawnsley and his son Noel to protect the breed. Beatrix was amused that she, a total abstainer, should be attending meetings usually held in bar parlours. She also related the tale of a jolly farmer who, in proposing a toast to the President at a dinner, compared her to a cow – with very neat legs – who had just won a first prize. She took her judging duties very seriously though. Always a respected figure at agricultural shows, she trudged round the sheep pens in a Herdwick tweed suit and brown felt hat kept in check with black elastic under her chin, completing the business of the day before greeting any friends. .

The Armitt Library in Ambleside was the eventual recipient of many of the show catalogues Beatrix accumulated over the years. She had been a library member since her marriage, William Heelis having been solicitor to the Armitt Library from its foundation in 1912 under the will of Mary L. Armitt. Beatrix had known the Armitt sisters, Mary Louisa, Sophia and Annie Maria, and approved of their aims. Living in Ambleside and always quietly involved in public works, they were loved and respected figures, close friends of the educational pioneer Charlotte Mason, the Rawnsleys and many writers and artists. They were themselves writers and enjoyed

425 *Lepiota procera* (Parasol Mushroom), Sawrey, September 1896

study. Mary Armitt was particularly inspired by Carlyle's famous London Library and founded the Armitt charity so that others could enjoy the kind of facilities found there and in old libraries like the Bodleian.

The library was intended to be a collection of local history, topography, natural history, archaeology and literature of the Lake Poets, and it succeeded in being even more than this. In time, with donors ranging from G. M. Trevelyan to Arthur Ransome, it came to reflect the social history of an area much influenced by poets, writers, social reformers and artists. The pictures and etchings held by the library are a record of the history of art in the Lake District over an era. One of the most important donors was Beatrix herself, who, in addition to a number of general reference books, gave the library a large collection of her fungi watercolours and other studies. The Armitt Library, in its own sphere, was as important to the artistic life of the Lake District as the Lake Artists' Society.

By the end of the twenties the Society was well established and its yearly exhibition at Grasmere was one of the highlights in the northern artistic calendar. The exhibitions were held in Grasmere Hall, also the venue of the famous Grasmere Dialect Plays, written and produced by Canon Rawnsley's widow Eleanor, which were eagerly awaited each January. Eleanor Rawnsley had persuaded Alfred Heaton Cooper to paint backdrops of Lake District scenery for these plays, wonderful panoramas of lake and fell stored on rollers from year to year. Alfred's son William was also becoming an established landscape painter, as well as being among the pioneers of British rock climbing. He came to know the Lake District mountains and valleys very well and he illustrated rock climbing guides.

Sheep farming and support for the National Trust shared first place in Beatrix's life, though. She continued to give to Trust appeals, but she was very quiet – almost mouselike – about her aims and ambitions for the Lake District. She made anonymous donations, so that the secret of how much she really gave to the Trust is not known.

In 1927 there was a particularly urgent appeal for money. A strip of Windermere's lake shore, Cockshott Point, near the

427 Pony Billy approaches Ing Bridge in Troutbeck, *The Fairy Caravan*, p. 114, 1929

ferry on the east shore, was coming up for sale and was sure to be bought by a property developer unless the Trust could step in first. Farming was in a particularly bad way that year and Beatrix was entirely unable to persuade her mother, though her house overlooked the Point, that there was any need to prevent the ownership of all the lake shore being in private hands. It then occurred to her that she might make a little money by selling some of her drawings in America, where, to her surprise, she seemed to be regarded as an important literary figure. She sent fifty signed copies of drawings of Peter Rabbit to the Editor of the *Horn Book Magazine*, Miss Bertha Mahony. Miss Mahony sold the drawings on behalf of the National Trust at a guinea each, there were requests for more and the final sum raised was £104, a substantial donation to the appeal.

In a letter to an American friend in 1929 Beatrix mentioned having been driven to Coniston by William to look at some land for sale. The evening had been lovely and the autumn colours very fine. She failed to mention that the 'land' was the Monk Coniston Estate stretching from the head of Coniston Water over into Little Langdale, extending to over 4,000 acres. Neither did she mention that she intended to buy the estate, the royalties from *The Fairy Caravan* and *The Tale of Little Pig Robinson* making this possible, and divide it between herself and the National Trust.

E.M.B.

9

BEATRIX POTTER'S LAKE DISTRICT

The National Trust Secretary, Mr S. H. Hamer, on being offered over half of the Monk Coniston Estate – nearly 3,000 acres of land which included, among much else, Tarn Hows, Tom Heights, Tilberthwaite, small farms on the south side of Little Langdale and the mountain ground running up to Wetherlam – accepted it immediately on behalf of the Trust. Mrs Heelis was offering the estate at cost, the money to be paid as and when possible, and Mr Hamer was optimistic about the results of an appeal for donations. His optimism was justified and the money was raised without difficulty.

One difficulty, however, did remain. The various voluntary committees who kept watch over the Trust properties in the Lake District were lacking in the experience necessary for the management of an agricultural estate. Mr Hamer asked Mrs Heelis if she would manage the Trust's half of the Monk Coniston land together with her own holdings until such time as the Trust could appoint a suitable land agent. Mrs Heelis, perhaps rather to her own surprise, accepted the job.

Nineteen-thirty was not an easy year in which to take on the work of an amateur land agent, which was how Beatrix saw herself. The world depression had brought agricultural prices tumbling and by 1932 some animals at the Westmorland autumn sheep sales were sold for as little as a shilling each.

428 *Tarn Hows*, part of the Monk Coniston Estate, Robert Thrift

429 *Yew Tree Farm in the 1930s*

Tenants were in difficulties and asked for rent reductions. Mrs Heelis was not unsympathetic but took measures to economize on general costs. She used her own car, nicknamed the 'Noah's Ark', to transport workmen for farm repairs, she distinguished real need from mere grumbling when it came to faulty ranges or damp walls and she made some progress in sorting out good tenants from the less efficient.

Another measure to improve farm economy was the suggestion to tenants that they might take advantage of the number of visitors to the Lake District. Mrs Heelis thought Yew Tree Farm near Coniston, being directly on the Ambleside–Coniston road, particularly suitably placed to offer visitors tea, and she gave some of her own surplus furniture to improve the parlour in which teas should be served. A mahogany table and ten chairs, a folding oak table, a bible box, a glass-fronted corner cabinet containing Victorian china and other items and a grandfather clock were among the pieces.

One contrivance of farmers during the depression did not meet with the approval of Mrs Heelis. Whilst encouraging farmers' wives to keep a few hens, she was much against the whole farm being turned over to poultry. As she once complained in a letter to Eleanor Rawnsley, it was the last resort of poor farmers who had stripped their land of all assets.

The work involved at Monk Coniston was considerable and Mrs Heelis was in some ways relieved when Bruce Thompson was appointed National Trust Agent for the North in 1936 and she was asked to turn over the management of Trust farms to the new Agent. She also had her regrets. In a letter to the Banners just before the official hand-over she said: 'Perhaps there will be a little less to do after another fortnight but much of it is interesting – even drains and deficiencies of shippons.'

The caretaking might be over, but the transfer of responsibility was no light task. Mrs Heelis still had reservations about the ability of the National Trust, in the shape of young Mr Thompson, to manage an agricultural estate. She made it her business to put him in the way of it.

430 Sawrey village and Coniston Old Man,
The Fairy Caravan, p. 103, 1929

431 Mixed poultry and cattle in Hill Top farmyard, *The Tale of Jemima Puddle-Duck*, p. 11, 1908

Long careful letters were written to the new Agent with lists of the tradesmen, with their virtues and faults, whom Mrs Heelis had employed for work on the estate. 'For Coniston Mr Bonny (elderly and a trifle slow) understands the complicated pipe supply at Thwaite. The Wilsons can dig up an ordinary burst; remember that all plumbers are expensive excavators.'

Tenants continued to bring their problems to Mrs Heelis and she conveyed these to Mr Thompson with appropriate instructions.

The Yew Tree tenant is asking about a broken fence against the Beck . . . It is much patched and wants re-erecting. It is usual to put *round* wire near flood water, because woven wirenetting gets clogged with drift . . . You want 1 cwt No. 9 . . . You can get round wire from Mr W. Middleton, 21 Stricklandgate, Kendal, or Hoggarths, Sandes Avenue or possibly Musgrave's Windermere, (but do not be put off with anything thinner than 9. You understand 10 is thinner and 8 is thicker).

Some problems were not agricultural. They had anxious consultations on the difficulties of granting public access to Trust land. Bathing at Tarn Hows was the subject of considerable correspondence. '*Bathing* is most perplexing,' Mrs Heelis wrote. 'It seems cruel to refuse in hot weather; but they should not do it at the exposed end of the lake.' There were other difficulties too. 'I was displeased one hot summer to see people going down from cars to the Tarn. It is so difficult with rules. The Miss Scotts took a gramophone to walse [sic] on the ice: a general habit of gramophoning and wirelessing would be a great nuisance.'

A few misunderstandings and differences of opinion occurred over the years. 'I am always glad to give you any information which I can about the Coniston estate or about elementary details of estate repairs,' Mrs Heelis wrote in January 1938 after a 'comment' had resulted in action of which she disapproved, 'but it is manifestly not fair to *either* of us for me to interfere by comments that might amount to advice upon any matter . . . In future I think I had better confine myself to minding my own business.' Nevertheless 'comments that might amount to advice' were still being offered – and received with gratitude – even in 1942, principally on compulsory acquisition of woodlands for the war effort, though there were also complaints about the high wages paid by the Trust compared with the Heelis rates of pay. The relationship had become an easy one, with Mrs Heelis now advising the Agent not to be out in this weather with a bad cold.

The fact of the matter was that this supposedly simple transfer of management of the Coniston farms was something far more complicated. Through the instigation of Mrs Heelis, and with her help and advice, the Trust was taking the first big step from being a mere holding company for buildings and land

432 *Harter Fell*, William Hartley
Waddington

to becoming an important influence on both the life and the
landscape of the Lake District.

There was, though, 'a little less to do' after the official
transfer and Beatrix had more time for her own affairs. Though
she had ceased to paint, she continued to interest herself in the
work of local artists. These included William Heaton Cooper
and William Hartley Waddington, who became President of
the Lake Artists. He came from Bolton to live in the Lake
District in 1914, at Hawkshead Hill, but Beatrix found him a
cottage in Sawrey and allowed him to extend it with a studio.

Delmar Banner was another artist who was encouraged by
Beatrix. He and his sculptor wife Josephine were 'incomers'
who came to live in the Lake District because it held such
attraction for them. They spent a good many years looking for
a house that would suit them, spending their holidays staying
in farmhouses or rented houses. They looked at property when
not climbing the high fells for Delmar to make preparatory
sketches for both his watercolour and oil landscapes. His main
preoccupation was with light and its effect on mountain
scenery and Beatrix bought some of his Coniston landscapes
whilst she was helping them look for a home. Delmar was of
the opinion, though, that if Beatrix had been the one who
found the cottage in Little Langdale that eventually became
their home, she would have bought the house herself and then
let it to them. 'I believe she regarded it as not only her duty, but
her right, to preserve old houses,' he said. He also painted her
portrait both in youth and old age.

Her friendship with Delmar and Josephine Banner had
begun in 1935, through an introduction by a mutual friend, a
farmer. Delmar's account of the meeting gives an affectionate
picture of Beatrix during this phase of her life.

433 *Castle Cottage, Sawrey*, R. Potter, 1912

434 'They crossed it hand in hand', *The Tale of
Pigling Bland*, p. 82, 1913

We knocked on the door of Castle Cottage one October afternoon. It opened, and we beheld one of her own characters, yet better than any: short, plump, solid, with apple-red cheeks; she looked up at us with keen blue eyes and a smile. On her head was a kind of tea-cosy, and she was dressed in lots of wool. 'Cum in,' she said in a snug voice, and led the way. There was drugget on the floor, and silver-mounted guns on the wall. In the room into which we followed her bent and venerable figure there were book-shelves, a mahogany dining table, silver candlesticks; and a cheerful fire. She sat down on a red plush armchair on one side, and we sat on stiff-backed eighteenth-century mahogany chairs on the other. We noticed a fine Girtin on the wall; her husband's slippers warming on the fender; and (for her age) a rather naughty quantity of silver chocolate paper on a little table. Two windows from floor to the low ceiling opened on to the old garden. She took us in; and during that searching silence we neither spoke nor moved.

The Banners asked to see the original illustrations for the books and Beatrix agreed, going upstairs to get them from their keeping place in the airing cupboard.

We heard the creaking of the stairs as she climbed slowly up, and then, after an interval of little noises, down again, armed with bundles in brown paper, fastened with blue ribbon. We saw how exquisite – beyond our hopes and beyond the means of colour-production – the pictures are. She identified all the places; every scene can be found, mostly of Near Sawrey and Hawkshead; some further off, like those in *Mrs. Tiggy-Winkle* in Newlands, Pigling and Pig-wig Bland go to live in Little Langdale; it is Colwith Bridge that they 'crossed hand in hand' like a human pair. In the house itself the chimney up which Tom climbed, the staircase up which Mrs Whiskers ran with provisions: the windows, beds, and dresser: and the chair on which sat a 'perfectly beautiful little Berkshire Pig'. She said, 'I can't invent, I only copy.' Yet nothing could be more invented.

435 (above left) 'Plenty of room for a little Tom Cat', *The Tale of Samuel Whiskers*, p. 37, 1908

436 (above centre) 'He made a second journey for the rolling-pin', *The Tale of Samuel Whiskers*, p. 56, 1908

437 (above right) Anna Maria stealing some of the dough, *The Tale of Samuel Whiskers*, p. 29, 1908

438 'They were not in bed: *not in the least*', *The Tale of Tom Kitten*, p. 52, 1907

439 *Heathwaite Farm, Coniston*, Delmar Banner, 1944

In 1937 there is a record of lunch with the Banners, staying at Heathwaite Farm above Coniston. Her 'Noah's Ark' was now not up to climbing steep hills, so 'I am not too proud to come up in a milk float provided you can haul me into it,' she wrote, and then went on to comment on weather and its effect on the fells from the point of view of both a farmer and of an artist, as she often did in her letters. 'I was at Coniston this morning and looked up towards Heathwaite and the lights and shadows in Mines Ghyll – it is rather beautiful weather.'

Delmar Banner has left an account of this visit.

She came to lunch with us at Heathwaite Farm in 1937, below the Old Man of Coniston. She met us at Church Bridge: and clambered into the milk-float, in which she made her progress up the steep lane, while we walked on each side . . . after which [dinner] she inspected the ship-pons, and then my pictures, with a professional eye for both. Her criticisms were practical in her insistence on the structure. She bought one of my watercolours – the second.

In her next letter Beatrix enclosed the cheque for the picture and explained why she had bought it.

What I tried to say is that these typographically-exact-in-detail are a stage in the artistic career; which usually is left behind (for better or worse) when a painter goes forward . . . So I seized on that landscape while I could get it, because for better or worse you may possibly not paint like that a few months or years hence. The clouds were wonderful in some of the landscapes.

She goes on to say: 'I had a most enjoyable visit, thanks to you and Josephine . . . what a pleasant house and float and charioteer.'

440 *Beatrix Potter in old age*, Delmar Banner, c.1950

Interest in more than landscapes is expressed in another letter to Josephine.

> It is curious how graphic children can be, up to a certain age, and then they lose it, or it is wiped out by teaching. A shepherd's child about 5 years old showed me a remarkable crayon scribble of two lambs kicking up their heels. I asked for another specimen. Now, six months later she gives me a 'picture' done at school; outline traced from an elaborate scene in Kate Greenaway style all carefully coloured; and consigned to the fire by me.

Beatrix liked children. She kept a few rabbits at Hill Top so visiting children would not be disappointed, assuring them these were at least the descendants of Peter Rabbit. Even so, she felt the younger generation should be seen but not heard too much, disliking noise on principle. She approved of Tom Storey's son Geoff as he had an instinctive understanding of Herdwick sheep.

Tom had improved the land at Hill Top as well as the Herdwicks, so the meadows produced good sweet hay. Beatrix liked to help in the hayfield, raking and turning the cut grass and making sure it was thoroughly dry before being carted. Tom said she had a horror of damp hay causing a barn fire. On hot hay days she would wear a rhubarb leaf on her head to keep off the sun, not heeding the disapproval of the village at such oddities. Tom remembered how she dressed round the farm:

> She always wore clogs and a tweed costume down to her ankles. Then she had a sacking apron and a sack round her shoulders if it was wet and an old felt hat. She was going to Miss Gregory's at the shop over the hill in Far Sawrey one bad morning, dressed like that with a butter basket over her arm and a cowcake sack round her shoulders and she met this old pedlar at the top of the hill, called Croft, and he looked at her and said 'It's a bad day for the likes of me and thee, Missis.' He thought she was a pedlar too, one of the same mark as he. She told the tale herself, you know, it did make her laugh.

Before her hysterectomy operation in 1939 in the Women's Hospital in Liverpool Beatrix instructed Tom on the disposal of her ashes. 'She asked me to do it you know. But she said whatever you do tell nobody: I want it kept a secret.' She recovered from the operation but the instructions remained in force. She also talked to Tom about buying land for the Trust: 'When she bought the Wray farms, Beyond the Fields, High Wray and Tock How . . . and gave them to Mr Heelis, she told me then: "Well, after my day, Storey, every farm that I own will go to the National Trust." She would talk at times to me about all that sort of thing you know.'

By 1940 Beatrix found herself for the second time faced with the task of keeping farms going amid a welter of wartime red

441 Beatrix Potter's clogs

442 *February Fields, Little Langdale*, William Heaton Cooper, *c.* 1958

tape, shortages of every kind and the difficulties of dealing with Government officials who had little idea of local problems and conditions.

In her last letter to Josephine Banner, who had settled in Little Langdale with Delmar in 1939, Beatrix comments on the difficulties of the times. She mentions that she had been inundated with inquiries from people unable to buy the Peter Rabbit books because of the paper quotas and says that the very wet winter had thrown back farm work awkwardly. 'This spell of fine weather has been most welcome. It's just too early for sowing corn and seeds, though tempting. Snowdrops have been very pretty, just going over.' After a digression on the ravages of the 'bracken clock grubs' she wonders how things are in Little Langdale. 'You have not had much snow to look at on the fells, but sunsets have been very beautiful this winter. I wonder if the wild swans have been on the tarn.' The letter finishes: 'What with shortage of petrol and flu, farming is a bit of a problem! But keep smiling!' Attached to the letter is a 'self portrait', a caricature, with the wartime motto 'Keep Smiling' written below.

The last time Josephine ever saw her was in August 1943. She was very bent and confessed to having overtaxed her strength in the hayfield. When Josephine left, she leant on the little gate, with her head on one side, smiling and waving goodbye with a cloverleaf she had just picked – the same gate from which Timmy Willie had waved his daisy.

Beatrix died on 22 December 1943, having lived long enough to know that the war was being won by the Allies and the ownership of her little farms would not pass into alien hands. Tom Storey was very shocked by her death, 'because I'd been talking to her an hour or more the night before, about the farm and everything'. He discharged his duty of scattering her ashes, telling only his son where they had been scattered. 'He's

443 *Letter from Beatrix Potter* to Josephine Banner

444 Timmy Willie waving a daisy, *The Tale of Johnny Town-Mouse*, p. 57, 1918

445 *Hill Top porch in Snow*

farming the farm and I thought he should just know. He's a good lad and she thought a lot about him.'

The shepherd who remarked at her funeral that it was a bad day for farmers expressed the general opinion of the farming world of Cumberland and Westmorland on the death of Mrs Heelis. The Trust, too, had lost a friend, and Willie Heelis only lived another eighteen months and died in August 1945.

In her will Beatrix had left the Trust 4,000 acres of land, including Hill Top, and the farms she had given to Willie came to the Trust on his death in 1945. The complete estate was called the Heelis Bequest, the largest gift of land the Trust had so far received.

The contents of Castle Cottage, which included Beatrix's book illustrations, were left to her cousin Stephanie, whose untimely death brought them into the possession of Stephanie's husband Captain K. W. G. Duke RN. (The rights in the books themselves were left to Norman Warne's nephew.) In 1947 Captain Duke generously presented the Trust with all the original Beatrix Potter drawings for the Peter Rabbit series with the exception of *The Tale of Peter Rabbit* itself (given to the publishers), *The Tailor of Gloucester* (given to the Tate Gallery) and *The Tale of the Flopsy Bunnies* (given to the British Museum). The National Trust thus became the owner and custodian of the majority of the drawings and decided to display some of them at Hill Top. The house was opened to the public in the summer of 1946, to all intents and purposes exactly as Beatrix Potter had left it.

In the first season there were a mere 1,800 adult visitors and 300 children visiting Hill Top between July and the end of September, but in 1947 there were three times that number and in 1978, when the figures rose to almost 90,000 visitors in one season, it was clear that something must be done to

446 *Beatrix Potter's house in Sawrey*, William Heaton Cooper, 1960

447, 448, 449 Hawkshead: *W. H. Heelis office*, Robert Thrift (top), Tabitha Twitchit's shop from *The Pie and the Patty-Pan*, p. 25, 1905 (above) – now the *National Trust Information Office*, Robert Thrift (above centre)

preserve Beatrix Potter's house and possessions from damage. The entrance fee was raised and the house shut on Fridays – found to be the most popular day.

A year later it was decided that, though the drawings had been looked after carefully, there would be inevitable continued deterioration if they were not kept in a properly controlled environment, with absence of dust, the correct humidity, not too much light and at the right temperature. The drawings were removed from Hill Top and a new introductory exhibition was put in the Entrance Lodge. Work is now under way to adapt the old W. H. Heelis office in Hawkshead to house the drawings. This eighteenth-century building has the right scale for the drawings and contains a perfect and extensive collection of late eighteenth-century built-in furniture and fittings. It was also where William Heelis worked, and Hawkshead has many associations with Beatrix. The Trust's Information Office there is the building Beatrix sketched as Tabitha Twitchit's Shop in *The Pie and the Patty-Pan*.

The Heelis Bequest as a whole was of considerable importance to the National Trust, not only for the actual number of acres it gave it, but also for the type and quality of the land and buildings acquired. Canon Rawnsley, whose work for the National Trust had helped to persuade Beatrix Potter to leave her lands in its care, had seen only beautiful countryside as being under threat; farms and cottages were incidental. Beatrix had understood that Lake District countryside could only survive if the traditional way of life survived with it, farms and farming particularly. Her bequest made it possible for the Trust to begin protecting the way of life in the Lake District valleys.

Farms which came to the Trust through the Heelis Bequest formed the beginnings of what are now several extensive agricultural estates protected by Trust ownership from unacceptable development. The flocks of Herdwick sheep which Beatrix specified in her will should remain with the farms have also been important to the Trust and it is now the largest overall owner of this breed. This has resulted in the double responsibility of maintaining the breed for its stamina and of making the breed an asset, not a liability, to tenant farmers. Improvement in sheep-handling methods, in which the Trust has become an acknowledged leader, has been some help; involvement in the seventies in the promotion of ethnic wools brought higher prices for the wool clip.

The high value of the buildings included in the Heelis Bequest has become more apparent in recent years. Most, if not all, of the several hundred farms, cottages and barns which the Trust owns in the Lake District were accepted not for their architectural merit, but as elements in a landscape of high scenic beauty. Over the years the Trust began to realize the value of this collection of traditional rural buildings, not least those which came from Beatrix Potter. In a recent Vernacular Survey, during which a comprehensive record was made of

450 *Moss Eccles Tarn*, Robert Thrift. Part was included in the Heelis Bequest, the remainder purchased outright by the National Trust in 1977

every building the Trust owns in the region, several unusual building trends came to light and it was found that Beatrix Potter's farms are amongst the most important examples of Lake District vernacular buildings.

The Trust's estates in the Lake District have lately become the focus of considerable attention. As an example, the setting up of Sites of Special Scientific Interest (SSSIs) by the Nature Conservancy Council means that areas of land so designated are, in effect, 'frozen' against all future development in order to protect their species environment. There are several such areas

451 *Ruin near Ambleside* (Bridge House), John Ruskin

452 *Slater's Bridge, Little Langdale*, William Heaton Cooper, 1970. An ancient packhorse bridge on land bought by the National Trust in 1947 (High Birk How farm) with help from the Heelis Bequest endowment

within the Lake District, including part of the shore of Esthwaite Water, Beatrix Potter's favourite small lake.

In addition, the national change of attitude to conservation has meant the Trust no longer acts in isolation, and with tighter controls on land, together with the development control exercised over the National Park as a whole, the Trust has been able to give more thought to the protection of the land and buildings it already owns.

One conclusion the Trust has come to is that there is a need to look in detail into the landscape, culture and way of life that brought the Lake District landscape, now almost entirely man-made, into being. This would give a better understanding of the balance that must be achieved between the natural and the man-made to maintain the landscape. A further conclusion in the light of this research is that the maintenance of the landscape, footpaths, lakesides, walls, woodlands and traditional buildings is of first importance. A Lake District Landscape Appeal has been launched to provide a fund both to carry out a backlog of jobs and for future needs.

454 Jemima above Esthwaite Water, *The Tale of Jemima Puddle-Duck*, p. 16, 1908

In the Lake District the Trust, now the largest landowner with nearly one third of the National Park coming under its protection, is primarily protecting the landscape: the lakes, fells and woodlands, and particularly the mosaic of small farms with traditional buildings. It is on these farms, which base their interests on sheep and some cattle, that many landscape features and the traditional valley life depend.

It is a measure of Beatrix Potter's foresight that her early vision of protecting the Lake District landscape by the practical means of ownership and good estate management should now have such general acceptance. With her beloved countryside, Beatrix Potter bequeathed to the Trust and the nation a policy for the future.

E.M.B.

AN APPRECIATION

In August 1939 a New Zealand journalist, John 'Jock' Stone, brought up on Beatrix Potter's books and on his first visit to England, wrote to the author through her publishers asking for a brief guide to the setting of the books that he so loved. Unaware that she rarely responded to such approaches, he was therefore not surprised to receive a prompt reply. It began: 'Your letter has amused me so much that I am answering it (with my address, in spite of the alarming "journalist"). I hate publicity; and I have contrived to survive to be an old woman without it, except in the homely atmosphere of Agricultural Shows.' Beatrix then answered his enquiries about the settings of the books and ended her letter with an invitation. 'If you come north during your visit to England – ring Hawkshead 16 and I will show you Tom Kitten's house.'

Two weeks later war was declared and seven months went by before John Stone was able to visit the Lake District and to follow up Beatrix's invitation. It was in the early spring of 1940 that he telephoned Hawkshead 16 from his hotel in Ambleside. 'A business-like feminine voice replied,' he later reported. 'At the age of 74, Beatrix Potter's voice, like her beautiful Victorian handwriting, was clear and full of decision and she instantly recalled my timid application made to her in August.'

The following morning, promptly at the agreed time of eleven o'clock, a large car drew up at the White Lion. The uniformed chauffeur had two passengers – Miss Mills, a friend and neighbour of Beatrix's, and Mrs Heelis herself: 'a little, round woman, much wrapped up against the chill in the spring air, with shrewdly observant eyes and the rosy cheeks that seem to stay with Englishwomen who love the open air.' During the drive to Near Sawrey the New Zealander was gently chided for not bringing a raincoat ('you should never come to this region without one!') and then treated to a discourse on how the road they were on had been spoiled after the First World War, 'widened and at some points straightened for the convenience of servants of the internal combustion engine'.

It was a day that John Stone would never forget. A conducted tour of Hill Top and then of the village was followed by lunch at Castle Cottage, during which there was much talk about the National Trust. In the afternoon the two of them pored over the original illustrations for 'the little books', with Beatrix giving a running commentary on each one and laughing loudly over the picture of Jemima Puddle-Duck trying to fly. 'That is what I used to look like to Sawrey people. I rushed about, quacking industriously!' Among the pictures were a number of variants ('I don't remember why' was Beatrix's comment) and one of them, the frontispiece for *Benjamin Bunny*, was signed and given to the visitor to take home.

A month or so later, on his return to New Zealand, John Stone sent Beatrix an account of his travels, expressing his particular delight at the beauty of the countryside. Her long reply was written on 5 June 1940. The previous few weeks had seen the capitulation of both Holland and Belgium to the Germans, and in the previous few days the greater part of the British army had been safely evacuated from the beaches of Dunkirk.

We have been through anxious days since you saw the English primroses and daffodils, now droughted with the fierce heat. Under a cloudless blue sky, we are longing for thunder and rain. April was lovely; showers and green grass; May was full of flowers, sheets of bluebells in our northern woods and the hawthorn hedges and big thorn bushes in the valleys have been like snow drifts . . . You found *some* of England that is still unspoilt. It is most unfortunate how much has been wilfully destroyed in the English country side. I have tried to do my humble bit of preservation in this district.

The rest of her letter ranged over the lack of domestic antiquity in the Border country prior to the Union (of England and Scotland) 'because it was continu-ally harried and burnt by the Scots'; the state of her health after a serious operation, 'at present I am able to get about again and superintending work in the woods and on the farms'; and the progress of the war, 'the colonies will carry on the cause of freedom if we go under . . . If things get worse I think I'll bury some tins of biscuits in the woods!'.

This meeting and exchange between Beatrix and her admirer from the other side of the world touch on many of the qualities for which this remarkable woman is remembered nearly half a century later, in particular her sense of humour, her love of the countryside and her determination to protect and to preserve it. Beatrix Potter was not only the creator of some of the best-loved children's books that have ever been published, she was also a gifted painter, a scientist, a farmer, a conservationist and a benefactor. Her shy, and sometimes gruff, exterior hid a kind and generous spirit, and never was it better demon-strated than when she was showing off her beloved Lake District.

J.T.

455   ICAA Christmas card, 1932

SOURCES AND CREDITS

All sizes given refer to the image size of the illustration unless otherwise stated.

Some of the sources are given in full, but the following is the key to those that are abbreviated.

AT	The Armitt Trust
BM	British Museum
LT	The Trustees of the Linder Collection, Book Trust
NAL	National Art Library, Victoria and Albert Museum
NT	The National Trust
TG	Tate Gallery
V&A	The Board of Trustees of the Victoria and Albert Museum
WA	Frederick Warne Archive

1 pencil, pen-and-ink and watercolour on card 186 x 235 mm V&A
2 sepia ink and watercolour 158 x 128 mm NT
3 pen-and-ink 27 x 129 mm WA
4 photograph NT
5 photograph NT
6 photograph V&A
7 photograph Jean Holland
8 photograph Joan Duke
9 pencil and pen-and-ink 97 x 112 mm V&A
10 pen-and-ink 55 x 107 mm WA
11 watercolour 100 x 145 mm V&A
12 photograph Jean Holland
13 photograph Joan Duke
14 watercolour 278 x 228 mm LT
15 photograph Joan Duke
16 photograph Joan Duke
17 watercolour 231 x 294 mm LT
18 detail, pencil, pen-and-ink and sepia wash 110 x 118 mm LT
19 photograph Joan Duke
20 photograph Joan Duke
21 photograph Rosalind Rawnsley
22 photograph Joan Duke
23 pencil and watercolour 350 x 205 mm LT
24 photograph Joan Duke
25 photograph V&A
26 watercolour 120 x 200 mm AT
27 photograph WA
28 pencil and watercolour 103 x 125 mm V&A
29 watercolour 500 x 360 mm WA
30 photograph V&A
31 sepia ink and watercolour 102 x 90 mm NT
32 pen-and-ink and watercolour 208 x 175 mm NT
33 watercolour 200 x 91 mm V&A
34 pencil and watercolour 88 x 74 mm V&A
35 photograph Winifred Boultbee
36 pencil and watercolour 190 x 165 mm private collection
37 pen-and-ink and watercolour 116 x 202 mm V&A
38 pen-and-ink and watercolour 115 x 95 mm NT
39 pen-and-ink and watercolour 168 x 128 mm NT
40 photograph WA
41 detail, pencil and watercolour 245 x 158 mm LT
42 photograph Joan Duke
43 pen-and-ink, sepia ink and watercolour 90 x 110 mm NT
44 photograph Joan Duke
45 printed cover WA
46 photograph WA
47 pen-and-ink 88 x 124 mm NT
48 photograph John Heelis
49 photograph NT
50 sepia ink and watercolour 112 x 93 mm NT
51 pencil and watercolour 120 x 180 mm V&A
52 photograph WA
53 pen-and-ink and watercolour 168 x 133 mm NT
54 photograph *The Horn Book*
55 pen-and-ink, sepia ink and watercolour 82 x 85 mm NT
56 photograph Jean Holland
57 photograph Betty Hart
58 pencil 190 x 160 mm LT
59 pencil 184 x 134 mm LT
60 watercolour 230 x 292 mm V&A
61 watercolour 350 x 254 mm V&A
62 pen-and-ink 180 x 115 mm V&A
63 sepia pen-and-ink 126 x 167 mm V&A
64 sepia pen-and-ink 126 x 167 mm V&A
65 pencil over fawn wash on card 85 x 120 mm V&A
66 watercolour 155 x 150 mm V&A
67 watercolour 100 x 50 mm V&A
68 pen-and-ink 220 x 158 mm V&A
69 pencil and watercolour on blue-grey paper 162 x 53 mm V&A
70 ink 169 x 56 mm V&A
71 pencil 50 x 80 mm V&A
72 pencil 178 x 110 mm V&A
73 pen-and-ink 78 x 178 mm V&A
74 violet ink transfer 115 x 118 mm V&A
75 watercolour 85 x 160 mm V&A
76 pencil and watercolour 130 x 152 mm LT
77 photograph V&A

78 etching 225 x 350 mm private collection
79 watercolour 168 x 240 mm V&A
80 colour printed 180 x 180 mm (page size) NAL
81 watercolour 150 x 150 mm V&A
82 printed page 204 x 237 mm (page size) NAL
83 printed page 204 x 237 mm (page size) NAL
84 printed page 230 x 200 mm (page size) NAL
85 photograph V&A
86 printed illustration 100 x 100 mm NAL
87 pencil and watercolour 200 x 230 mm V&A
88 pencil 180 x 83 mm V&A
89 pen-and-ink and watercolour 90 x 60 mm (card size) WA
90 pen-and-ink and watercolour 90 x 60 mm (card size) V&A
91 watercolour 106 x 83 mm WA
92 pen-and-ink and watercolour mounted on card 152 x 112 mm V&A
93 pen-and-ink and watercolour 66 x 66 mm (mouse in nest) 68 x 115 mm (open nest) V&A
94 crayon 200 x 180 mm V&A
95 pen-and-ink with grey wash and chalky highlights 189 x 144 mm V&A
96 pen-and-ink and grey wash 189 x 146 mm V&A
97 pen-and-ink and watercolour mounted on card 150 x 150 mm V&A
98 pen-and-ink and watercolour mounted on card 150 x 150 mm V&A
99 pencil and pen-and-ink 85 x 175 mm V&A
100 pen-and-ink 200 x 160 mm V&A
101 pen-and-ink and watercolour mounted on linen with silk tassled loop 175 x 252 mm V&A
102 pen-and-ink and watercolour mounted on linen with silk tassled loop 175 x 252 mm V&A
103 watercolour 92 x 111 mm TG
104 watercolour 86 x 127 mm V&A
105 watercolour 87 x 127 mm V&A
106 watercolour 92 x 47 mm LT
107 sepia ink and watercolour 95 x 85 mm NT
108 watercolour 102 x 68 mm V&A
109 pen-and-ink and watercolour 110 x 72 mm V&A
110 watercolour 93 x 68 mm V&A
111 watercolour 84 x 144 mm V&A
112 pen-and-ink and watercolour 68 x 60 mm V&A
113 pencil and watercolour 114 x 70 mm V&A
114 printed cover 246 x 185 mm NAL
115 pencil and watercolour 75 x 70 mm V&A
116 pencil and pen-and-ink 52 x 140 mm V&A
117 pen-and-ink and watercolour 90 x 60 mm V&A
118 pen-and-ink and watercolour 132 x 116 mm NT
119 pencil and pen-and-ink 138 x 107 mm V&A
120 sepia ink, pen-and-ink and sepia wash 180 x 240 mm WA
121 pen-and-ink and watercolour 139 x 278 mm V&A
122 pen-and-ink 50 x 118 mm WA
123 sepia ink, pen-and-ink, sepia wash and watercolour 212 x 167 mm V&A
124 pen-and-ink 132 x 173 mm LT

125 pen-and-ink and watercolour 115 x 72 mm V&A
126 pen-and-ink and watercolour 100 x 77 mm V&A
127 pen-and-ink and watercolour with white highlights 80 x 65 mm V&A
128 sepia ink, sepia wash and watercolour 115 x 200 mm LT
129 pen-and-ink 130 x 127 mm WA
130 sepia ink and watercolour 93 x 73 mm NT
131 pen-and-ink and watercolour 95 x 77 mm V&A
132 pen-and-ink and watercolour 190 x 130 mm LT
133 pen-and-ink 116 x 144 mm WA
134 pencil and pen-and-ink 242 x 224 mm LT
135 pencil and pen-and-ink 175 x 268 mm LT
136 pencil, pen-and-ink and watercolour 150 x 203 mm LT
137 pen-and-ink and watercolour 228 x 160 mm V&A
138 pen-and-ink and watercolour 84 x 70 mm LT
139 pen-and-ink and watercolour 84 x 70 mm LT
140 pen-and-ink 156 x 104 mm V&A
141 detail, pencil and pen-and-ink 23 x 45 mm V&A
142 pencil, pen-and-ink and watercolour 100 x 155 mm V&A
143 watercolour 28 x 109 mm LT
144 pen-and-ink and watercolour 214 x 267 mm V&A
145 pen-and-ink and watercolour 168 x 128 mm NT
146 pen-and-ink and grisaille with white highlights 81 x 115 mm V&A
147 grisaille with white highlights 218 x 288 mm LT
148 pen-and-ink and watercolour 256 x 190 mm V&A
149 sepia ink and watercolour 85 x 78 mm NT
150 pencil and ink 162 x 150 mm V&A
151 pencil, pen-and-ink and watercolour 302 x 250 mm V&A
152 detail, pen-and-ink and watercolour 140 x 233 mm LT
153 lithograph 353 x 212 mm V&A
154 detail, pen-and-ink 76 x 118 mm LT
155 pencil and watercolour 61 x 71 mm V&A
156 pencil 240 x 152 mm LT
157 pen-and-ink 207 x 182 mm V&A
158 pencil and pen-and-ink 108 x 110 mm V&A
159 pen-and-ink and watercolour 52 x 72 mm LT
160 detail, pencil and sepia ink 167 x 110 mm V&A
161 watercolour 157 x 100 mm LT
162 pencil and watercolour 190 x 120 mm V&A
163 pen-and-ink and watercolour 101 x 75 mm NT
164 pen-and-ink 65 x 117 mm WA
165 pencil 163 x 114 mm LT
166 pen-and-ink 32 x 95 mm WA
167 pencil 199 x 252 mm V&A
168 pencil, pen-and-ink and watercolour 69 x 217 mm LT
169 pen-and-ink and grisaille with white highlights 187 x 138 mm V&A
170 watercolour 127 x 102 mm WA
171 watercolour 127 x 102 mm WA
172 sepia ink and watercolour 243 x 193 mm LT
173 pen-and-ink and watercolour 83 x 84 mm NT
174 detail, watercolour 96 x 150 mm AT
175 pencil and watercolour 283 x 210 mm V&A
176 pen-and-ink and watercolour 168 x 128 mm NT
177 pencil, pen-and-ink and watercolour 145 x 248 mm V&A

178 pen-and-ink and watercolour 168 x 128 mm NT
179 watercolour 106 x 110 mm LT
180 pen-and-ink and grisaille with white highlights 105 x 147 mm NT
181 pen-and-ink and watercolour 157 x 182 mm NT
182 pen-and-ink and watercolour 230 x 148 mm private collection
183 detail, pencil and watercolour 216 x 364 mm LT
184 watercolour 201 x 170 mm NT
185 watercolour 176 x 203 mm AT
186 watercolour 157 x 252 mm AT
187 watercolour 157 x 248 mm AT
188 pen-and-ink 144 x 108 mm WA
189 watercolour 150 x 188 mm AT
190 watercolour 133 x 138 mm AT
191 watercolour 234 x 187 mm AT
192 watercolour 264 x 260 mm AT
193 pencil and watercolour 185 x 165 mm V&A
194 watercolour 100 x 140 mm V&A
195 wash, pencil and watercolour 240 x 275 mm V&A
196 pen-and-ink and watercolour 90 x 60 mm V&A
197 watercolour 93 x 182 mm LT
198 pen-and-ink, monochrome wash and white highlights 75 x 122 mm V&A
199 ink WA
200 printer's proof with ink 140 x 100 mm V&A
201 printed cover WA
202 printed pages WA
203 oil on canvas 1156 x 641 mm TG
204 watercolour 98 x 74 mm WA
205 watercolour 60 x 75 mm V&A
206 watercolour [size unknown] WA
207 watercolour 87 x 78 mm WA
208 watercolour 85 x 70 mm LT
209 printed cover WA
210 pen-and-ink and watercolour 161 x 124 mm V&A
211 watercolour [size unknown] WA
212 watercolour [size unknown] WA
213 watercolour 70 x 70 mm WA
214 watercolour 100 x 82 mm WA
215 watercolour 102 x 80 mm NT
216 photograph WA
217 printed card 132 x 190 mm V&A
218 printed pages WA
219 pen-and-ink and watercolour 80 x 91 mm NT
220 pen-and-ink and watercolour 155 x 180 mm NT
221 pen-and-ink and watercolour 95 x 106 mm NT
222 watercolour 111 x 92 mm TG
223 pencil 181 x 110 mm NT
224 watercolour 112 x 83 mm WA
225 pen-and-ink and watercolour 83 x 99 mm V&A
226 pencil and watercolour 130 x 130 mm; 145 x 145 mm V&A
227 watercolour 111 x 92 mm TG
228 watercolour 111 x 92 mm TG
229 watercolour and pen-and-ink 98 x 82 mm V&A
230 watercolour 80 x 77 mm NT
231 pen-and-ink 225 x 178 mm V&A

232 watercolour 82 x 104 mm WA
233 watercolour 125 x 90 mm WA
234 watercolour 140 x 227 mm NT
235 watercolour 108 x 88 mm NT
236 pen-and-ink and watercolour 93 x 85 mm NT
237 pencil and sepia ink 145 x 264 mm V&A
238 detail, colour wash with pencil 168 x 111 mm V&A
239 photograph NT
240 watercolour 90 x 130 mm NT
241 pencil 100 x 80 mm V&A
242 pen-and-ink and watercolour 93 x 77 mm NT
243 watercolour 226 x 190 mm LT
244 watercolour 228 x 190 mm V&A
245 pen-and-ink and watercolour 106 x 86 mm NT
246 pencil and pen-and-ink 70 x 43 mm V&A
247 sepia ink and watercolour 188 x 280 mm V&A
248 pen-and-ink and watercolour 206 x 160 mm V&A
249 pencil, pen-and-ink and watercolour 104 x 88 mm V&A
250 pen-and-ink and watercolour 132 x 116 mm NT
251 pen-and-ink and watercolour 94 x 113 mm NT
252 pen-and-ink and watercolour 86 x 102 mm NT
253 pencil, pen-and-ink and watercolour on card 120 x 110 mm V&A
254 detail, pencil and watercolour 135 x 98 mm V&A
255 pencil and watercolour 130 x 80 mm NT
256 watercolour 123 x 102 mm NT
257 sepia pen-and-ink 270 x 206 mm LT
258 pencil, pen-and-ink and watercolour 190 x 225 mm V&A
259 pen-and-ink and watercolour 136 x 124 mm NT
260 pencil 118 x 95 mm V&A
261 pencil 74 x 70 mm NT
262 pen-and-ink 90 x 125 mm NT
263 pen-and-ink and watercolour 50 x 47 mm V&A
264 sepia ink and watercolour 156 x 181 mm V&A
265 pen-and-ink and watercolour 168 x 128 mm NT
266 pencil and sepia ink 188 x 197 mm V&A
267 pen-and-ink and watercolour 168 x 128 mm NT
268 detail, pencil 204 x 168 mm (sheet-size) V&A
269 pen-and-ink 80 x 170 mm V&A
270 pencil 111 x 93 mm WA
271 watercolour 110 x 94 mm NT
272 ink 42 x 90 mm V&A
273 ink 38 x 124 mm V&A
274 pen-and-ink and watercolour 227 x 290 mm V&A
275 pen-and-ink and watercolour 97 x 95 mm V&A
276 pencil 118 x 108 mm WA
277 sepia ink and watercolour 105 x 85 mm NT
278 sepia ink and watercolour 93 x 80 mm NT
279 sepia ink and watercolour 103 x 90 mm NT
280 sepia ink and watercolour 55 x 40 mm V&A
281 pen-and-ink, sepia ink and watercolour 107 x 87 mm NT
282 pen-and-ink, sepia ink and watercolour 108 x 86 mm NT
283 pen-and-ink, sepia ink and watercolour 110 x 92 mm NT

284 pen-and-ink, sepia ink and watercolour 106 x 90 mm NT

285 sepia ink and watercolour 106 x 89 mm NT

286 pen-and-ink and watercolour 112 x 90 mm NT

287 pencil 87 x 71 mm WA

288 pen-and-ink and watercolour 110 x 85 mm NT

289 pen-and-ink and watercolour 90 x 111 mm NT

290 pen-and-ink and watercolour 120 x 98 mm NT

291 pen-and-ink and watercolour 103 x 110 mm NT

292 pencil 123 x 29 mm private collection

293 pen-and-ink and watercolour 130 x 70 mm NT

294 pen-and-ink 89 x 149 mm V&A

295 pen-and-ink 60 x 90 mm WA

296 watercolour 155 x 126 mm NT

297 photograph V&A

298 watercolour 162 x 126 mm NT

299 watercolour on card 160 x 130 mm V&A

300 printed page 204 x 237 mm NAL

301 watercolour 132 x 152 mm NT

302 pen-and-ink 65 x 95 mm V&A

303 watercolour 96 x 86 mm BM

304 sepia ink and watercolour 157 x 126 mm NT

305 sepia ink and watercolour 152 x 128 mm NT

306 sepia ink 85 x 108 mm NT

307 watercolour 254 x 178 mm LT

308 watercolour 150 x 125 mm NT

309 watercolour 118 x 140 mm V&A

310 pencil 85 x 140 mm NT

311 sepia ink 83 x 108 mm NT

312 pencil and pen-and-ink 34 x 58 mm V&A

313 watercolour 57 x 65 mm V&A

314 pen-and-ink and watercolour 90 x 70 mm NT

315 watercolour 105 x 85 mm NT

316 pencil and sepia ink 80 x 200 mm LT

317 sepia ink and watercolour 112 x 93 mm NT

318 sepia ink and watercolour 93 x 113 mm NT

319 pencil and sepia ink 76 x 91 mm V&A

320 printer's proof 41 x 56 mm V&A

321 sepia ink and watercolour 112 x 93 mm NT

322 pencil 117 x 95 mm V&A

323 pencil, sepia ink and watercolour 91 x 77 mm LT

324 sepia ink and watercolour 93 x 113 mm NT

325 sepia ink 68 x 105 mm NT

326 sepia ink 54 x 99 mm NT

327 watercolour 147 x 210 mm V&A

328 sepia ink 59 x 103 mm NT

329 pen-and-ink 140 x 250 mm V&A

330 sepia ink and watercolour 112 x 92 mm NT

331 sepia ink and watercolour 158 x 127 mm LT

332 sepia ink 66 x 102 mm NT

333 sepia ink and watercolour 111 x 93 mm NT

334 pencil, pen-and-ink and watercolour 112 x 93 mm V&A

335 pen-and-ink 158 x 123 mm V&A

336 pen-and-ink and watercolour 118 x 115 mm V&A

337 pen-and-ink and watercolour 136 x 84 mm V&A

338 sepia ink and watercolour 108 x 90 mm NT

339 pencil and sepia ink 118 x 96 mm NT

340 watercolour mounted on board 115 x 160 mm V&A

341 sepia ink and watercolour 149 x 190 mm NT

342 watercolour 92 x 115 mm LT

343 watercolour 90 x 114 mm LT

344 pen-and-ink, sepia ink and watercolour 75 x 94 mm NT

345 pen-and-ink and watercolour 185 x 157 mm LT

346 pen-and-ink and watercolour 196 x 167 mm LT

347 pencil, sepia ink and watercolour 202 x 152 mm LT

348 pen-and-ink, sepia ink and watercolour 92 x 79 mm NT

349 pen-and-ink, sepia ink and watercolour 85 x 80 mm NT

350 pen-and-ink and watercolour 94 x 139 mm NT

351 pen-and-ink and watercolour 158 x 205 mm LT

352 pen-and-ink and watercolour 227 x 278 mm NT

353 pen-and-ink and watercolour 157 x 181 mm NT

354 pen-and-ink and watercolour 157 x 183 mm V&A

355 pen-and-ink and watercolour 157 x 181 mm NT

356 pen-and-ink and watercolour 157 x 182 mm LT

357 pen-and-ink 50 x 72 mm V&A

358 pen-and-ink 55 x 78 mm WA

359 pen-and-ink 55 x 78 mm WA

360 pen-and-ink 164 x 123 mm WA

361 pencil 200 x 160 mm WA

362 pen-and-ink [size unknown] WA

363 pen-and-ink and watercolour 177 x 134 mm NT

364 pen-and-ink 132 x 107 mm WA

365 pen-and-ink 130 x 125 mm WA

366 pen-and-ink 51 x 104 mm WA

367 pen-and-ink and watercolour 169 x 134 mm NT

368 pencil and pen-and-ink 155 x 135 mm V&A

369 printed page 136 x 92 mm V&A

370 sepia ink 57 x 100 mm NT

371 watercolour 70 x 74 mm WA

372 pencil and watercolour 101 x 65 mm V&A

373 photograph V&A

374 pastel 275 x 210 mm NT

375 photograph V&A

376 watercolour 432 x 584 mm TG

377 watercolour 240 x 165 mm The John Ruskin Museum, Brantwood

378 pencil and sepia ink 252 x 206 mm V&A

379 pencil and watercolour 161 x 205 mm LT

380 pencil and watercolour 291 x 228 mm V&A

381 watercolour 250 x 115 mm V&A

382 watercolour 240 x 413 mm The Whitworth Art Gallery

383 coloured engraving 120 x 244 mm AT

384 pen-and-ink and watercolour 227 x 291 mm V&A

385 sepia ink and watercolour 293 x 228 mm LT

386 pencil and watercolour 255 x 355 mm V&A

387 pencil and sepia ink 132 x 215 mm LT

388 photograph V&A

389 photograph NT

390 pen-and-ink and watercolour 122 x 110 mm NT

391 sepia ink and watercolour 86 x 79 mm NT

392 pen-and-ink, sepia ink and watercolour 106 x 89 mm NT

393 sepia ink and watercolour 72 x 69 mm NT

394 pencil and watercolour 254 x 178 mm V&A

395 pencil and watercolour 239 x 185 mm V&A

396 pencil and watercolour 255 x 186 mm V&A

397 pencil and watercolour 202 x 179 mm V&A
398 oil on canvas 600 x 900 mm The John Ruskin Museum, Brantwood
399 pencil and watercolour 228 x 190 mm LT
400 photograph NT
401 pen-and-ink and watercolour 112 x 90 mm NT
402 pencil and watercolour 176 x 251 mm V&A
403 photograph NT
404 sepia ink and watercolour 159 x 128 mm V&A
405 pencil and watercolour 255 x 179 mm LT
406 pen-and-ink and watercolour 115 x 95 mm NT
407 oil on canvas 1010 x 1680 mm NT
408 pen-and-ink and watercolour 168 x 128 mm NT
409 printer's proof 43 x 52 mm V&A
410 pen-and-ink 74 x 130 mm WA
411 pencil and watercolour 186 x 253 mm V&A
412 pen-and-ink and watercolour 104 x 92 mm NT
413 pencil 228 x 202 mm V&A
414 pencil 132 x 147 mm V&A
415 photograph NT/Robert Thrift
416 watercolour 400 x 295 mm Abbot Hall Art Gallery
417 watercolour 380 x 300 mm Abbot Hall Art Gallery
418 photograph NT/Robert Thrift
419 pen-and-ink 87 x 132 mm WA
420 photograph NT
421 pen-and-ink 83 x 135 mm WA
422 pastel on brown paper 210 x 168 mm V&A
423 pencil and sepia ink 76 x 90 mm LT
424 pen-and-ink 130 x 130 mm WA
425 watercolour 195 x 190 mm AT
426 photograph NT/Robert Thrift
427 pen-and-ink 50 x 120 mm WA
428 photograph NT/Robert Thrift
429 photograph NT
430 pen-and-ink 60 x 133 mm WA
431 pen-and-ink and watercolour 110 x 100 mm NT
432 watercolour 310 x 385 mm Abbot Hall Art Gallery
433 photograph V&A
434 sepia ink 66 x 102 mm NT
435 sepia ink and watercolour 158 x 127 mm NT
436 sepia ink and watercolour 115 x 135 mm NT
437 sepia ink and watercolour 133 x 154 mm NT
438 pen-and-ink, sepia ink and watercolour 107 x 88 mm NT
439 oil on canvas 630 x 760 mm Robert Steele Gilchrist
440 watercolour 760 x 630 mm NT
441 photograph NT
442 watercolour 375 x 550 mm Heaton Cooper Studio
443 pen-and-ink 67 x 75 mm V&A
444 pen-and-ink, sepia ink and watercolour 90 x 75 mm NT
445 pencil and watercolour 178 x 148 mm LT
446 watercolour 250 x 375 mm private collection
447 photograph NT/Robert Thrift
448 photograph NT/Robert Thrift
449 pen-and-ink 85 x 117 mm NT
450 photograph NT/Robert Thrift
451 pencil reduced to photogravure 34 x 26 mm Ruskin Museum, Coniston
452 watercolour 360 x 470 mm private collection
453 watercolour 127 x 182 mm V&A
454 pen-and-ink and watercolour 98 x 118 mm NT
455 pen-and-ink 87 x 146 mm WA

BIBLIOGRAPHY

BATTRICK, ELIZABETH: *The Real World of Beatrix Potter*, National Trust and Jarrold, 1986.

BROOKE, HENRY: *Leslie Brooke and Johnny Crow*, Frederick Warne, 1982.

CAVALIERO, GLEN (ed.): *Beatrix Potter's Journal* (abridged), Frederick Warne, 1986.

CROUCH, MARCUS: *Beatrix Potter*, The Bodley Head, 1960.

GODDEN, RUMER: *The Tale of the Tales*, Frederick Warne, 1971.

GREENE, GRAHAM: *Collected Essays*, The Bodley Head, 1969.

HOBBS, ANNE STEVENSON and WHALLEY, JOYCE IRENE: *Beatrix Potter: The V&A Collection*, The Victoria and Albert Museum and Frederick Warne, 1985.

LANE, MARGARET: *The Magic Years of Beatrix Potter*, Frederick Warne, 1978.

LANE, MARGARET: *The Tale of Beatrix Potter*, revised edition, Penguin, 1985.

LINDER, LESLIE: *The Art of Beatrix Potter*, Frederick Warne, 1955; revised edition, 1972.

LINDER, LESLIE: *The History of the Writings of Beatrix Potter*, Frederick Warne, 1971; revised edition, 1987.

LINDER, LESLIE: *The Journal of Beatrix Potter*, Frederick Warne, 1966.

MALONEY, MARGARET CRAWFORD (ed.): *Dear Ivy, Dear June: Letters from Beatrix Potter*, Toronto Public Library, 1977.

MILLAIS, JOHN GUILLE: *The Life and Letters of Sir John Everett Millais*, 2 vols. Methuen, 1899.

MITCHELL, W. R.: *Beatrix Potter Remembered*, Dalesman Books, 1987.

MORSE, JANE CROWELL (ed.): *Beatrix Potter's Americans: Selected Letters*, The Horn Book, 1982.

PARKER, ULLA HYDE: *Cousin Beatie*, Frederick Warne, 1981.

RAWNSLEY, ELEANOR F.: *Canon Rawnsley*, Maclehose, Jackson, 1923.

TAYLOR, JUDY: *Beatrix Potter: Artist, Storyteller and Countrywoman*, Frederick Warne, 1986.

TAYLOR, JUDY: *That naughty rabbit: Beatrix Potter and Peter Rabbit*, Frederick Warne, 1987.

WHALLEY, JOYCE IRENE and BARTLETT, WYNNE K.: *The Derwentwater Sketchbook*, Frederick Warne, 1984.

All the Little Books are currently in print with Frederick Warne, and so are *The Fairy Caravan*, *The Tale of Tuppenny*, *The Sly Old Cat*, *The Tale of The Faithful Dove*, *Country Tales* and *Wag-by-Wall*.

INDEX

Figures in **bold** refer to illustrations

A., Mrs, *art teacher*, 13, 39
Abraham, George (*Motorways in Lakeland*), 185
Ackland, Judith, 189; **416**
Aesop, 29, 64–6, 153, 156; *see also* fables
Aesthetic Movement, 45
agricultural shows, sales and fairs, 31–2, 190, 192, 195, 207; **52, 56, 420**
agriculture, in general, 177, 195–6, 203; farm economy, 196; estate management, 195–7; *see also* National Trust; crops inc. peat, 176–7, 191, 201, 202; *see also* Lake District; National Trust; Potter, H. B. (as farmer) *and under names of livestock*
algae, 90
Alice's Adventures in Wonderland, 55, 69–70, 72, 77, 121; **136–9**
almanac, *see* Peter Rabbit's Almanac
alphabet designs, 88
Ambleside, 161, 162, 163, 171, 192, 196, 207; Bridge House, **451**; The Croft, 170; Centenary Exhibition, 88; Ginnet's Travelling Circus, 162; *see also* Armitt Library
Ancrum, Roxburghshire, 29
Andersen, Hans Christian, 62
Angel, Marie, 168; **371**
animals, *see under book titles and names of animals*; exotic, 7, 39, 162; **63**; stuffed, 42, 73–4; **147**
Appley Dapply's Nursery Rhymes, 8, 28, 55, 58, 59, 124, 129, 153–6, 159, 160; **110, 117, 263, 341–3**; privately printed edition (idea for), 154; 1905 Book of Rhymes, 59, 62, 70, 129, 153–5, 160; **329, 335–40, 347**; *see also* rhymes
'*Arabian Nights, The*', 63–4; 'Forty Thieves', 63–4; **128**
archaeology, 7, 15, 93–4, 170, 193; Lake District, 180, 189, 193, Cumberland and Westmorland Antiquarian and Archaeological Society, 180; London, 93–4; **190–92**, Bucklersbury, 93–4; **190–92**, Walbrook, 94; **192**
Aris, Ernest A., 130, 153
Armitt, Annie Maria, 192–3; Mary Louisa, 192–3; Sophia, 192–3
Armitt Library, Ambleside, 89, 185, 192–3; Beatrix Potter and, 89, 185, 193
Art of Flower Painting, The, 39
Ashieburn, Roxburghshire, 45
astronomy, 94
Auden, Wystan Hugh, 107
Aulnoy, Marie Catherine de la Motte, Countess of, 63

Baddeley, J. B., 172
badgers, 80, 145–8; **318–19, 322, 423**
Banner, Delmar H., 196, 198–200, 202; **29, 439–40**; Josephine (*née* De Vasconcellos), 185, 196, 198–201, 202; **443**
Baring Gould, Sabine, Rev, 60
baths and tubs, as motif, 137, 149; **327**
bats, 14, 16, 42, 77, 81, 82; **76**, long-eared, 42, 77; **155**
Bayliss, Wyke, PRSBA, 100
bears, 144, 145
Beckett, –, *coachman, and family*, 177
Bedford Square, *see* London
Bedford Street, *see* London
beds and bedrooms, as motif, *see* dream and sleep; furniture; interiors
Bedwell Lodge, Hertfordshire, 52, 104; **94–6**
beetles, *see* insects
Benjamin Bounce(r) (Benjamin Bunny), *see* rabbits
Benjamin Bunny, The Tale of, 23, 24, 26, 30, 65, 69, 83, 84, 101, 104, 115–18, 139, 140, 160, 207; **172, 210, 219, 241–9**; toy picture, 82; **101–102**
Bennett, Charles Henry, 64
Berwickshire, 88; Berwick, 92, 104; *see also* Coldstream; Dryburgh Abbey; Lennel
Bewick, Thomas, 72
Bible, 107
Bingham, Clifton [i.e. C.B.], 54
birds, 13, 39, 62, 72, 77, 82, 85, 95, 134, 144, 164, 168; **62–4, 92, 202, 217, 315, 369, 455**; crows, 65–6, 168; **131**; doves and pigeons, 62, 66, 168; **123, 132, 371**; *see also* Faithful Dove, The Tale of the; hawfinches, 72; jackdaws, 57, 72, 124; **112**; jay, 42, 72, 77; kestrel, 72; magpies, 72, 124; **145**; owls, 70, 81, 111–12, 114, 166; **124, 137, 141, 231, 238, 352**; parrots, 72, 77, 164; **419**; peregrine, 168; puffins, 81; robins, 102; **208, 348**; starling, **410**; stork, 66; **34**; thrush, 72; **144**; eggs, 74
Birds' Place, *see* Camfield Place
Birmingham, 181
Birnam, 72, 80, 86; *see also* Heath Park
Blackburn, Jane [i.e. Jemima], 39, 72; *Birds drawn from Nature*, 39, 72; *Pipits, The*, 39; **68**
Blackpool, 34
'Bland, Alexander', 151
'Bluebeard', *see* fairy tales; Sister Anne
boats and boating, 17, 127; **20, 221**; *see also* fish and fishing; 'I saw a ship'; Lear, E.; Little Pig Robinson, The Tale of; picture letters; sea and ships; Windermere
Bodleian Library, 193

Bolton, 198
Bolton, Mr, 158
Bolton Gardens, *see* London
Bonny, Mr, 197
book illustration, in general, 55, 69, 98
Book of Nonsense, The, *see* Lear, E.
Book of Rhymes (1905), *see* Appley Dapply's Nursery Rhymes
Bookshop for Boys and Girls, Boston, 161
borders, decorative, 62, 64, 67, 78, 154, 155; **1, 120, 123–4, 128, 134–5, 137, 157, 335, 338–9, 345–7**
Borrowdale, 172, 177, 187; Borrowdale stone, 180
Boston, 161
Boston, U.S.A., Bookshop for Boys and Girls, 161
Bowness, *see* Windermere
Braithwaite, nr Keswick, 172
Brandelhow Park Estate, Derwentwater, 181
Brantwood, Coniston, 171; **398**
Brathay Bridge, nr Windermere, 149; Brathay Hall, 173
Brefeld, Julius Oscar, 90
'Brer Rabbit', *see* Uncle Remus
bridges, 149, 164, 199, 200; **364, 427, 434, 452**
Bright, John, 9, 12, 66–7
British Aluminium Co., 175
British Museum, 59, 203
British Museum (Natural History), *see* Natural History Museum
Brooke, Leslie L. (*Johnny Crow's Garden*), 123
Browne, Hablot K. ('Phiz'), 46, 55
Browning, Robert, 173
Bucklersbury, City of London, *see* archaeology (London)
buildings, 59, 108, 121, 123, 178, 329; *see also under names of places*
Bull Banks, *see* Sawrey
Bunsen, Robert Wilhelm von, 86, Bunsen burner, 86, 159; **182**
Burlington House, 93; *see also* Royal Academy
Burns, Margaret, 187
Burton, *family*, 19, 131; Fred, *uncle*, 25, 26, 140; Harriet, *aunt*, 80, 140
Burton, Sir Richard Francis, 63
butterflies and moths, *see* insects

Caldecott, Randolph, 11, 45–6, 65, 107, 129, 130, 138–9, 153–4; *Babes in the Wood, The*, 154; *Frog He Would A-Wooing Go, A*, 45–6, 129, 138–9, 154; **82–3, 300**; *Queen of Hearts, The*, 46; **84**; *Sing a Song for Sixpence* [at Hill Top], 45; *Three Jovial Huntsmen*, 45

calico printing, 9, 11, 114; *see also* cotton trade
Calvin, John, 10
Cameron, Miss, *art teacher*, 13, 39
Camfield Place, nr Hatfield, 11–12, 18, 56, 60, 77, 78, 104, 159, 164, 165; **9, 16, 157, 168**, Birds' Place, 79, 165; **10**
cancer, treatments for, 81, 89
candle, as motif, 159; **71, 310, 351**
Cannon, *family*, 26; John, 25, 26, 133, 150–51, 177; Mrs, 133, 177, 184; **406**; Ralph, 133; Betsy, 133
caricatures, by Beatrix Potter, 66, 79, 80–81, 104, 127, 150, 158, 159, 202; **67, 166, 346, 443**; by Bertram Potter, 40; **71**; by Rupert Potter, 37; **63–4**
Carlisle, 9, 21, 180
Carlyle, Thomas, 193
carpet industry, 26, 191
Carr, Rev Mr, 121; Lucie, 121–2; **257**; *see also* Mrs. Tiggy-Winkle, The Tale of
carriages, coaches and carts, *see* travel
'Carrier's Bob', 152
Carroll, Lewis, 55, 69–70; *see also* Alice's Adventures in Wonderland
Carter, Annie B., *see* Moore, Annie B.
Castle Cottage (Castle Farm), Sawrey, 26, 27, 31, 145, 148, 183–4, 187, 191, 199, 203, 207; **49, 433**
Cat Bells, nr Keswick, 121
cats, 24, 46, 62–3, 70, 79, 81, 108, 116, 120, 123–6, 129–33, 134, 136–9, 140–43, 153, 160, 163, 164, 166, 199; **39, 84, 105, 115, 124–7, 141, 162, 217, 219, 266–7, 276–7, 279–84, 295, 299, 302, 304, 306, 308, 329, 334, 355, 392, 408, 424, 435, 438, 448**; Tomasine ('Mary Ellen'), 163, 164; **360, 363**
cattle, 29, 33, 68, 73, 76–7, 133, 150, 206; **2, 39, 55, 154, 401, 427, 431**; *see also* agricultural shows
Cecily Parsley's Nursery Rhymes, 30, 55, 59, 79, 84, 85, 136, 156, 158–61; **181, 220, 350–56**
chairs, *see* furniture
Chambers, Robert, 60
Changing Pictures, 57; **113–14**
Chantrey Bequest, 100
Charles, *see* chickens'
'Cherry Tree Camp', 167
chickens, 124, 133–5, 141, 142, 149, 151, 163, 164, 165, 196; **50, 309, 329, 332, 406, 419, 430–31**; Charles (cock), 152, 163; **332**; Henny Penny, 133, 163; *see also* poultry
children, *see* miniature letters; picture letters; Potter, H. B. (Beatrix Potter and children); toy pictures
children's books, inc. attitudes to, 30, 49, 67, 98, 107–08, 120, 161; *see also* Potter, H. B. (Beatrix Potter and children)
china and pottery, *see* pottery
chipmunks, 144–5; **217, 315, 455**
Christmas and greetings cards, 7, 17, 50–51, 52, 57, 62, 79, 80, 82, 105, 136, 159, 165; **91–3, 110–11, 161, 170–71, 196, 233, 455**; collecting card, 105; **217**

Christmas inc. presents, 22, 30, 32, 78, 82, 85, 109, 111, 129, 150, 158, 165, 168; **110, 159, 167**; carols, 22; stocking; **91**; Father Christmas, **92**; *see also* Rabbits' Christmas Party, The
Christmas tree, 165; **455**
Chuleh, *see* dogs
'Cinderella', *see* fairy tales
circuses, 162; Ginnet's Travelling Circus, 162; *see also* Fairy Caravan, The
Clark, Francis William, of Ulva [*son of cousin Caroline, née Hutton*], 148
clocks, *see* furniture
clogs, 162; **441**
Coates, Henry, 89
Cobden, Richard, 9
Cockermouth, 172
code writing, 14, 40, 161; **70**; *see also* Potter, H. B. (as writer . . . journal)
Coldstream, 88, 91–2; Hatchednize Wood, 88; **185**; *see also* Lennel
collecting card, *see* Christmas and greetings cards
Collingwood, W. G., 178, 180; **398**; William, RWS, 180
Colwith Bridge, nr Little Langdale, 149, 199; **434**
Commons Preservation Society, 172, 175
Coniston inc. Coniston Water, 21, 32, 84, 172, 178, 180, 194, 196, 198, 200; **398**; Coniston Bank, 22; Coniston farms, 197; Coniston Fells, 180; Coniston Hunt, 190; Old Man of Coniston, 125, 164, 200; **43, 377, 430**; *see also* Brantwood; Heathwaite Farm; Mines Ghyll; Monk Coniston Estate; Tarn Hows; Thwaite; Tilberthwaite; Yew Tree Farm
conservation, *see* Lake District; National Trust; Potter, H. B. (as farmer and conservationist)
Constable, John, RA, 47, 107, 173–4; **381**
Coolidge, Henry P., 162
Cooper, Alfred Heaton, 178, 193; William Heaton, 193, 198; **442, 446, 452**
Coronation, 145; *see also* pottery and china
cotton trade, 9; *see also* calico printing; textile industry; wool trade
country dancing, *see* dance
Country Life (journal), 152
cows, *see* cattle
cowslip wine, 85, 145, 160; **181**
Crabtree & Evelyn, 136
Crane, Walter, 45, 46, 64, 153–4, 170; *Baby's Bouquet, The*, 153; *Baby's Opera, The*, 39, 45, 153, 154; **80–81**; *Baby's Own Aesop, The*, 153; *Frog Prince, The*, 153; *Sleeping Beauty, The*, 153
Cridland, Margery, (*née* McKay), *see* McKay, M.
Croft, – , 201
Crompton, Abraham, *great-grandfather*, 14, 32; Alice, *great-grandmother*, 32; Jessie, *see* Potter, J.
Crossland, J. H., 180
Crosthwaite, nr Keswick, 21, 172, 187
Cruikshank, George, 129
Cumberland, 203; **416**; *see also* Lake District

Cumberland and Westmorland Antiquarian and Archaeological Society, *see* archaeology (Lake District)
Cupboard Love (B. Rivière), 40, 125; **265**

Dalguise House, nr Dunkeld, 12–13, 14, 18, 38, 42, 60, 71, 74, 77, 85, 86, 91, 169; **13, 85, 375**
dance, as motif, 57, 61, 62, 105, 130, 150, 151, 152, 162, 165, 168; **3, 31, 107, 116, 122, 158, 229–30, 328–9, 333**; country dancing, 29, 165, 185; *see also* Tales of Beatrix Potter, The (ballet film)
Dawson, Dr and Mrs, 169
deer, 12, 72–4, 81, 165; **146**; *see also* hunting
De la Mare, Walter, 62
'Demerara Sugar', 165
Denbighshire, 19, 92; *see also* Gwaynynog
Depression, The, 195, 196
Derwentwater, 17, 84, 111, 115, 121, 132, 172, 176, 181; **234–7, 240, 399**; Derwent Bay, 112, 114, 115; **234–5**; Friar's Crag, 172, 180; St Herbert's Island ('Owl Island'), 17, 111–12; **236–7**; Walla Crag, 17, 164; **421**; Derwentwater sketchbook, 115, 118, 120, 121, 122; **234, 240, 255, 261**; *see also* Brandelhow Park Estate; Fawe Park; Gutherscale; Lingholm; Skelgill
Dickens, Charles, 69
dinner, place- and menu cards, 50, 70; **89–90**
Dinting Lodge, Glossop, 37
dogs, 40, 66, 72, 79, 124, 133, 134, 136, 158, 162, 163, 167; **65, 205–06, 304–05, 308, 424**; Spot (spaniel), 79–80; **22**; sheepdogs, 66, 79, 163, 192; **421, 424**, Kep, 133, 134, 136, 161; **2, 49, 403, 412**, Nip, 163; **424**, Scotch Fly, 163; **361, 424**; hounds, 134, 136, 167; **72, 366, 412**; Pekinese, 32; **57**, Chuleh, 32, 34; **54, 57**, Tzusee, 32, 34; **54, 57**; Pomeranians, 24, 124, Darkie, 124, Duchess, 24, 85, 124–5; **176, 178, 262, 265**; terriers, 134, 137, 140–41; **154**, Sandy, 163, 164; **364**
dolls, 23, 55, 105, 119, 136, 151; **38, 308, 311**; *see also* doll's house; merchandise; Two Bad Mice, The Tale of
doll's house, inc. furniture, 24, 83, 118–19; **38, 118, 250–51**; *see also* Tale of Two Bad Mice, The
donkeys, 64; **128, 424**
Doré, Gustave, 46–7, 55
dormice, *see* mice
Dover, Kent, 168
Doyle, Richard, 46
dream and sleep, as motif, 62, 67, 78, 86, 149, 160, 164, 166; **37, 50, 75, 91, 118, 120, 123, 134, 138–9, 157, 160, 182, 194, 353, 363**
'Dream of Toasted Cheese, A', 78, 86, 159; **182**
Dryburgh Abbey, Berwickshire, 60
Duchess, *see* dogs
ducks, 37, 68, 132–6; **2, 43, 44, 72–3, 80–81, 89, 163, 210, 217, 285–8, 290–3, 316,**

401, 406, 431, 454–5; *see also* poultry
Duke, Captain Kenneth W. G., 203; National Trust and, 203; Mary Stephanie (*née* Hyde-Parker), *see* Hyde-Parker, S.
Dunkeld, 12, 18, 86, 126, 169; *see also* Dalguise House; Eastwood

Eastbourne, 72
Easter customs inc. eggs, 136, 152; Easter Ledger Pudding, 85
Eastwood, Dunkeld, 18, 21, 86, 97; **199**
Edinburgh, 16
Edwards, Mary Stella, 189; **417**
Eesbridge, Sawrey, 364
Eeswyke (Ees Wyke), Sawrey, *see* Lakefield
Elterwater Common, 80
Ennerdale, Show, 190
Eskdale, 80, 190; Woolpack Show, **52**; *see also* Penny Hill Farm
Esthwaite Water, 20, 63, 128, 134–5, 145, 147, 206; **187**, **274**, **316**, **320**, **334**, **386**, **423**, **453–4**
Evans, Edmund, 102

fables, 29, 59, 64–6, 133, 156, 158; 'Ant and Grasshopper' ('Grasshopper Belle and Susan Emmett'), 66; 'Belling the Cat', 66, 162; **133**; 'Fox and Crow' ('Folly of Vanity', 'Tale of Jenny Crow'), 65–6, 168; **131**; 'Fox and Grapes', 66; **132**; 'Fox and Stork' ('King Stork'), 66; **34**; 'Tale of the Birds and Mr. Tod', 65–6; 'Town and Country Mouse', 130; **345–6**, *see also* Johnny Town-Mouse, The Tale of; 'Wolf in Sheep's Clothing' ('Tale of Daisy and Dumpling'), 65, 162, 164; **129**; 'Wolf! Wolf!', 66
Fairy Caravan, The, 32, 57, 61, 62, 64, 65, 66, 79, 80, 84, 91, 152, 161–8, 191–2, 194; **3**, **10**, **122**, **129**, **133**, **164**, **188**, **357**, **359–60**, **362–6**, **410**, **419**, **421**, **424**, **427**, **430**; privately bound edition, 161, 162, 163; **359**; sequel to, *see* 'Cherry Tree Camp'; Sister Anne; 'Solitary Mouse, The'; 'Walk Amongst the Funguses, A'
'Fairy Clogs, The', 152
'Fairy in the Oak, The', 64, 82, 163
fairy painting, 55
fairy tales and legends, fairies, magic and hauntings, 10, 55, 59–64, 66, 82, 108, 111, 153, 162, 164, 165, 167, 185; 'Bluebeard', 64, 167; *see also* Sister Anne; 'Bonny Annot', 162; 'Cinderella', 60, 61, 62; **120–21**; 'Forty Thieves', 63–4; **128**; 'Frog Prince', 63, 153; 'Puss in Boots', 60, 62–3, 69, 153; **124**; 'Red Riding Hood', 60, 63, 64, 133, 167; 'Sleeping Beauty', 62, 153; **123**; 'Tom Thumb', 63; 'White Cat', 63; **125–7**; 'Yellow Dwarf', 63; *see also* Fairy Caravan, The; 'Fairy Clogs, The'; 'Fairy in the Oak, The'; 'Kitty-in-Boots'; 'Oakmen, The'; Peermingle'; Sister Anne; Wag-by-Wall
Faithful Dove, The Tale of the, 62, 168; **371**
Falmouth, 70, 72
fantasy pictures, 39, 49–70 *passim*, 78, 82, 85, 86, 95, 112, 159; **95–8**, **106**, **112**,

157, 167, 169, 180, 182; *see also* alphabet designs; Christmas and greetings cards; fungi (in fantasy); picture letters; toy pictures, *etc*
farm buildings, *see* buildings; interiors; Lake District (vernacular buildings); National Trust *and also under names of places*
farming, *see* agricultural shows; agriculture; Potter, H. B. (as farmer)
Far Sawrey, *see* Sawrey
Fawe Park, Derwentwater, 115, 116–17, 121, 140, 172; **240–45**, **247**, **378**
ferns, 86, 87, 162, 164; **184**
ferrets, 165
Fielding, Henry, 119
Fierce Bad Rabbit, The Story of A, 26, 83, 129–30; **278**
Findlay, Dr W. P. K. (*Wayside and Woodland Fungi*), 88
fireplaces, *see* interiors
fish and fishing, 12, 17, 18, 55, 67, 68, 72, 127, 129; **11**, **13**, **269**, **337**; *see also* 'Frog he would a-fishing go, A'; Mr. Jeremy Fisher, The Tale of
Flaxman, John, 55
'Flittermouse and Fluttermouse', 77
Flodden Field, Northumberland, 93
Flopsy Bunnies, The Tale of the, 26, 83, 104, 139–40, 146, 203; **210**, **303**
flowers, *see* plants and flowers
Folkestone, 168
folklore, 55; *see also* fairy tales
Footpath Association, 182
fossils, 19, 21, 72, 74, 91–3; **32**, **189**; *see also* geology
foxes, 65–6, 67–9, 71, 80, 81, 133–6, 145–8, 164; **34**, **89**, **129**, **131–2**, **134–5**, **286–9**, **316–18**, **322**, **365**, **423**; *see also* hunting
Foyers, Falls of, 175
'Frog he would a-fishing go, A', 54, 126–7; **99**, **269**
Frog He Would A-Wooing Go, A, *see* Caldecott, R.
frogs, 14, 16, 26, 45–6, 54, 72, 126–9; **82–3**, **99**, **210**, **217**, **221**, **268**, **270–71**, **275**, **300**, **304**, **337**, **455**; Punch, 16; *see also* fairy tales
Froswick, 189; **410**
fruit, 66, 71, 83–4, 102, 160; **17**, **60**, **101–102**, **132**, **173–4**, **356**; *see also* trees
fungi, 7, 8, 19–20, 21, 49, 85–91, 92, 93, 94, 165, 182, 193; **26**, **33**, **183–8**, **425**; dry rot (*Serpula lacrymans*), 89; *Penicillium*, 89; spores, germination of, 19–20, 87, 90–91; as environmental indicators, 89; hallucinogenic effects of, 91; **187**; in fantasy, 60, 62, 91; **188**, **336**, **339**; *see also* 'Walk Amongst the Funguses, A'
furniture, 49, 123, 125, 187, 196, 199, 204; **227**, **265**, **324**, **330**, **354**, **413–14**, **437**; collected by Beatrix Potter, 31, 187, 199; beds, 78, 146, 148, 160, 164, 178; **9**, **37**, **47**, **157**, **319**, **363**, **391**, **438**; chairs, 56, 150, 151, 196, 199; **104–105**, **113**, **180**, **279**, **282**, **330**, **344**, **378**, **437**; clocks, 39,

61, 196; **68**, **120**, **224**, **299–300**, **354**, **408**, **414**; *see also* Wag-by-Wall; mirrors, 124; **262–3**; *see also* doll's house; interiors

Gaddum, Walter, *cousin*, 54; **195**
'Game of Peter Rabbit, The', *see* merchandise
gardens and gardening, 26, 52, 55, 68, 69, 83–5, 104, 116–17, 125, 130–31, 133, 140, 158, 159, 165, 178, 184, 187, 199; **10**, **136**, **213–14**, **240–5**, **264**, **281**, **283–4**, **303**, **349–50**, **384–5**, **392**; *see also* fruit; plants and flowers; trees; vegetables
Gaskell, William, 12, 95; **12**
geese, 59, 160; **92**, **353**; *see also* poultry
geology, 15, 49, 81, 91–3, 94; *see also* fossils
Gerard, John (*Herbal*), 85
Gilpin, William (*Picturesque Tours*), 174
Ginger and Pickles, 26, 104, 140–43, 144, 159, 163; **304–311**; *see also* Sawrey ('Ginger and Pickles')
Girtin, Thomas, 199
Glossop, 9; *see also* Dinting Lodge
Gloucestershire, 19, 22; Gloucester, 108, 109–110; *see also* Harescombe Grange; Hutton, *family*; Tailor of Gloucester, The
'Goosey, goosey, gander,' 160; **353**
Gowbarrow Park, Ullswater, 181, 182; **382**
Grahame, Kenneth, 67
Grandville, J. J., 66
Grasmere, Hall, 193; Allan Bank, 187; Grasmere Dialect Plays, 193
Graythwaite, 167
Greenaway, Kate, 155–6, 201
Greene, Graham, 107, 145, 151
greetings cards, *see* Christmas and greetings cards
Gregg, Joe, 190
Gregory, Miss, 201
Grimm, Jacob Ludwig Carl and Wilhelm Carl, 62, 63, 64
Grosvenor Gallery, 47
Grosvenor House, 175
guinea fowl, 59, 69; **136**; *see also* poultry
guinea pigs, 32, 59, 69, 79, 81, 91, 159, 162, 163; **119**, **121**, **136**, **161**, **350**, **357–9**; Henry P., 162; 'Amiable Guinea-Pig, The', 124, 159; **263**; 'Picture story about a guinea pig', 81, 162; **358**; Tuppenny, *see* 'Tale of Tuppenny, The'
guns, *see* hunting and shooting
Gutherscale, nr Derwentwater, **257**
Gwaynynog, Denbighshire, 25, 26, 64, 77, 131, 140; **303**

Halliwell, James Orchard, *later* Halliwell-Phillipps, 60
Hamer, S. H., 195
Hamleys, 119
Hammond, Miss, *governess*, 13, 15
Hammond, Margaret, 87
Happy Pair, A, 17, 57; **108–109**
Hard Cragg, nr Newby Bridge, 150
Harden, John, 173–4; Jessy, 173–4
Harescombe Grange, nr Stroud, **108**, **118**; *see also* Gloucestershire

Harris, Joel Chandler, 66; *see also* Uncle Remus
Harrods, 23
Hart, Alison, **57**; Reginald, **57**
Harter Fell, **432**
Hastings, Sussex, 118, 124, 162, 166, 168
Hawkshead, 28, 29, 124, 158, 176, 177, 178, 187, 199, 204; **447–9**; Hawkshead Hill, 198; Sun Inn, 148; Thimble Hall, 164; Show, 190
Hawkshead and District Nursing Association (Nursing Trust), 29, 187
Heath Park, Birnam, 17–18
Heathwaite Farm, Coniston, 200; **439**
hedgehogs, 7, 24, 60, 120–23; 210, 217, 253–4, 259, 305, 340–41, 390, 455; Mrs Tiggy-winkle, 24, 80, 120, 122
Heelis, *family*, 32; Arthur, 31; Helen Beatrix (*née* Potter), *see* Potter, H. B.; William, 26–8, 29, 31, 32, 33, 34, 130, 148, 151, 158, 183, 184, 185, 186, 192, 194, 199, 201, 203, 204; **48**; W. H. (& Co.), 26, 28, 183, 204; **447**; Heelis Bequest, *see* Potter, H. B. (as property owner . . . charities, gifts and bequests)
Henny Penny, *see* chickens
Hentschel & Co., 98
herbals and herbal remedies, 85, 100
Herdwick Sheepbreeders' Association, 26, 32, 192; *see also* sheep
Hertfordshire, 104; *see also* Bedwell Lodge; Camfield Place
High Birk How Farm, Little Langdale, **452**
Highgate Cemetery, 25
High Street, 189
Hildesheimer & Faulkner, 17, 50–51, 156; **92–3, 108–110, 196**
Hill, Octavia, 175, 181, 187
Hill Top Farm, 25, 26, 31, 45, 68, 124, 125, 128, 130–31, 133, 136, 137–8, 140, 144, 150–51, 152, 159–60, 161, 163, 167, 169, 177–8, 181, 182, 183, 184, 187, 190, 191, 199, 201, 203, 204, 207; **2, 39–40, 281, 299, 301, 330, 370, 372, 387–9, 401, 404–406, 413, 414, 431, 445–6**
Hogarth, William, 109
Hoggarths, 197
Holehird, *see* Windermere
holidays, *see under* names of places
Holman Hunt, William, 170; **376**
Honister, 172
Horn Book Magazine, 55, 161, 162, 168, 194
horses and ponies, 29–30, 61, 62, 79, 80, 162, 165; **72, 92, 145, 424**; Old Diamond, 158; **163, 412**; Pony Dolly ('Pony Billy'), 62, 159, 162, 163, 164, 165; **122, 164, 364, 410, 424, 427**; *see also* travel (by carriage, coach and pony-cart)
Hudson, Nancy (*née* Nicholson), *see* Nicholson, N.
Hunca Munca, *see* mice; Two Bad Mice, The Tale of
Hunter, Sir Robert, 175, 181, 187
hunting and shooting, inc. guns, 12, 29, 63, 65, 68, 130, 164–5, 181, 183, 186, 189, 190, 199; **125–7, 135, 278, 334, 366, 375**

hutches, hampers, cages, *see* pets
Hutton, *family*, 19, 92, 118; Caroline, *cousin*, 22, 108, 148; Crompton, *uncle*, 80–81; *Putney Park cousins*, 132
Hyde-Parker, *family*, 32, 49, 60; Stephanie, *cousin*, 22, 32, 111, 114, 121, 128, 203; Ulla, Lady, 78; *see also* Melford Hall

'I saw a ship a-sailing', 58–9; **119**
ICAA (Invalid Children's Aid Association), 105, 136, 165; **217, 455**
Ilfracombe, Devon, 70, 71, 165
insects, spiders *etc*, 19, 66, 74, 76, 94, 127, 143–4, 183, 202; ants, 66, 76; bee(hive)s, 164, 178; **419**; beetles, 70, 74, 76; **23, 28, 151**; butterflies, moths, caterpillars, 39, 74, 76, 132, 143; **66, 148–50, 284, 312**; house-fly, 83; mites, 76; **152**; spiders, 76; **153, 188**; woodlice, 71, 143–4
interiors, 36, 52, 55, 56, 66, 122, 123, 125–6, 136–8, 142, 148, 180; **61–2, 82, 96, 98, 138–9, 180, 227, 265–6, 299–301, 304–308, 356, 379, 413–14, 436–7**; barns and outbuildings, 52, 189; **94–5, 298, 416–17**; bedrooms, 56, 78; **9, 37, 47, 322, 363, 438**; kitchens, fire-places, ovens, 111, 122, 126, 138, 146, 148, 149, 151, 160, 163; **61–2, 82, 117, 135, 181, 197, 223–4, 258–9, 267, 318, 324, 354, 355, 360, 388–9, 408–409, 435**
Inverness, 175
Ireland, Northern, 175

Japanese prints, 39
Jemima Puddle-Duck, The Tale of, 26, 37, 66, 133–6, 147, 207; **64, 89, 175, 210, 286–91, 401, 406, 412, 431, 454**
Jemima Puddle-Duck's Painting Book, 28, 133, 135, 136; **292–3**
Jeremy Fisher, The Tale of, *see* Mr. Jeremy Fisher, The Tale of
Johnny Crow's Garden (L. L. Brooke), 123
Johnny Town-Mouse, The Tale of, 29, 65, 80, 81, 85, 152, 153, 156, 158, 184, 202; **55, 130, 163, 173, 344, 348–9, 444**
journal, Beatrix Potter's, *see* Potter, H. B. (as writer . . . journal)

Kelso, 80; Archaeological Museum, 93
Kendal, 171, 197, Lords of, 189
Kep, *see* dogs
Keswick, 17, 21, 104, 171, 172, 181; **261**; Show, 190; **56**; School of Industrial Art, 21, 170; *see also* Braithwaite; Cat Bells; Crosthwaite; Derwentwater
Kew Gardens, 19, 20, 86, 90–91, 144
Kipling, Rudyard, 67
'Kitty-in-Boots', 63, 147, 153; **334**

La Fontaine, Jean de, 66
Lake Artists' Society, 180, 193, 198
Lake District, 14, 15, 17, 20, 21, 22, 23, 25, 26, 29, 34, 84, 85, 89, 92, 96, 111, 114, 118, 123, 138, 140, 144, 161, 167, 169–84, 185–94, 195–206, 207, 208; *see also* landscapes *and under* names of places;

antiquities, *see* archaeology (Lake District); customs and way of life, 85, 124, 125, 152, 172, 177, 178, 186, 187, 193, 204, 206; **390–91**; dialect and place-names, 152, 162, 193; vernacular buildings, 169, 180, 184, 186, 187, 189, 198, 204–205, 206; *see also* buildings; interiors *and under names of places*; monasteries, 191; guides to, 21, 185, 193; rights of way and tracks, 182, 189; rock climbing in, 193, 198; railways and travel, *see* travel; tourism and visitors, 15, 170–71, 174–5, 182, 187, 189, 196, 197, 203–204; property development, 15, 170–71, 172, 181, 186, 187, 189, 194, 205–206; ecology, 187, 189, 191; preservation of buildings and landscape, 15, 170, 171–3, 186, 187, 198, 204–206; 'Defend the Lake District' party, 171; 'Defence Association', 172, (Permanent) Lake District Defence Society, 15, 173; National Park, 206; Lake District Landscape Appeal, *see* National Trust; artists, 173–5, 178, 180, 192, 193, 198, *and see* Lake Artists' Society; *see also* agriculture; Cumberland; Lake Poets; Lancashire; National Trust; Potter, H. B. (as farmer and conservationist; as property owner, *etc*); Westmorland *and under other names of places*
Lakefield (*later* Eeswyke), Sawrey, 20, 23, 124, 176, 183; **384–5**; Lakefield cottages, 123, 124, 125–6; **265–6**
Lake Poets, 170, 193
Lamb, Harry, 52
Lancashire, 9, 149, 171, 178; *see also* Blackpool; Bolton; Lake District; Manchester; Stalybridge
landscapes, 8, 11, 18, 44, 46, 49, 52, 108, 112, 113, 115, 121, 134, 145, 173, 178, 193, 198, 200–201; **55, 78–9, 92, 125, 127, 221, 234, 236–7, 240–41, 255–6, 291, 320–21, 325, 328, 331, 333–4, 365–7, 376–7, 381–6, 392, 394–9, 402, 405, 407, 410–11, 415, 417, 421, 423, 427, 429–30, 432, 439, 442, 452–4**; *see also* Lake District (artists, *etc*); Peter Rabbit Books; photography; Potter, H. B. (as artist, *etc*)
Lane, Margaret (*The Magic Years*), 100
Langdale, *see* Elterwater Common; Little Langdale
Lankes, J. J., 168
Lear, Edward, 55, 70; **140**; *Book of Nonsense, The*, 70; 'Owl and the Pussy Cat, The', 70, 166; **140–41**
Leech, Helen, *see* Potter, H.
Leech, John, *artist*, 46
Leech, John, *grandfather*, 9
Leeds, 181
Lennel, 93; **189**; *see also* Coldstream
lichens, 19, 87, 89, 90; **184**; *see also* fungi
Lincoln's Inn, *see* London
Linder, Leslie (*A History of the Writings of Beatrix Potter*), 109, 110; Linder Bequest, Victoria and Albert Museum (National Art Library), 47, 118, 138

Lindeth How(e), *see* Windermere

Lingholm, Derwentwater, 17, 20–21, 24, 77, 88, 104, 111, 112, 115, 121, 132, 172, 176; **21**, **183**, **200**, **379–80**

Linnean Society, 20; *see also* Massee, G.

'Little Black Kettle, The', 167

Little Langdale, 32, 149, 194, 195, 198, 199, 202; **442**; *see also* Colwith Bridge; High Birk How Farm

Little Pig Robinson, The Tale of, 32, 70, 151, 159, 163, 165–6, 167, 194; **53**; **367–8**

Little Songs for Me to Sing (J. E. Millais), 48; **85**

Little Town, Newlands Valley, 121, 122; **256–7**

Liverpool, 169, 181

lizards, 14, 16, 61, 69, 71–2, 185; **136**; Judy, 71–2; **17**, **142**

'Llewellyn's Well', 64

lobster, 72

Lockhart, John Gibson, 78

London, 9ff, 12, 13, 19, 20, 26, 28, 29, 31, 32, 71, 90, 92, 115, 144, 177, 178, 183; Bayswater, 17; Bedford Square, 22–3, 25; **36**; Bedford Street, Covent Garden, 22; Bolton Gardens inc. No. 2, 9–10, 12, 13, 17, 18, 19, 22, 23, 25, 45, 86, 89, 138, 178; **6**, **62**, **87**, **197**, **200**; The Boltons, 89; Bucklersbury, City, *see* archaeology (London); Kensington, 10, 28, 183; Lincoln's Inn, 9; Upper Harley Street, 9; Walbrook, City, *see* archaeology (London); Wandsworth Common, 20; *see also under names of clubs, houses, museums, galleries, libraries, societies*

London Library, 193

Longmire, William, 174–5

Lord, Mrs, 123

Love Locked Out (A. L. Merritt), 100, 125; **203–204**

Loweswater, Show, 190

Lowther, Hon. J. W., 181

Lucy, Mr, 92

Lunt, Joseph, 85–6; **182**

Lyme Regis, Dorset, 166

McDonald, Kitty, 121

McGregor, Mr, 21, 83, 85, 87, 98, 100, 101, 104, 116, 139; **202**, **213–14**, **242**; Mrs, 101, 103, 104; **205–206**

McIntosh, Charles, 86–7, 89, 90, 91

McKay, Alexander, 32, 161, 162, 166, 167; David, Co., 32; Margery, 162

McKenzie, Nanny, 10, 11, 36, 60

Mackereth, John, 163

Mahony, Bertha, *see* Miller, B. M.

Manchester, 12, 181; Corporation, 172; New College, 9; *see also* Stalybridge

Marley, Elsie, 160–61, 164

Martineau, Miss, 76

Mason, Charlotte, 192

Massee, George, 20, 86–7, 90, 91, 92; *see also* Kew Gardens

Melford Hall, Suffolk, 22, 66, 111, 114, 128; **34**, **37**, **89–90**; *see also* Hyde-Parker, *family*

menu cards, *see* dinner cards

merchandise, 27, 105–106, 136; **46**, **216**; board game ('The Game of Peter Rabbit'), 24, 105; table mats, 136; wallpaper, 24, 105; *see also* Christmas and greetings cards; painting books; Peter Rabbit's Almanac

Merritt, Anna Lea (*Love Locked Out*), 100, 125; **203–204**

mice, 7, 20, 23–4, 39, 42, 51, 52, 55–7, 58–9, 60, 61, 69, 71, 77, 78–9, 81, 82, 83, 86, 108, 110, 111, 112, 118–20, 129–30, 137, 139, 140, 141, 143–4, 149, 155, 156, 158, 163, 164, 165, 167, 168; **3**, **31**, **37**, **68**, **88**, **93**, **96**, **103–107**, **116–18**, **120–21**, **130**, **136**, **158–9**, **180**, **182**, **204**, **210**, **217**, **223–5**, **228**, **250–52**, **276–7**, **306**, **310**, **312**, **342–6**, **351**, **363**, **391**, **393**, **455**; Hunca Munca, 118–20; Tom Thumb, 118–19; *see also* Two Bad Mice, The Tale of; dormice, 14, 77, 78–9, 165; **160**; Xarifa, 78–9; **160**; *see also* Fairy Caravan, The; voles, 78, 156, 158, 202; **55**, **130**, **173**, **344–9**, **444**; *see also* rhymes

microscopes and microscopic studies, 7, 19, 60, 74, 76, 87, 90, 91; **23**, **148**, **151–3**

Middleton, W., 197

Millais, *family*, 12; Sir John Everett, PRA, 7, 11, 12, 13, 38, 43–4, 47–8, 55, 138, 170; **85**, **375**; *Little Songs for Me to Sing*, 48; **85**; John Guille, 47

Miller, Bertha Mahony (née Mahony), 161, 168, 194

Mills, Cecily, 207

Milne, Dr, 183

Milne, Alan Alexander, 67, 145

Minehead, Somerset, 72

Mines Ghyll, nr Coniston, 200

miniature letters, 127–8, 133, 140, 149; **272–3**

mirrors, *see* furniture

Miss Moppet, The Story of, 26, 57, 69, 129–30, 155; **31**, **276–7**

'Mole Catcher's Burying, The', 152

moles, 62, 83, 152; **121**, **338**

Monk Coniston Estate, 32, 194, 195, 196; **428**

moon(light), as motif, 59, 61–2, 91, 146, 149; **121–2**, **164**, **328**, **339**, **352**

Moore, Anne Carroll, 30, 167

Moore, *family*, 17, 18, 20, 49, 72; Annie B. (née Carter), 15–16, 17, 18, 20, 48, 49, 97; Beatrix, 124; Edwin, 17, 20; Eric, 70, 114, 126; **141**; Freda, *see* Winifred(e); Joan, 124; **30**; Marjorie, 20, 54, 59; **30**, **100**; Noel, 17, 18, 21, 87, 97, 111, 160; **27**, **199**, **354**; Norah, 22, 111, 112; **30**, **231**; Winifred(e) (Freda), 22, 109; **30**

Moscrop, Joseph, 167

Moss Eccles Tarn, nr Sawrey, 128; **450**

mosses, 86, 87, 88; **184**; *see also* fungi

'movables', *see* toy pictures

Mr. Jeremy Fisher, The Tale of, 25–6, 46, 54, 72, 76, 81, 83, 126–9, 272–3; **210**, **221**, **270–75**; *see also* frogs; newts; tortoises

Mrs. Tiggy-Winkle, The Tale of, 24, 25, 60, 85, 104, 115, 118, 119, 120–23, 178, 199; **210**, **253–4**, **256–60**, **305**, **390**; *see also* hedgehogs

Mrs. Tittlemouse, The Tale of, 27, 46, 57, 72, 74, 78, 80–81, 83, 91, 143–4, 147, 178; **107**, **149**, **312–13**, **391**, **393**; *see also* Flopsy Bunnies, The Tale of the; mice

Mr. Tod, The Tale of, 8, 27, 62, 65, 69, 80, 81, 84, 104, 145–8, 151; **89**, **316–23**, **409**, **423**; *see also* fables; foxes; Jemima Puddle-Duck, The Tale of

Musgrave's, Windermere, 197

mycology, *see* fungi

National Art Library, *see* Victoria and Albert Museum

National Park (Lake District), 206

National Trust, 8, 15, 21, 32, 34, 170, 175–6, 181–2, 187, 189, 193–4, 195–8, 204–206, 207; **449–50**, **452**; National Trust Act, 181; Vernacular Survey, 204–205; Lake District Landscape Appeal, 8, 206; Beatrix Potter and, 8, 32, 34, 181–2, 187, 189, 193–4, 195–8, 201, 203–206, 207, 208; **449–50**, **452**; *see also* Potter, H. B. (as farmer and conservationist)

natural history, in general, 45, 71–94; *see also under individual subjects*

Natural History Museum, 19, 73–4, 76, 92, 93, 110

Nature Conservancy Council, Sites of Special Scientific Interest, 205–206

Near Sawrey, *see* Sawrey

Newcastle, Agricultural College, 183

New England, *see* Potter, H. B. (success and popularity . . . friends and visitors from U.S.A.)

Newlands (Valley), 121, 122, 164, 178, 199; **78**, **255–6**; *see also* Little Town

Newton, Sir Isaac, 72; *see also* Mr. Jeremy Fisher, The Tale of

newts, 14, 72, 81, 127; **143**, **271**

New York, Public Library, 30

New Zealand, 104; *see also* Stone, J.; Tuckey, Dr R. P.

Nicholson, Nancy, 153

'Nid nid noddy', 91; **339**

'Ninny Nanny Netticoat', 159, 161; **351**

Nip, *see* dogs

Nister, Ernest, 17, 54, 57, 63, 126–7; **99**, **112–15**

nursery rhymes, *see* rhymes

Nursing Trust, *see* Hawkshead and District Nursing Association

'Oakmen, The', 64, 82, 153

Oatmeal Crag, *see* Sawrey

'Over the hills and far away', 150, 152, 162, 164; **325**, **328**, **333**

'Owl and the Pussy Cat, The', *see* Lear, E.

Oxenholme, 170

Oxford, 18, 50, 69, 170, 172, 180; *see also* Bodleian Library

'Pace Eggers', 152

Paget, *family*, 79; Mr, 79; Elizabeth Ann, 159

painting books, 136; *Peter Rabbit's*, 27, 105, 136, 144; **45**; *Tom Kitten's*, 28, 133, 136; *Jemima Puddle-Duck's*, 28, 133, 135, 136; **292–3**

palaeontology, *see* fossils

panoramic editions, *see* Peter Rabbit Books

Parker, *see* Hyde-Parker

parodies, 40, 100, 109, 125; **204, 265**

Parsons, Dr, 158

Parton, –, [*coachman's son*], 110, 111; **226**

Pasteur, Louis, 89

pattens, 125; **178**

peat (moss), 88, 177; peat cart, **417**

Peel, John, 164–5

'Peermingle, the story of a cockle-shell fairy', 64

Penicillium, *see* fungi

Penny Hill Farm, Eskdale, 189; **415–16**

Penrith, 172

Perrault, Charles, 61, 62, 64, 167; *see also* fairy tales

Perthshire, 12, 39, 73, 89, 104, 169; *see also* Birnam; Dalguise House; Dunkeld; Eastwood; Strathallan, Woods of

pet animals, *see* pets

Peter of New Zealand, *see* Tuckey, Dr R. P.

Peter Piper (Peter Rabbit), *see* rabbits

Peter Rabbit Books, 8, 21–30, 32, 52, 57, 59, 65, 70, 83, 93, 94, 95, 103–104, 106, 107–61, 162, 165, 166–7, 168, 169, 177, 178, 184, 199, 202, 203, 207, 208; de luxe editions, 114; panoramic editions, 26, 129–30; **276–9**; foreign editions, 30, 106; **210**, **218**; piracies and imitations, 68, 106; illustrations, in general, 46, 199, 203, 204, 207; preservation of, 204; title pages, 101, 135, 143, 160; **292, 312**, (*Fairy Caravan*) 161; frontispieces, 98, 100–101, 109, 118, 125, 135, 153, 156, 160, 207; **39, 110, 200, 215, 281, 331, 334, 354, 363, 405**, (*Fairy Caravan*) 164; **363**; endpapers, 102, 103–104, 114, 124, 130, 136, 148, 162; **210, 211–12**; bindings and jackets, 86, 99, 100–01, 102, 103, 104, 109, 114, 124, 125, 129, 136, 148, 160; **45, 201, 209, 221, 230, 253, 280, 293, 314**; proofs, 200, **409**; *see also* Potter, H. B. (as artist); sales *etc*, *see* Potter, H. B. (success and popularity); copyrights and royalties, 23, 28, 34, 161, 177, 183, 194; *see also* painting books *and under titles*; in other media, *see* merchandise; Tales of Beatrix Potter, The (ballet film)

Peter Rabbit, The Tale of, 22–3, 26, 30, 54, 68, 69, 70, 83, 85, 95–106, 107, 115, 118, 125, 126, 127, 130, 136, 139–40, 145, 154, 158, 194, 201, 203; **90, 204–209, 211–14, 218**; picture letter, 18, 21, 54, 87, 97; **199**; privately printed edition, 8, 21–2, 95, 98–101; **200–202**; *see also* merchandise

Peter Rabbit's Almanac, 31, 105; **215**

Peter Rabbit's Painting Book, 27, 105, 136, 144; **45**

pets, 7, 13–14, 16, 17, 18, 20, 23–4, 42, 49, 71–2, 77, 80, 81, 96, 119, 120, 127, 159, 162; **62, 161, 195, 197**; *see also* Potter, H. B. (as artist . . . natural history artist; as naturalist) *and under names of animals*

'Phiz', *pseud.*, 46, 55

photography, in general, 11, 43, 81; Photographic Society of London, 11; photographs by Beatrix Potter, 18, 19, 43, 89, 92, 124, 138; **297, 388**; by Rupert Potter, 11, 18, 37, 43–4, 47, 114, 138; **6–8, 12–13, 15–16, 19–22, 24, 42, 48, 77, 85, 87, 373, 375, 389, 400, 403, 433**; by Norman Warne, 119; by others, 4, 5, 25, 27, 30, 35, 40, 44, 46, **49, 52, 54, 56–7, 216, 239, 415, 418, 420, 426, 428–9, 447, 449–50**; *see also* Potter, H. B. (photographs and portraits)

picture letters and stories, 8, 18, 20, 21, 22, 54, 57, 59, 70, 87, 88, 96–7, 108, 109, 111, 112, 114, 119, 126, 133, 153, 168; **100, 141, 199, 231**; 'Picture story about a guinea pig', *see* guinea pigs

Picturesque, The, 174; **383**

Picturesque Tours (W. Gilpin), 174

Pie and the Patty-Pan, The (later *The Tale of the Pie and the Patty-Pan*), 24, 25, 72, 81, 84, 85, 118, 123–6, 133, 141, 160, 204; **39, 145, 176, 178, 262, 264–7, 408, 448**

pigeons, *see* birds (doves and pigeons)

Pigling Bland, The Tale of, 27, 28, 60, 125, 144, 148–52, 160, 199; **2, 47, 50, 324–6, 328, 330–33, 370, 404–05, 434**; *see also* pigs

Pig Robinson, *see* Little Pig Robinson, The Tale of

pigs, 25, 30, 55, 59, 70, 79, 80, 91, 125, 133, 144, 148–52, 155, 159–60, 162, 163, 165, 166, 167, 199; **2, 41, 47, 50, 53, 140, 166, 188, 324–3, 352–3, 367–8, 370, 404, 434**; Aunt Dorcas, 151; Aunt Pettitoes, 125, 151; **47, 370, 404**; Aunt Susan, 151; Old Sallie, 159–60; Black Berkshires, 79, 150–51; Pig-wig, 79, 150–51, 199; **324–5, 328, 330, 333**; *see also* Pigling Bland, The Tale of

Pinkie, Winkie, and Wee, 63

place-cards, *see* dinner cards

plants and flowers, 13, 39, 55, 59, 62, 76, 83–5, 87, 94, 95, 118, 125–6, 131, 140, 143, 154, 156, 160, 165, 176, 208; **14, 58, 64, 69, 73, 123, 172, 175–81, 220, 233, 248–9, 266, 274, 444**; bluebells, 55, 84, 165, 208; **220**; corn, ears of, 156; **96, 347**; daisies, 62, 85, 250; **179–80, 444**; elder, 83, 85; foxgloves, 84, 135; **175**; geraniums, 84, 123; **83, 95, 215, 294**; roses, 62, 131; **1, 123, 136, 244**; tiger lilies, 84, 125, 131; **176**; water-lilies, 128; **274, 337**; *see also* algae; cowslip wine; ferns; fruit; fungi; gardens; herbals; lichens; mosses; seaweed; trees; vegetables

Portland, Dorset, 92

Postlethwaite, *Farmer* ('Farmer Potatoes'), 137, 138; **297–8**; Mary, **297**; Ruth, **297**

Potter, Helen Beatrix (Mrs Heelis)

photographs and portraits, 36, 37, 40, 43; **7–8, 12–13, 15–16, 19–22, 24–5, 40, 42, 44, 48–9, 52, 54, 56–7, 373, 400, 403, 420**; by Bertram Potter, 40; **71–2**; by Delmar Banner, 198; **29, 440**; self-portraits and caricatures, 80, 137, 150, 151, 160, 202; **2, 47, 166, 296, 443**; *see also* photography (by Beatrix Potter)

life, in general, 9–34; early life, 9–18, 35–43, 45–8, 49, 55, 60, 66–7, 69, 71–3, 85, 86, 95; creativity and originality, 55, 81, 89 *and passim*; gift of memory, 81; memories of, 198–203, 207–208; character, costume, appearance, 186–7, 192, 193, 199, 201, 207; **441**; health, 17, 27, 32–3, 34, 145, 148, 183, 201, 202, 208; eyesight, 8, 32, 65, 87, 130, 156, 184; in old age, 32–4, 81, 89, 136, 168, 198–202, 207–208; **54, 56, 57, 440**; death, 34, 202–203; *see also* photography; travel (by carriage *etc*; by car)

as artist, in general, 7–8, 48, 107–108, 178; in context, 7, 107, 178; early influences, 7, 11, 13, 15, 35–41, 43, 45–8, 52, 55, 60, 62, 64, 85, 129, 134, 153–4, 170, 174; *see also* Caldecott, R.; Crane, W.; Lear, E.; Millais, Sir J. E.; Tenniel, Sir J.; exhibitions and galleries visited by Potter family, 7, 11, 16, 17, 36, 40, 45, 46, 47, 100; works of art collected by Potter family inc. Beatrix, 11, 45, 199; *see also* Caldecott, R.; furniture; pottery and china; formal training, 13, 39–40, 43, 47, 48, 55, 84; juvenile work, 11, 12, 15, 16, 35–42, 45, 47, 48, 49, 71, 72, 74, 84, 95–6, 170; **17, 58–61, 66–9, 74–5, 81, 87, 150, 194**; sketchbooks (juvenile and adult), 38–9, 49, 74, 95, 111, 112, 115, 118, 120, 121, 122; **66–8, 81, 150, 234, 240, 255, 261**; copies, 7, 38, 39, 41, 45, 46, 47, 55, 62, 72, 74, 164, 174; **28, 68, 81, 154**, (by Bertram, 41, by Rupert, 37, 41; **65**); figure drawing, 7, 40, 55, 62, 63–4, 69, 101, 103, 110, 111, 122, 149; **81, 205–206, 213, 224, 226–7, 256, 260–61, 278, 298, 368, 390, 421**; still life, 16, 71; **17, 60**; works in various media, etchings, 41, (by Bertram, 45, 164; **78**), lino cuts, 41, lithographs, 76; **153**, oils, 41–2, (by Bertram, 44–5), 48, transfer prints, 41; **74**, watercolours, 8, 39, 42, 45 *and passim*; early commercial productions, 7, 17, 22, 49–51, 54, 57–8, 62, 63, 96, 100, 126–7, 156; *see also* Christmas and greetings cards; Happy Pair, A; Peter Rabbit, The Tale of; book illustrations, 7–8, 52, 55–70, 106; *see also* fantasy pictures *and other special subjects*; parodies; Peter Rabbit Books *and under names of animals and plants*

comments on art, 7, 40, 46–7, 55, 72, 93, 170, 200, 201; comments on own art, 16, 51, 55, 65, 67, 76, 101, 107, 114, 117, 122, 129, 143, 144–5, 151, 154, 156, 163, 164, 167, 168, 207; style, technique and working methods, 7–8, 16, 17, 19, 26, 42, 46, 48, 49, 51, 52, 54, 55, 56, 65, 67, 72, 74, 78, 79, 80, 84–5, 92, 99, 101,

102, 107–108, 110, 111, 112, 114, 116–17, 118, 119, 120, 121, 122, 125, 126, 129, 130, 132, 136, 138, 140, 142, 143, 145, 147, 148, 150, 151, 152, 154, 155, 166, 168, 178, 191, 199; **177, 226, 298**; knowledge of printing and design, 19, 50, 51, 98, 99, 101, 102, 103, 114, 118, 123, 124, 154, 155; **124**; as natural history artist, 7–8, 14, 17, 18, 19, 39, 42, 49, 51, 52, 55, 57–8, 59, 63, 64–5, 69–70, 71–4, 76–93, 94, 95–6, 108, 117–18, 143, 145, 150, 151, 163, 191; *see also* Peter Rabbit Books; pets *and under names of animals and plants* collections of works, 37, 38, 47, 89, 95–6, 118, 138, 193, 203–204; exhibitions of works, 8, 88, 204

as writer, early reading, 8, 11, 36, 39, 45, 48, 55, 60, 64, 66, 67, 69, 70, 72, 153; interest in dialect and oral tradition, 60, 67, 107, 152, 162; *see also* Lake District (dialect and place-names); prose style and use of language, 8, 55, 60–61, 64, 66, 67, 69, 70, 91, 99, 103, 107–108, 114, 118, 127, 130, 135–6, 139, 144, 146–7, 151, 156, 158, 163, 164, 166, 167, 168; journal, 7, 8, 14, 16, 17, 36, 39, 40, 45, 46–7, 49–50, 55, 60, 62, 65, 72, 81, 121, 166, 170, 187; **70**, correspondence, **443** *and passim*; *see also* miniature letters; picture letters; articles and essays, 72, 82, 152; *see also* Peter Rabbit Books

success and popularity, 7, 22, 23, 28, 100, 102, 103, 106, 107, 115, 136, 142–3, 161, 162, 165, 203, 204, in U.S.A., 30, 31, 32, 34, 68, 104, 144, 161, 165, 194; friends and visitors from U.S.A., 30, 31, 33–4, 158, 161, 162, 194; attitudes to publicity and success, 30, 65, 146, 163, 165, 187, 207

as naturalist and scientist, 7, 14, 16, 18, 19–20, 21, 29–30, 39, 42, 49, 71–4, 76–93, 94, 143, 208; *see also under names of animals and plants*

as lover of the country, 11–13, 14, 26, 64, 71, 108, 156, 169, 176–7, 208

as farmer and conservationist, 8, 25, 26, 28, 29–32, 33, 42, 80, 105, 133, 144, 146–7, 150, 151, 152, 158, 167, 169, 182–3, 184, 185, 186, 189–91, 192, 193, 194, 195–7, 200, 201–202, 203, 204, 206, 208; *see also* agricultural shows; agriculture; Lake District; National Trust *and under names of livestock*

as property owner, 7, 23, 25, 26, 31, 32, 34, 138, 169, 177–8, 183–4, 186, 187, 189–90, 193–4, 195–8, 201, 202, 203, 204–206; *see also* National Trust

charities, gifts and bequests, 32, 34, 105, 165, 193–4, 203; Heelis Bequest, 203, 204; **450, 452**; *see also* ICAA; National Trust

Beatrix Potter and children, 17, 18, 20, 21, 22, 24, 25, 30, 49, 54, 58–9, 65, 70, 81, 97, 100, 101, 105, 107, 108, 112, 114, 118, 121, 124, 127–8, 129, 130–31, 134, 135, 136, 137, 140, 141, 148, 151, 152, 153, 158, 160, 162, 163, 165, 167, 168,

201; **276**; *see also* Coolidge, H. P.; Gaddum, W.; miniature letters; Moore, *family*; picture letters; toy pictures; Warne, *family*

Potter, *family*, 7, 9, 12, 14, 16, 17–18, 20–21, 24, 36, 38, 40, 43, 45, 49, 50, 67, 73, 96, 111, 114, 115, 121, 126, 144, 166, 169, 170, 172, 176, 177, 186; holidays, *see under names of places*

Potter, Bertram, *see* Potter, Walter Bertram

Potter, Clara, *aunt*, 177

Potter, Crompton, *uncle*, 9

Potter, Edmund, *grandfather*, 9, 11, 12, 114

Potter, Edmund, and Company, 9, 114

Potter, Helen (*née* Leech), *mother*, 9–11, 13, 14, 15, 16, 17, 18, 19, 22, 23, 24, 25, 26, 27, 28, 29, 31, 32, 36–7, 40, 45, 49, 55, 77, 89, 119, 144, 148, 177, 178, 182, 183, 184, 194; **5, 7, 13, 20, 71, 79**

Potter, Helen Beatrix, *see* Potter, H. B. *above*

Potter, Jessie (*née* Crompton), *grandmother*, 9, 11, 16, 18

Potter, Kate, *cousin*, 40, 125

Potter, Lucy (*née* Potter), *aunt*, *see* Roscoe, L.

Potter, Mary (*née* Scott), *sister-in-law*, 45, 183

Potter, Rupert, *father*, 9–12, 13, 14, 15, 16, 17, 18, 19, 22, 24, 25, 26, 27, 28, 36, 37–8, 39, 40, 42, 43–4, 45, 47, 49, 55, 67, 69, 86, 89, 90, 92, 95, 127, 138, 144, 148, 169, 170, 177, 178, 182, 183, 184; **4, 8, 13, 22, 42, 65, 85**, sketchbook, 37, 134; **63–4**, collections of works, 38; *see also* photography

Potter, Walter, *uncle*, 11

Potter, Walter Bertram, *brother*, 7, 11–14, 15, 16, 17, 18, 21, 27, 29, 40–41, 42, 44–5, 49–50, 71, 72, 74, 77, 114, 127, 183, 184; **16, 20, 22, 42, 73, 78, 373, 407**, sketchbooks, 40; **71–2**

pottery and china, 64, 124, 125, 148; **31, 55, 128, 190, 224, 267, 279, 281, 318, 340–42, 348, 354, 356, 408, 437**; designed by Rupert Potter, 38; collected by Beatrix Potter, 31, 196; Coronation tea-pot, 126; **267**; *see also* archaeology; interiors; merchandise; Roman antiquities and art

poultry, 29, 82, 158, 196; **167**; *see also* chickens; ducks; guinea fowl; turkeys

Pre-Raphaelites, 74

printing, style and technique, 7, 51, 99, 101; *see also* Potter, H. B. (as artist . . . knowledge of printing and design)

privately printed editions, *see* Peter Rabbit Books

Punch (journal), 37, 46, 172, 175

Putney Park, 79, 132, 151

quarries, 92, 146, 172; *see also* slate mining

rabbits, 7, 13, 20, 29, 33, 39, 42, 49, 51, 52, 55, 57, 59, 60, 61, 66–70, 77–8, 79, 81, 85, 95–9, 100, 101, 102, 103, 104–105, 116, 117, 118, 119, 120, 127,

129, 130, 136, 139–40, 141, 144, 145–6, 147, 148, 149–50, 156, 160–61, 201; **45–6, 67, 74–5, 88, 90–91, 95, 97–8, 100–102, 108–111, 113–14, 119–21, 134–9, 156–7, 181, 193–202, 204, 207, 209–218, 220, 241–2, 245–6, 249, 278, 303–304, 309, 320–21, 323, 328, 354, 356, 455**; Tommy, 95; Benjamin Bounce(r) (Benjamin Bunny), 17, 18, 19, 50, 54, 71, 77, 96; **24, 75, 156**; Peter Piper (Peter Rabbit), 18–19, 55, 77–8, 81, 96, 101; **157, 194, 197–8**

'Rabbits' Christmas Party, The', 52, 85; **97–8**

Ransome, Arthur, 193

rats, 46, 57, 59, 61, 66, 78, 130, 134, 135–6, 136–7, 138–9, 162, 177, 199; **82, 133, 217, 229, 279, 294–6, 300–302, 304, 309, 436–7, 455**; Sammy, 78, 137; *see also* Roly-Poly Pudding, The; Tom Kitten, The Tale of

Rawnsley, *family*, 170, 172, 192; *cousin*, 170; Edith (*née* Fletcher), 21, 170, 187; Eleanor (*née* Simpson), 187, 193, 196; Canon Hardwicke D., 15, 21–2, 26, 98–9, 170, 172, 173, 175, 176, 180, 181–2, 186, 187, 191, 192, 193, 204; **21, 374, 400**; Noel, 192; **21**

Reform Club, 10

'Remus, Uncle', *see* Uncle Remus

Renoir, Pierre Auguste, 52

rhymes, 22, 29, 55–6, 57, 58–60, 65, 74, 91, 107, 109, 119, 149, 153, 154, 155, 156, 158, 162, 164; **37, 70, 80–81, 84, 86, 103–105, 116–117, 119, 181, 220, 363**; collections by Baring Gould, Chambers, Halliwell, Sharp, 60; *see also* Appley Dapply's Nursery Rhymes; Caldecott, R.; Cecily Parsley's Nursery Rhymes; Crane, W.; Lear, E.; Millais, Sir J. E. (*Little Songs for Me to Sing*); *and under individual titles*; 1905 Book of Rhymes, *see* Appley Dapply's Nursery Rhymes

Richter, (Adrian) Ludwig, 55, 62

riddles, 60, 112, 159

Rivière, Briton (*Cupboard Love*), 40, 125; **265**

Rogerson, Mary, 124, 125, 158

Roly-Poly Pudding, The (later *The Tale of Samuel Whiskers*), 26, 46, 66, 70, 134, 136–9, 141, 142, 151, 199; **294–6, 298–9, 301–302, 435–7**; *see also* Tom Kitten, The Tale of

Roman antiquities and art, 93–4, 189; 190–2

Roscoe, *family*, 85; Dora, *cousin*, 85; Sir Henry, FRS, *uncle*, 19, 50, 72, 85–6, 90; **182**; Lucy, *aunt* (*née* Potter), 52, 85

Rowlandson, Thomas (*The Tour of Dr. Syntax*), 174; **383**

Royal Academy, 17, 40, 100, 170, 180; *see also* Burlington House

Royal Society of British Artists, 100

Ruskin, John, 170, 171–2, 173, 180–81, 187; **377, 451**

Rye, Sussex, 62, 80, 168; **371**

salamanders, 14
Salisbury, Antiquarian Museum, 93
Sammy (Samuel Whiskers), *see* rats
Samuel Whiskers, The Tale of, *see* Roly-Poly Pudding, The
Sawrey, Near Sawrey, 20, 23, 25–6, 27, 28, 29, 31, 32, 33, 64, 66, 80, 119, 122, 123, 124, 128, 131, 138, 143, 145, 158, 163, 164, 176, 177, 178, 183, 184, 186, 198, 199, 207; **43, 57, 264, 296, 307–308, 331, 395–6, 402, 405, 425, 430, 444,** Belle Green, 130; Buckle Yeat (post office), 124, 125; **176;** Bull Banks, 145, 146, 147, 191; **321, 423;** 'Ginger and Pickles' (shop), 119, 125, 140, 142; **304–308, 311, 444;** *see also* Ginger and Pickles; Oatmeal Crag, 60, 145; Tower Bank Arms, 136, 187; **412;** Far Sawrey, 201, Spout House, 151; *see also* Castle Cottage; Eesbridge; Esthwaite; Hill Top Farm; Lakefield (Eeswyke); Moss Eccles Tarn
Sayers, Dorothy L. (*The Documents in the Case*), 88
Scales, Sally, 167
Schwendener, Simon, 90
Scotch Fly, *see* dogs
Scotland, 12, 14, 17–18, 39, 60, 82, 96, 97, 176, 208; Scottish Borders, 44, 60, 208; Scottish Highlands, 10, 60; *see also* Edinburgh; Perthshire *and under other names of places*
Scott, Mary, *see* Potter, M.
Scott, The Misses, 197
Scudder, Frank, 86
sea and ships, 12, 54, 70, 72, 166; **100, 140–41, 368, 376**
seaweed, 72
Shakespeare, William, 19, 55, 107
Sharp, Cecil J., 60
sheep, sheep farming and shepherds, 26, 29, 30–31, 33, 70, 74, 79, 80, 81, 152, 162, 163–4, 167, 182–3, 186, 193, 201, 206; **53, 71, 86, 129, 147, 165, 367, 376, 397, 421;** Herdwicks, 26, 31, 64, 80, 133, 136, 162, 163–4, 177, 189–92, 204; **51, 56, 362, 420, 422;** Hill Top Queenie, 164, 192; Saddleback Wedgewood, 164; **362;** *see also* agricultural shows; dogs (sheepdogs); Gregg, J.; Mackereth, J.; Moscrop, J.; Potter, H. B. (as farmer); Storey, T.
shells, 64, 72, 92; *see also* fossils
ships, *see* fish and fishing; 'I saw a ship', Lear, E.; Little Pig Robinson, The Tale of; photography; picture letters; sea and ships
shoes and boots, 58, 62, 80, 148, 155; **116, 192, 208, 340–41;** *see also* clogs; pattens
shooting, *see* hunting and shooting
Sidmouth, Devon, 166; **367**
Silchester, Hampshire, 93
Sister Anne, 64, 167; **369**
Sites of Special Scientific Interest, 205–206
Skelgill, nr Guthersacle, 122; **257**
sketchbooks, *see* Potter, H. B. (as artist); Potter, W. B.; Potter, R.

Skiddaw, 121; **421**
skulls and skeletons, 14, 68, 71, 76–7; 18, **135, 154**
slate mining, 172
Slater's Bridge, Little Langdale, **452**
sleep, as motif, *see* dream and sleep
'Sleeping Beauty, The', *see* fairy tales
Sly Old Cat, The, 130; **279**
Smailholm Tower, Roxburghshire, 88
snails, 71; **270**
snakes, 14
snow, as motif, 57, 62, 84, 111, 156, 164, 165; **97, 109–111, 113–14, 125–7, 364, 372, 377, 394–7, 410, 442, 445, 453;** *see also* weather
'Solitary Mouse, The', 167
Somerville, Robert, 171
South Kensington Museum, *see* Victoria and Albert Museum
Speckter, Otto, 55, 62; **124**
spiders, *see* insects, spiders *etc*
spores, germination of, *see* fungi
Squire, Tom, 93
Squirrel Nutkin, The Tale of, 22, 60, 83, 103, 111–12, 114–15, 130–31; **230–32, 235–6, 238–9**
squirrels, red, 7, 17, 22, 82, 111–12, 114, 144; **169–71, 217, 230–33, 235–6, 455;** grey, 144–5; **217, 314, 455**
Stalybridge, nr Manchester, 9
Stephens, Frederick Warne, 34, 203
Stevens, Walter, *coachman and chauffeur*, 185, 207
Stevenson, Rev John, of Glamis, 86
Stevenson, Robert Louis, 60, 153
still life, *see* Potter, H. B. (as artist)
stoats, 82
Stone, John, 207–208
Storey, Tom, 31, 34, 163, 177, 183–4, 190–92, 201, 202–03; **420;** Mrs, 190; Geoff, 201, 202–203
story-letters, *see* picture letters
Stott Farm, Graythwaite, 167
Strangeways & Sons, 98
Strathallan, Woods of, Perthshire, 88
Stroud, Gloucestershire, 92, *see also* Harescombe Grange
Sturges, Katharine, 167; **369**
Sty Head Tarn, Borrowdale, **381**
Sunday Herald (newspaper), 150
Surbiton, Surrey, 24
Swanage, Dorset, 92, 93
'Syntax, Dr.', 174; **383**

Tailor of Gloucester, The, 22, 55, 57, 59–60, 62, 86, 103, 108–111, 115, 123, 135–6, 161, 163, 168, 203; **103, 222–9;** privately printed edition, 22, 59–60, 108–109; **225, 229;** costumes for, 110; **222, 225, 228**
'Tale of Daisy and Dumpling, The', 162; **129;** *see also* fables ('Wolf in Sheep's Clothing')
'Tale of Jenny Crow, The', *see* fables ('Fox and Crow')
'Tale of Tuppenny, The', 118, 162; **357, 359;** *see also* Fairy Caravan, The; guinea pigs

Tales of Beatrix Potter, The (ballet film), 106
'Tales of Country Life', 152
Tarn Hows, Coniston, 195, 197; **428;** Tom Heights, 195
Tate Gallery, 8, 17, 203
Tay, River, 12, 121, 126
Taylor, John, of Sawrey, 140; **307**
Teignmouth, Devon, 166
Tenby, Pembrokeshire, 54, 104; **77, 100**
Tenniel, Sir John, 69, 70; **53**
Tennyson, Alfred, Lord, 173, 175
textile industry, 172; *see also* cotton trade; wool trade
'There was an old woman who lived in a shoe', 58, 155, 156; **37, 116–17**
Thirlmere, 172
Thiselton-Dyer, Sir William, 19, 90–91
'This little pig', 159–60; **352**
Thompson, Bruce, 196–7
Thorburn, Archibald, 168
'Three blind mice' (round), 101, 158
'Three little mice sat down to spin', 55–6, 74; **103–105**
Thring, Edward, of Uppingham, 170
Thwaite, Coniston, 197
Tilberthwaite, Coniston, 195
Times, The, 72
Timmy Tiptoes, The Tale of, 27, 144–5, 156; **314–15**
'Tingle, Dingle, Dousy', 57
toads, 46, 72, 80–81, 144; **107, 188, 313;** 'Toads' Tea Party', 91; **336**
Tom Heights, *see* Tarn Hows
Tom Kitten, The Tale of, 26, 74, 81, 84, 130–33, 137, 142, 178; **43, 280–85, 392, 438;** *see also* Roly-Poly Pudding, The
Tom Kitten's Painting Book, 28, 133, 136
Tommy Thumb's Pretty Song Book, 59
Torquay, Devon, 76
tortoises and terrapins, 14, 66, 68, 127; **62, 135, 217, 271;** *see also* fables
Tour of Dr. Syntax, The, 174; **383**
Townley, *Farmer*, 150
toy pictures, 54, 82; **101–102, 195**
travel, by carriage, coach and pony-cart, 10, 12, 17, 18, 21, 80, 121, 172, 178, 185; **163, 412;** in fairy tales, 61, 62; **120–21, 124;** *see also* 'Carrier's Bob'; horses and ponies; by railway, 16, 72, 77, 170–72, 173, 174, 185, Railway Bill, 172, Oxenholme-Windermere line, 170, Cockermouth, Keswick and Penrith Railway, 172, 'Steam Dragon of Honister', 172, 'The Flying Scotsman', 16, railway advertisements, 148; by car, 185, 196, 200, 207
trees and woodland, 12, 64, 68, 82, 84, 88–9, 91, 103, 104, 111–12, 114, 115, 116, 162, 165, 187, 191, 197, 206, 208; **10, 33, 87, 122, 124, 169–71, 177, 187–8, 212, 220, 231–5, 239, 244–5, 286, 290, 315–17, 321, 336, 340–41, 364, 411,** acorns, 335; pine-cone, 84; **174;** *see also* Christmas tree; fungi; plants and flowers
Trevelyan, George Macaulay, 193
Troutbeck, 31, 33, 164, 189; **362, 410;**

Broad How, 164; **78**; High Buildings, 167; Ing Bridge, 164; **427**; Nanny Lane, 92; **32**; Pinfold, 164; **410**; Townend Farm, 190; Troutbeck Park Farm, 31, 163, 164, 167, 189–90; **418–19**; Troutbeck Tongue, 21, 164, 165, 189; **362, 366, 410, 418**, Tongue Ghyll, **366**; Woundale, **365**

Troutbeck, nr Caldbeck, 164–5

Tuck, Raphael, 50

Tuckey, Dr R. P. ('little Peter of New Zealand'), 158

Tuppenny, see Fairy Caravan, The; guinea pigs; 'Tale of Tuppenny, The'; 'Walk Amongst the Funguses, A'

turkey, 163; see also poultry

Turner, Joseph Mallord William, RA, 55, 174; **382**

Twain, Mark, 66

Two Bad Mice, The Tale of, 24, 58, 83, 118–20, 123, 143; **38, 118, 210, 250–52**

Tzusee, see dogs

Ullswater, 181; **382**; see also Gowbarrow Park

Uncle Remus, 55, 66–9, 80, 168; **134–5**

United States of America, 33, 96, 111, 167–8; see also Boston; Coolidge, H. P.; Fairy Caravan, The; Harris, J. C.; Horn Book Magazine; McKay, Alexander; Merritt, A. L.; Miller, B. M.; Moore, A. C.; New York Public Library; Potter, H. B. (success and popularity . . . in U.S.A.); Sister Anne; Twain, M.; Uncle Remus; Wag-by-Wall

vegetables, 68, 83, 149, 156; **101–102, 214, 218**; broad beans, 83; **172**; carrots, 83, 130; **113–14, 278**; lettuce, 83, 116, 127, 139; **214, 271**; onions, 83, 101, 116, 117–18, 134; **247**; radishes, 83; **46**

verses, see rhymes

Victoria and Albert Museum, 47, 110, National Art Library, 37, 38, 47, 95–6, 118, 138; Department of Textiles, 110

Virgil, 71

voles, see mice

Waddington, William Hartley, 198; **432**

Wag-by-Wall ('Wag-by-the-Wall', 'Wag-by-Wa'), 167–8

Walbrook, City of London, see archaeology (London)

Wales, 25, 182; see also Denbighshire; Gwaynynog; Tenby

'Walk Amongst the Funguses, A', 91, 167

Walla Crag, see Derwentwater

War, First World, 28, 30, 33, 152, 184, 186, 187, 207; Second World, 32, 33–4, 197, 201–202, 207–208

Ward, Marcus, 50

Ward, Rowland, 144

Warne, family, 22–3, 24, 168; **36**; see also Stephens, F. W.

Warne, Amelia (Millie), 22–3, 25, 136, 142–3

Warne, Edith, 24

Warne, Frederick, 22

Warne, (W.) Fruing, 22, 28, 154–5, 156, 168

Warne, Harold E., 22, 25, 27, 28, 126, 130, 132, 140, 143, 144–5, 146–7, 168

Warne, Louie, 130, 140, 143

Warne, Louisa (Mrs Frederick), 22–3

Warne, Mary (Mrs Fruing), 105

Warne, Nellie, 130, 143

Warne, Norman Dalziel, 22–3, 24–5, 26, 34, 59, 85, 93, 110–11, 114, 115, 117, 119, 120, 122, 123–4, 125, 126, 127, 140, 154, 177, 203; **35**

Warne, Winifred M. L., 24, 25, 119

Warne, Frederick (& Co.), firm, 17, 22, 25, 26, 27, 28, 30, 31, 32, 60, 65, 70, 88, 95, 98–9, 101, 102–103, 104, 105, 108–109, 110, 114, 123, 124, 126, 135–6, 140, 143–4, 146, 148, 150, 153, 154, 158, 160, 161, 166, 168, 203, 207; **205–206, 208–209, 225**; see also Peter Rabbit Books

Watford, Hertfordshire, 87

Watts, George Frederick, 175

weasels, 80, 82; **167–8**

weather and seasons, 64, 80, 116, 158, 162, 180, 191, 197, 200, 202, 207, 208; **377, 380**; see also landscape; snow

Weatherly, Frederic E., 17, 57; see also Happy Pair, A

Webb, Mrs Sidney (née Beatrice Potter), 150

West & Newman, 76

Westminster, Duke of, 173, 175

Westmorland, 149, 203, sales, 195; *Westmorland Gazette*, 172; see also archaeology (Lake District); Lake District

Wetherlam, 195

Weymouth, Dorset, 19, 72; **11**

Wilson, Professor [Oxford friend of Rupert Potter], 69

Wilsons, 197

Winchelsea, Sussex, 119, 168

Windermere inc. Lake, 14, 20, 31, 130, 152, 169, 170–1, 181, 187, 189, 193–4, 197; **20, 426**; Bowness, 31; Cockshott Point, 193–4; **426**; Holehird, 20; Lindeth How(e), 29, 32, 144, 184; **42**; Queen Adelaide's Hill, 181–2, 187; ferry, 31, 184, 193–4; see also Brathay; Wray (Castle)

wolves, 63, 64, 67–8; see also fables

Woodcote, Horsley, 72, 85; **144**

Woodward, Dr Henry, 92; Alice [artist friend], 98

wool trade, 26, 176, 191, 204; see also carpet industry; cotton trade; textile industry

Woolpack Inn, see Eskdale

Wordsworth, William, 170, 176, 177

Wray, Windermere, 15, 21, 170; farms, 201; Wray Castle, 14–15, 36, 88, 169, 170, 187; **61, 186, 373**

Xarifa, 78; see also Fairy Caravan, The; mice; 'Walk Amongst the Funguses, A'

Yates, Frederick, 170; **374**

Yew Tree Farm, Coniston, 196, 197; **429**

Zoological Gardens and other zoos, 72–3, 114, 144; **146**